THE 100 MOST INFLUENTIAL
RELIGIOUS
LEADERS
OF ALL TIME

THE 100 MOST INFLUENTIAL
RELIGIOUS
LEADERS
OF ALL TIME

EDITED BY PHILIP WOLNY

Britannica
Educational Publishing
IN ASSOCIATION WITH

ROSEN
EDUCATIONAL SERVICES

Published in 2017 by Britannica Educational Publishing (a trademark of Encyclopædia Britannica, Inc.) in association with The Rosen Publishing Group, Inc.
29 East 21st Street, New York, NY 10010

Distributed exclusively by Rosen Publishing.
To see additional Britannica Educational Publishing titles, go to rosenpublishing.com.

First Edition

Britannica Educational Publishing
J.E. Luebering: Executive Director, Core Editorial
Anthony L. Green: Editor, Compton's by Britannica

Rosen Publishing
Philip Wolny: Editor
Nelson Sá: Art Director
Michael Moy: Designer
Cindy Reiman: Photography Manager
Philip Wolny: Photo Researcher
Introduction and supplementary material by Mary-Lane Kamberg

Library of Congress Cataloging-in-Publication Data

Names: Wolny, Philip, editor.
Title: The 100 most influential religious leaders of all time / edited by
  Philip Wolny.
Description: First Edition. | New York : Britannica Educational Publishing,
  2017. | Series: The EB guide to the world's most influential people |
  Includes bibliographical references and index.
Identifiers: LCCN 2016003420 | ISBN 9781680482775 (library bound : alk. paper)
Subjects: LCSH: Religious leaders--Biography--Juvenile literature.
Classification: LCC BL72 .A15 2016 | DDC 200.92/2--dc23
LC record available at http://lccn.loc.gov/2016003420

Manufactured in the United States of America

CONTENTS

138

146

307

320

337

INTRODUCTION

The wounded hunter lay burning with fever on a bed of horse hide and wooly rhinoceros fur on the cave floor. The smell of wood smoke filled the air as sparks from the fire at the cave mouth rose into the night. The tribe's religious leader, who was believed to serve as a connection between the natural and supernatural world, held a cup of medicinal tea to the patient's lips. After the hunter drank, the healer shook a rattle filled with dried seeds and began his magical chant, asking divine spirits to intervene and heal the hunter.

Before the hunt, the leader painted reindeer, ibex, musk ox, and aurochs on the cave wall to ensure a successful hunt. He or she also served as the tribe's storyteller, with stories that explained what the people encountered in their world, told about creation, and revealed a sense of order in the universe. In some tribes, these leaders, known in some cultures as shamans, medicine men, or witch doctors, were the most respected members of the group.

Archeological evidence from the Stone Age shows that as early as 300,000 years ago, the human experience has included burial rites and other signs of religious practices among the Neanderthals, humans sometimes known as cavemen. The prehistoric human groups sought help from spiritual beings through visions and other communication that led to such practices as healing through magic, predicting the future, and controlling spiritual beings and future events. The spiritual leader directed these activities.

As humans gathered together into larger groups, forming clans, towns, cities, and larger societies, the roles of religious leaders remained important. Healing the sick remained important. Some leaders established laws for religious practices or social and personal behavior. Others founded new religions or priesthoods. Some interpreted spiritual communication received through visions and prophecy. Still others became known for defending their faith or spreading it to new believers.

HEALING THROUGH FAITH

Healing has always been an important part of religious activities. Even today many religious organizations sponsor hospitals, health clinics, and other healing activities in both modern and developing countries. Jesus Christ, for example, was said to have cured people with leprosy, palsy, blindness, paralysis, and dropsy, and even to have raised Lazarus, Jairus's daughter, and the widow's son at Nain from the dead. So from the beginning, Christianity accepted healing through spiritual connection as part of its doctrine.

In China during the first and second centuries CE, during the reign of Shundi of the Dong (Eastern) Han dynasty, Zhang Daoling founded a movement within Daoism called Tianshidao, the "Way of the Celestial Masters." Zhang taught that sickness resulted from sinful mindedness. Through faith and confession to a priest, an ill person could be purified and cured.

During the early thirteenth century CE, Francis of Assisi tended the poor and sick, including lepers. His Franciscan order continues missionary work today caring for the poor and providing educational opportunities.

In 1866, Mary Baker Eddy, born in New Hampshire, in 1821, suddenly recovered from a serious injury. That experience led her to study Christ's healings in the Bible and later to found the Church of Christ Scientist. Its followers, known as Christian Scientists, believe in healing through faith. The religion is based on Christ's healings and teachings, but Eddy never claimed to be divine herself.

NEW IDEAS AND DOCTRINES

Other religious leaders brought laws and doctrines that established rules for religious, social, and personal behavior. For instance, more than 3,000 years ago, Moses, according to the Biblical account, came down from Mount Sinai and delivered to his people two stone tablets bearing the Ten Commandments. He then oversaw the creation and development of the first Israelite systems of worship, as well as civil laws for the community. These laws still form the basis of civil governance and religious practices among many Western countries.

Like Moses, Zoroaster (also known as Zarathushtra) introduced a new belief system around 600 BCE. He presented the ideas of *asa* (truth) and *druj* (lie) as the foundation of Zoroastrian doctrine, a religion that predates Islam in what today is Iran. Its three basic tenets are good thoughts, good words, and good deeds. Zoroaster also promoted the ideas of free will to choose right or wrong and individual responsibility for one's actions. His ideas influenced Judaism and Middle Platonism, a philosophy based on the thought of the ancient Greek philosopher Plato.

About the same time Zoroaster was founding Zoroastrianism, Mahavira was teaching the precepts of Jainism in India. He led a simple life with the goal of attaining the stage of highest perception. Teaching a doctrine of austerity, Mahavira advocated nonviolence in all circumstances and the acceptance of the five "great vows," renouncing killing, lying, greed, sexual pleasure, and attachment to objects and living beings. He also established rules of religious life for Jain monks, nuns, and lay practitioners that included vegetarianism, a form of "nonviolent" eating.

In the third century CE, Mani (also called Manes, or Manichaeus), founded the Manichaean religion in what is now Iran. He advocated a dualistic doctrine that saw the world as a mixture of spirit and matter, or good and evil. Twice, he saw in a vision an angel, who called him to preach the new religion.

In the twelfth century, Hildegard of Bingen brought a touch of what today is called feminism to the Catholic Church. Raised in a convent, she later became head of a convent and took steps to move it out from under the supervision of men.

In the late 18th century in the United States, Ann Lee led the United Society of Believers in Christ's Second Appearing, a Christian sect also called the Shakers. Their religious practices included dancing or shaking.

FOUNDING PRIESTHOODS

In a variety of the world's religions priests perform such rites as baptism and marriage and bless those who are ill. Priests are religious leaders who serve their congregations. Establishing a line of priesthood serves to further religious observance. Moses, for instance, did just that by anointing his brother Aaron's family line as priests. These priests saw to enforcement and furtherance of God's laws.

Among Catholics, the priesthood is said to have been started by Jesus Christ and continues today in the papacy, with Simon Peter as the first pope. Since the Middle Ages, popes have been elected by the College of Cardinals meeting in conclave.

In India in the 6th Century BCE, Siddhartha Gautama, the son of a Nepalese rajah, was "awakened to the truth" and became known as the Buddha, a teacher, but not a divine being. He, too, founded an order of monks who observed Buddhism's ideas and practices. Buddha traveled throughout India sharing his ideas, which included doing no harm to any creature, adopting vegetarianism, remaining chaste, and refraining from theft, lying, strong drink, and the taking of life. He developed an Eightfold Path of right views, right aspirations, right speech, right behavior, right mode of livelihood, right efforts, right thoughts, and right contemplation.

Judas Maccabeus also founded a line of priests. When Judas died in battle around 152 BCE, his brother Jonathan became the high priest in Jerusalem, despite the fact that he was not descended from Moses's brother Aaron. He thus became the first priest of the Hasmonean line.

VISIONS AND PROPHECY

Many religious leaders reported visions or displayed the gift of prophecy that led others to follow them. For instance, Isaiah's call to prophecy, found in the sixth chapter of the Book of Isaiah of the Old Testament, occurred about 742 BCE. He "saw" God and was overwhelmed by his contact with the divine glory and holiness. He became aware of God's need for a messenger to the people of Israel, and he offered himself to God's service: "Here am I! Send me." He was thus commissioned to give voice to the divine word. He told the Israelites that God's special bond with them depended on their own personal conduct. He told them that while God could intervene to rescue them from catastrophe, he could also visit catastrophe upon them. Isaiah worried that their society was headed for collapse and admonished his people to mend their ways.

Around 600 BCE Jeremiah was also known for prophecy. As a shy youth, he responded to Yahweh's (God's) call to prophecy by saying, "I do not know how to speak." According to the Book of Jeremiah, God said he would put his own words into Jeremiah's mouth and make him a "prophet to the nations." Jeremiah denounced social injustice and said weakness and corruption were the sources of sin. He also spoke about repentance, urging his followers to forsake evil and turn their loyalty to God. His New Covenant prophecy said Yahweh would write his law upon men's hearts, and all would know God directly and receive his forgiveness. This New Covenant lies behind words attributed to Jesus at the Last Supper, "This cup is the new covenant in my blood."

In the Middle Ages, Saint Joan of Arc led a French army against the British, following "instructions" she received through divine visions.

SPREADING THE WORD

Some religious leaders spread or defended their beliefs through warfare. Judas Maccabeus, who founded the Hasmonean priesthood, is best known as a military leader who defended Judea from invasion by the Seleucid king Antiochus IV Epiphanes. Judas Maccabeus's success in battle prevented the imposition of Hellenism and preserved the Jewish religion.

Ashoka, the last major emperor in the Mauryan dynasty of India, helped spread Buddhism throughout his country through conquest. However, later in life Ashoka renounced armed conflict and relied instead on a policy he called "conquest by dharma" ("right life").

In the 1950s, Ayatollah Khomeini advocated Islamic purity and gained a substantial following in Iran. He opposed Iran's ruler Mohammad Reza Shah Pahlavi and denounced Western influence. By the early 1960s he had become grand ayatollah, one of the supreme religious leaders of the Shiite sect in Iran. From exile in Paris, Khomeini inspired massive demonstrations, strikes, and civil unrest that led to the forced departure of the shah from Iran on Jan. 16, 1979. Two weeks later Khomeini arrived in Tehran in triumph and established an Islamic theocracy in Iran, becoming Iran's political and religious leader.

Many modern-day Christian evangelists, such as Billy Graham and Jerry Falwell, preached to large crowds in person and even bigger audiences through broadcast television. Joel Osteen, pastor of the Lakewood Church, a charismatic megachurch, from 1999, worked to spread his religion through persuasion.

Throughout history, humans have sought explanations for their existence and assistance from the supernatural. As various religions grew and changed, their leaders played key roles in defining creation, as well as providing rules of ethical conduct and religious practice and defending and spreading their faith. You'll find such men and women among *The 100 Most Influential Religious Leaders of All Time.*

MOSES

(flourished 14th–13th century BCE)

Revered as a prophet but even more importantly as a teacher and a lawgiver, Moses was the leader of the Israelite people 3,300 years ago during their journey from slavery in Egypt to freedom as a nation in the land of Israel. For 40 years Moses led the people through the desert on their way to Israel and helped shape them into a nation that could live under the laws of God. Moses oversaw the creation and development of the first Israelite systems of worship, the anointing of the family line of his brother Aaron as priests, and the creation of a legal system of governance for the community.

Ancient Israel had a long oral tradition of laws and legends, and it is likely that some parts of the story of Moses were written long after his lifetime. Modern scholarship recognizes that the core of the biblical story of Moses contains real history, but there is disagreement as to the accuracy of every action and every word attributed to Moses by the biblical writers. Whether one views the Bible as the revealed word of God or as the writing of inspired people, the figure of Moses towers over the early history of the Jewish people.

Jewish, Christian, and Muslim traditions revere Moses for his central role in communicating the Ten Commandments and the Torah (the first five books of the Bible) directly from God to the Jewish people soon after their escape from Egypt. Thus the Torah is also known as the Five Books of Moses.

According to Genesis, the first book of the Bible, the Israelite people first came to Egypt in search of food during a famine that affected the entire ancient Near East. At first welcomed by the Egyptians, after about 400 years the Israelites, or Hebrews, were perceived as a threat and were enslaved. In addition, the pharaoh, the ruler of Egypt, decreed that all newborn male Israelites were to be killed.

It was at this time that Moses was born. His older siblings, Aaron and Miriam, would join him later in his life to help lead the Israelite people. Moses was saved from death when his mother, Yocheved, floated him down the Nile River in a small basket, where he was discovered and saved by the daughter of Pharaoh. The name Moses is actually an Egyptian name.

Little is known about the childhood of Moses. Following his adoption into the royal household the Bible next mentions him as an adult who killed an Egyptian taskmaster for abusing an Israelite slave. Forced to flee Egypt, Moses became a shepherd in the neighboring land of Midian, where he met and married his wife, Zippora.

Moses Showing the Tables of the Law to the People, *oil painting by Rembrandt, 1659; in the Staatliche Museen Preussischer Kulturbesitz, Berlin.*

While tending his flock, as the Bible relates, Moses had his first encounter with God, who would ultimately free the Israelite people from Egyptian slavery. At a bush that miraculously burned but was not burnt up, Moses heard God call him to go to Pharaoh and demand that the Israelite people be set free. At first reluctant and afraid, Moses was convinced by a series of divine signs and was reassured by the presence of his brother Aaron, who came to assist him. Moses's first confrontation with Pharaoh was a failure. The Egyptians relied on slave labor for their massive building projects, and Pharaoh was reluctant to lose such a large number of workers. Angry at Moses, Pharaoh decreed that the Israelite slaves should work even harder. The consequent increasing oppression of the Israelites caused them to reject Moses as their deliverer.

The Bible then tells of God's visiting upon the Egyptians a series of divine punishments in the form of ten plagues. The final plague took the life of Pharaoh's own son. Pharaoh then relented and let the Israelites leave Egypt under the leadership of Moses. But Pharaoh soon regretted his decision and set out in pursuit with his army to bring the Israelite slaves back to Egypt. At the Sea of Reeds, with the Egyptians closing in on them, the Israelites miraculously passed through the divided waters to freedom, while the Egyptians were drowned. Moses and Miriam led the people in song and prayer, the words of which are preserved in the Bible in the Book of Exodus.

As the Bible next describes, Moses then led the Israelites to Mount Sinai, where God gave them the Ten Commandments and other laws contained in the Torah. Through these laws, God is said to have established a covenant with the Israelite people. The Israelites pledged to follow God's laws, and God promised to be their God forever. These laws were intended to establish the moral principles by which the new Israelite nation would govern itself and through which it would manifest God's hope for just and right relationships among people.

When Moses first came down from Mount Sinai he saw that many of the Israelites had made an image of a calf out of gold, which they were worshiping. In his anger, Moses smashed the tablets containing the Ten

Commandments. God was prepared to abandon the people for the sin of idolatry, but Moses interceded on their behalf. Soon after, he went back up Mount Sinai and was given a second set of the Ten Commandments.

Moses next prepared to lead the people from Mount Sinai to the promised land of Israel. However, the Israelite people, accustomed to slavery and uncertain of freedom, soon rebelled against God. They became convinced that they could not conquer the new land, and they constantly questioned Moses's leadership and their own faith in God. As a consequence, the generation that left Egypt was not allowed to enter the promised land. The Bible describes Moses himself as once losing patience with the people and seeming to doubt God: rather than speaking to a rock to get water as God commanded, Moses struck the rock with his staff. For this, Moses was also destined not to enter the new land.

Near the end of his life, Moses taught the laws of the Torah to the new generation that had grown up in the desert. He then transferred leadership to Joshua. The Torah ends with Moses's final blessing to the people, after which he ascended Mount Nebo, which is identified with Mount Pisgah, on the eastern edge of the Jordan River. Moses died there, able to see, but not to enter, the promised land.

AKHENATON

(b. 1353–d. 1336 BCE)

In the 14th century BC the Egyptian pharaoh Amenhotep IV undertook a religious reform by trying to displace all the traditional deities with the sun god Aton (also spelled Aten). In the god's honor, the pharaoh changed his name to Akhenaton (also spelled Ikhnaton), which means "beneficial to the Aton." Akhenaton ruled from 1353 to 1336 BC. His queen was Nefertiti, one of the most famous women in Egyptian history. A few years after his death, the boy-king Tutankhamen, the discovery of whose tomb in 1922 was an archaeological sensation, became ruler.

Akhenaton's reform was seen by some as one of the earliest attempts to enforce monotheism, the belief in one god, although the religion of the Aton may best be described as the worship of one god in preference to all others. At one time Akhenaton initiated a program to erase the name and image of the Theban god, Amon, from all monuments. To further enforce his views, Akhenaton moved the country's capital from Thebes to a site 200 miles (300 kilometers) north, which he called Akhetaton (now called Tell el-Amarna). His primary intention was to construct a city dedicated to the worship of the Aton separate from already established cults. Still, monotheism was not complete, as private homes have yielded numerous figurines of household deities, and stelae dedicated to traditional deities, such as Isis and Tausret, have been found in some of the private chapels.

Akhenaton's reforms, and the artistic and literary revival that accompanied them, did not survive for long. So much of his time was devoted to religion that the powerful Egyptian empire began to disintegrate. This, combined with the opposition of the priests of the displaced gods, worked to undermine the new religion. After Akhenaton's death the capital was moved back to Thebes and the former gods, never fully rejected by the general populace in the first place, were restored.

ISAIAH

(flourished 8th century BCE, Jerusalem)

Isaiah, Hebrew Yesha'yahu ("God Is Salvation"), was a prophet after whom the biblical Book of Isaiah is named (only some of the first 39 chapters are attributed to him) and a significant contributor to Jewish and Christian traditions. His call to prophecy in about 742 BC coincided with the beginnings of the westward expansion of the Assyrian Empire, which threatened Israel and which Isaiah proclaimed to be a warning from God to a godless people.

The earliest recorded event in his life is his call to prophecy as now found in the sixth chapter of the Book of Isaiah; this occurred about 742 BC. The vision (probably in the Jerusalem Temple) that made him a prophet is described in a first-person narrative. According to this account he "saw" God and was overwhelmed by his contact with the divine glory and holiness. He became agonizingly aware of God's need for a messenger to the people of Israel, and, despite his own sense of inadequacy, he offered himself for God's service: "Here am I! Send me." He was thus commissioned to give voice to the divine word. It was no light undertaking; he was to condemn his own people and watch the nation crumble and perish. As he tells it, he was only too aware that, coming with such a message, he would experience bitter opposition, willful disbelief, and ridicule, to withstand which he would have to be inwardly fortified. All this came to him in the form of a vision and ended as a sudden, firm, and lifelong resolve.

Presumably, Isaiah was already prepared to find meaning in the vision before the arrival of that decisive moment. Information about that period of his life is inconclusive, however, and consists mainly of inferences drawn from the biblical text.

At times the prophet's private life shows through the record as an aspect of his public message. Once when he went to confront a king, he took with him, to reenforce his prophetic word, a son with the symbolic name Shear-yashuv ("A Remnant Shall Return"). Again, to memorialize a message, he sired a son on the "prophetess" (his wife) and saddled the child with his message as a name:

Maher-shalal-hash-baz ("Speed-spoil-hasten-plunder"), referring to the imminent spoliations by the Assyrians. If the sons had not been wanted as walking witnesses to the prophet's forebodings, posterity would not know of this wife or these sons.

Of Isaiah's parental home it is known only that his father's name was Amoz. Since he often spoke with kings, it is sometimes suggested that Isaiah was an aristocrat, possibly even of royal stock. The same reasoning, however, might apply to any number of prophets; from Nathan in David's time onward, prophets had dealings with kings and were, like Isaiah, well informed about public affairs. Moreover, Isaiah's sympathies were emphatically with the victimized poor, not with the courtiers and well-to-do. Also, it is sometimes argued that he was of a priestly family, but his knowledge of cultic matters and the fact that his commissioning seemingly occurred in the Temple in Jerusalem are slender evidence for his priestly descent as against his unreserved condemnation of the priests and their domain: "I am fed up with roasting rams and the grease of fattened beasts," he has God proclaim in a famous passage in the first chapter.

One could argue with equal force that Isaiah is descended from a family of prophets (though his father, the otherwise unknown Amoz, is not to be confused with the prophet Amos). He is thoroughly schooled in the traditional forms and language of prophetic speech. It is an educated speech— strong, vivid, the finest of classical Hebrew. Isaiah is particularly well acquainted with the prophetic tradition known to his slightly older contemporary, Amos. Four eminent Hebrew prophets addressed themselves to the people of Israel and Judah in the latter half of the 8th pre-Christian century: Amos, Hosea, Micah, and Isaiah. Strangely, no evidence suggests that any of these knew in person any of the others. Seemingly, they were apart and alone, yet Isaiah and

Amos follow essentially the same lines of thought and differ significantly only in that Amos had addressed the northern kingdom (Israel) while Isaiah would emphatically include Judah and Jerusalem. The basic similarities in style and substance strongly suggest influence, direct or indirect, of the one on the other—and both invoke a recognizable Israelite tradition.

Isaiah's experience bridges the classes and occupations. Whatever his family circumstances, still in his youth he came to know the face of poverty—and the debauchery of the rich. He was at home with the unprotected, the widowed and orphaned; with the dispossessed, homeless, landless; and with the resourceless victims of the moneyed man's court. He was also acquainted with the rapacious authors of the prevailing misery: promulgators of discriminatory laws, venal judges, greedy landgrabbers, fancy women, thieving and carousing men of means, and irresponsible leaders, both civil and religious. In other words, he was intimately aware of the inequities and evils of human society—which may have been no worse in Israel in the 8th century before Christ than many critics believe they are almost everywhere in the 20th century after Christ.

JEREMIAH

(b. probably after 650 BCE, Anathoth, Judah—d. c. 570 BCE, Egypt)

Jeremiah, Hebrew Yirmeyahu, Latin Vulgate Jeremias, was a Hebrew prophet, reformer, and author of a biblical book that bears his name. He was closely involved in the political and religious events of a crucial era in the history of the ancient Near East; his spiritual leadership helped his fellow countrymen survive disasters that included the capture of Jerusalem by the Babylonians in 586 BCE and the exile of many Judaeans to Babylonia.

Jeremiah was born and grew up in the village of Anathoth, a few miles northeast of Jerusalem, in a priestly family. In his childhood he must have learned some of the traditions of his people, particularly the prophecies of Hosea, whose influence can be seen in his early messages.

The era in which Jeremiah lived was one of transition for the ancient Near East. The Assyrian Empire, which had been dominant for two centuries, declined and fell. Its capital, Nineveh, was captured in 612 by the Babylonians and Medes. Egypt had a brief period of resurgence under the 26th dynasty (664–525) but did not prove strong enough to establish an empire. The new world power was the Neo-Babylonian Empire, ruled by a Chaldean dynasty whose best-known king was Nebuchadrezzar. The small and comparatively insignificant state of Judah had been a vassal of Assyria and, when Assyria declined, asserted its independence for a short time. Subsequently Judah vacillated in its allegiance between Babylonia and Egypt and ultimately became a province of the Neo-Babylonian Empire.

According to the biblical Book of Jeremiah, Jeremiah began his prophetic career in 627/626—the 13th year of King Josiah's reign. It is told there that he responded to Yahweh's (God's) call to prophesy by protesting "I do not know how to speak, for I am only a youth," but he received Yahweh's assurance that he would put his own words into Jeremiah's mouth and make him a "prophet to the nations." A few scholars believe that after his call Jeremiah served as an official prophet in the Temple, but most believe that this is unlikely in view of his sharp criticism of priests, prophets, and the Temple cult.

Jeremiah's early messages to the people were condemnations of them for their false worship and social injustice, with summons to repentance. He proclaimed the coming of a foe from the north, symbolized by a boiling pot facing from the north in one of his visions, that would cause great destruction. This foe has often been identified with the Scythians, nomads from southern Russia who supposedly descended into western Asia in the 7th century and attacked Palestine. Some scholars have identified the northern foe with the Medes, the Assyrians, or the Chaldeans (Babylonians); others have interpreted his message as vague eschatological predictions, not concerning a specific people.

In 621 King Josiah instituted far-reaching reforms based upon a book discovered in the Temple of Jerusalem in the course of building repairs, which was probably Deuteronomy or some part of it. Josiah's reforms included the purification of worship from pagan practices, the centralization of all sacrificial rites in the Temple of Jerusalem, and perhaps an effort to establish social justice following principles of earlier prophets (this program constituted what has been called "the Deuteronomic reforms").

Jeremiah's attitude toward these reforms is difficult to assess. Clearly, he would have found much in them with which to agree; a passage in chapter 11 of Jeremiah, in which he is called on by Yahweh to urge adherence to the ancient covenant upon "the men of Judah and the inhabitants of Jerusalem," is frequently interpreted as indicating that the prophet travelled around Jerusalem and the villages of Judah exhorting the people to follow the reforms. If this was the case, Jeremiah later became disillusioned with the reforms because they dealt too much with the externals of religion and not with the inner spirit and ethical conduct of the people. He may have relapsed into a period of silence for several years because of the indifferent success of the reforms and the failure of his prophecies concerning the foe from the north to materialize.

Some scholars doubt that Jeremiah's career actually began as early as 627/626 BCE and question the accuracy of the dates in the biblical account. This view arises from the difficulty of identifying the foe from the north, which seems likely to have been the Babylonians of a later time, as well as the difficulty of determining the prophet's attitude toward the Deuteronomic reforms and of assigning messages of Jeremiah to the reign of Josiah. In the opinion of such scholars, Jeremiah began to prophesy toward the end of the reign of Josiah or at the beginning of the reign of Jehoiakim (609–598).

Early in the reign of Jehoiakim, Jeremiah delivered his famous "Temple sermon," of which there are two versions, one in Jeremiah, chapter 7, verses 1 to 15, the other in chapter 26, verses 1 to 24. He denounced the people for their dependence on the Temple for security and called on them to effect genuine ethical reform. He predicted that God would destroy the Temple of Jerusalem, as he had earlier destroyed that of Shiloh, if they continued in their present path. Jeremiah was immediately arrested and tried on a capital charge. He was acquitted but may have been forbidden to preach again in the Temple.

The reign of Jehoiakim was an active and difficult period in Jeremiah's life. That king was very different from his father, the reforming Josiah, whom Jeremiah commended for doing justice and righteousness. Jeremiah denounced Jehoiakim harshly for his selfishness, materialism, and socially unjust practices.

Near the time of the Battle of Carchemish, in 605, when the Babylonians decisively defeated the Egyptians and the remnant of the Assyrians, Jeremiah delivered an oracle against Egypt. Realizing that this battle made a great difference in the world situation, Jeremiah soon dictated to his scribe, Baruch, a scroll containing all of the messages he had delivered to this time. The scroll was read by Baruch in the Temple. Subsequently it was read before King Jehoiakim, who cut it into pieces and burned it.

Jeremiah went into hiding and dictated another scroll, with additions.

When Jehoiakim withheld tribute from the Babylonians (about 601), Jeremiah began to warn the Judaeans that they would be destroyed at the hands of those who had previously been their friends. When the king persisted in resisting Babylonia, Nebuchadrezzar sent an army to besiege Jerusalem. King Jehoiakim died before the siege began and was succeeded by his son, Jehoiachin, who surrendered the capital to the Babylonians on March 16, 597, and was taken to Babylonia with many of his subjects.

The Babylonians placed on the throne of Judah a king favourable to them, Zedekiah (597–586 BCE), who was more inclined to follow Jeremiah's counsel than Jehoiakim had been but was weak and vacillating and whose court was torn by conflict between pro-Babylonian and pro-Egyptian parties. After paying Babylonia tribute for nearly 10 years, the king made an alliance with Egypt. A second time Nebuchadrezzar sent an army to Jerusalem, which he captured in August 586.

Early in Zedekiah's reign, Jeremiah wrote a letter to the exiles in Babylonia, advising them not to expect to return immediately to their homeland, as false prophets were encouraging them to believe, but to settle peaceably in their place of exile and seek the welfare of their captors. When emissaries from surrounding states came to Judah in 594 to enlist Judah's support in rebellion against Babylonia, Jeremiah put a yoke upon his neck and went around proclaiming that Judah and the surrounding states should submit to the yoke of Babylonia, for it was Yahweh who had given them into the hand of the king of Babylonia. Even to the time of the fall of Jerusalem, Jeremiah's message remained the same: submit to the yoke of Babylonia.

When the siege of Jerusalem was temporarily lifted at the approach of an Egyptian force, Jeremiah started to leave Jerusalem to go to the land of the tribe of Benjamin. He was arrested on a charge of desertion and placed in prison. Subsequently he was placed in an abandoned cistern, where he would have died had it not been for the prompt action of an Ethiopian eunuch, Ebed-melech, who rescued the prophet with the king's permission and put him in a less confining place. King Zedekiah summoned him from prison twice for secret interviews, and both times Jeremiah advised him to surrender to Babylonia.

When Jerusalem finally fell, Jeremiah was released from prison by the Babylonians and offered safe conduct to Babylonia, but he preferred to remain with his own people. So he was entrusted to Gedaliah, a Judaean from a prominent family whom the Babylonians appointed as governor of the province of Judah. The prophet continued to oppose those who wanted to rebel against Babylonia and promised the people a bright and joyful future.

After Gedaliah was assassinated, Jeremiah was taken against his will to Egypt by some of the Jews who feared reprisal from the Babylonians. Even in Egypt he continued to rebuke his fellow exiles. Jeremiah probably died about 570 BCE. According to a tradition that is preserved in extrabiblical sources, he was stoned to death by his exasperated fellow countrymen in Egypt.

ZOROASTER

(b. c. 628 BCE, probably Rhages, Iran—d. c. 551, site unknown)

Zoroaster, Old Iranian Zarathushtra, or Zarathustra, was an Iranian religious reformer and founder of Zoroastrianism, or Parsiism, as it is known in India.

A major personality in the history of the religions of the world, Zoroaster has been the object of much attention for

A portrait of ancient Persian poet and prophet Zoroaster.

two reasons. On the one hand, he became a legendary figure believed to be connected with occult knowledge and magical practices in the Near Eastern and Mediterranean world in the Hellenistic Age (c. 300 BCE–c. 300 CE). On the other hand, his monotheistic concept of God has attracted the attention of modern historians of religion, who have speculated on the connections between his teaching and Judaism and Christianity. Though extreme claims of pan-Iranianism (i.e., that Zoroastrian or Iranian ideas influenced Greek, Roman, and Jewish thought) may be disregarded, the pervasive influence of Zoroaster's religious thought must nevertheless be recognized.

The student of Zoroastrianism is confronted by several problems concerning the religion's founder. One question is what part of Zoroastrianism derives from Zoroaster's tribal religion and what part was new as a result of his visions and creative religious genius. Another question is the extent to which the later Zoroastrian religion (Mazdaism) of the Sāsānian period (224–651 CE) genuinely reflected the teachings of Zoroaster. A third question is the extent to which the sources—the Avesta (the Zoroastrian scriptures) with the Gāthās (older hymns), the Middle Persian Pahlavi Books, and reports of various Greek authors—offer an authentic guide to Zoroaster's ideas.

A biographical account of Zoroaster is tenuous at best or speculative at the other extreme. The date of Zoroaster's life cannot be ascertained with any degree of certainty. According to Zoroastrian tradition, he flourished "258 years before Alexander." Alexander the Great conquered Persepolis, the capital of the Achaemenids, a dynasty that ruled Persia from 559 to 330 BCE, in 330 BCE. Following this dating, Zoroaster converted Vishtāspa, most likely a king of Chorasmia (an area south of the Aral Sea in Central Asia), in 588 BCE. According to tradition, he was 40 years old when this event occurred, thus indicating that his birthdate was 628 BCE. Zoroaster was born into a modestly situated family of knights, the Spitama, probably at Rhages (now Rayy, a suburb of Tehrān), a town in Media. The area in which he lived was not yet urban, its economy being based on animal husbandry and pastoral occupations. Nomads, who frequently raided those engaged in such occupations, were viewed by Zoroaster as aggressive violators of order, and he called them Followers of the Lie.

According to the sources, Zoroaster probably was a priest. Having received a vision from Ahura Mazdā, the Wise Lord, who appointed him to preach the truth, Zoroaster apparently was opposed in his teachings by the civil and religious authorities in the area in which he preached. It is not clear whether these authorities were from his native region or from Chorasmia prior to the conversion of Vishtāspa. Confident in the truth revealed to him by Ahura Mazdā, Zoroaster apparently did not try to overthrow belief in the older Iranian religion, which was polytheistic; he did, however, place Ahura Mazdā at the centre of a kingdom of justice that promised immortality and bliss. Though he attempted to reform ancient Iranian religion on the basis of the existing social and economic values, Zoroaster's teachings at first aroused opposition from those whom he called the Followers of the Lie (Dregvant).

LAOZI

(flourished 6th century BCE, China)

Laozi was the first philosopher of Chinese Daoism and is the alleged author of the Daodejing (q.v.), a primary Daoist writing. Modern scholars discount the possibility that the Daodejing was written by only one person but readily acknowledge the influence of Daoism on the development of Buddhism. Laozi is venerated as a philosopher by Confucians and as a saint or god in popular religion and was worshipped as an imperial ancestor during the Tang dynasty (618–907).

Despite his historical importance, Laozi remains an obscure figure. The principal source of information about his life is a biography in the Shiji ("Records of the Historian") by Sima Qian. This historian, who wrote in about 100 BCE, had little solid information concerning the philosopher. He says that Laozi was a native of Quren, a village in the district of Hu in the state of Chu, which corresponds to the modern Luyi in the eastern part of Henan Province. His family name was Li, his proper name Er, his appellation Dan. He was appointed to the office of *shi* at the royal court of the Zhou dynasty (c. 1046–256 BCE). *Shi* today means "historian," but in ancient China the shi were scholars specializing in matters such as astrology and divination and were in charge of sacred books.

After noting the civil status of Laozi, the historian proceeds to relate a celebrated but questionable meeting of the old Daoist with the younger Confucius (551–479 BCE). The story has been much discussed by the scholars; it is mentioned elsewhere, but the sources are so inconsistent and contradictory that the meeting seems a mere legend. During the supposed interview, Laozi blamed Confucius for his pride and ambition, and Confucius was so impressed with Laozi that he compared him to a dragon that rises to the sky, riding on the winds and clouds.

No less legendary is a voyage of Laozi to the west. Realizing that the Zhou dynasty was on the decline, the philosopher departed and came to the Xiangu Pass, which was the entrance to the state of Qin. Yinxi, the legendary guardian of the pass (*guanling*), begged him to write a book for him. Thereupon, Laozi wrote a book in two sections of

Laozi.

5,000 characters, in which he set down his ideas about the Dao (literally "Way") and the *de* (its "virtue"): the Daodejing. Then he left, and "nobody knows what has become of him," says Sima Qian.

After the account of the journey of Laozi and of the redaction of the book, Sima Qian alludes to other persons with whom Laozi was sometimes identified. One was Lao Laizi, a Daoist contemporary of Confucius; another was a great astrologer named Dan. Sima Qian adds, "Maybe Laozi has lived one hundred and fifty years, some say more than two hundred years." Since the ancient Chinese believed that superior men could live very long, it is natural that the Daoists credited their master with an uncommon longevity, but this is perhaps a rather late tradition because Zhuangzi, the Daoist sage of the 4th century BCE, still speaks of the death of Laozi without emphasizing an unusual longevity.

To explain why the life of Laozi is so shrouded in obscurity, Sima Qian says that he was a gentleman recluse whose doctrine consisted in nonaction, the cultivation of a state of inner calm, and purity of mind. Indeed, throughout the whole history of China, there have always been recluses who shunned worldly life. The author (or authors) of the Daodejing was probably a person of this kind who left no trace of his life.

The question of whether there was a historical Laozi has been raised by many scholars, but it is rather an idle one. The Daodejing, as we have it, cannot be the work of a single author; some of its sayings may date from the time of Confucius; others are certainly later; and a version of the text has been recovered in an archaeological find at Guodian that dates to before 300 BCE. Owing to these facts, some scholars have assigned the authorship of the Daodejing to the astrologer Dan; while others, giving credit to a genealogy of the descendants of the philosopher, which is related in the biography by Sima Qian, try to place the life of Lao Dan at the end of the 4th century BCE. But this genealogy can hardly be considered as historical. It proves only that at the time of Sima Qian a certain Li family pretended to be descended from the Daoist sage; it does not give a basis for ascertaining the existence of the latter. The name Laozi seems to represent a certain type of sage rather than an individual.

MAHAVIRA

(b. c. 599 BCE traditional dating, Kshatriyakundagrama, India—d. 527 traditional dating, Pavapuri)

Mahavira was the the last of the 24 Tirthankaras ("Ford-makers," i.e., saviours who promulgated Jainism), and the reformer of the Jain monastic community. According to the traditions of the two main Jain sects, the Shvetambara ("White-robed") and the Digambara ("Sky-clad," i.e., naked), Mahavira became a monk and followed an extreme ascetic life, attaining *kevala*, the stage of omniscience or highest perception. Teaching a doctrine of austerity, Mahavira advocated nonviolence (*ahimsa*) in all circumstances and the acceptance of the *mahavratas*, the five "great vows" of renunciation.

Although tradition dictates that Mahavira was born about 599 BCE, many scholars believe this date to be as much as 100 years early, in that Mahavira probably lived at about the same time as the Buddha, whose traditional birth date has also been reassessed. The son of a Kshatriya (warrior caste) family, he grew up in Kshatriyakundagrama, a suburb of Vaishali (modern Basarh, Bihar State), where both Jainism and Buddhism originated. His father was Siddhartha, a ruler of the Nata, or Jnatri, clan. According to one Jain tradition, his mother was Devananda, a member of the Brahman (priestly) caste; other traditions call her Trishala, Videhadinna, or Priyakarini and place her in the Kshatriya caste.

The 7th to 5th century BCE was a period of great intellectual, philosophical, religious, and social ferment in India, a time when members of the Kshatriya caste opposed the cultural domination of the Brahmans, who claimed authority by virtue of their supposed innate purity. In particular, there was growing opposition to the large-scale Vedic sacrifices (*yajna*) that involved the killing of many animals. Because of the popularity of the doctrine of continual rebirth, which linked animals and humans in the same cycle of birth, death, and rebirth, unnecessary killing had become objectionable to many people. Economic factors may also have encouraged the growth of the doctrine of nonviolence. The leaders of the anti-Brahman sects came to be regarded as heretical. Mahavira and his contemporary Siddhartha Gautama, the Buddha, were two of the greatest leaders in this movement.

Although accounts of the life of Mahavira vary for the two Jain sects, he apparently was reared in luxury, but because he was a younger son he could not inherit the leadership of the clan. At the age of 30, after (according to the Shvetambara sect) marrying a woman of the Kshatriya caste and having a daughter, Mahavira renounced the world and became a monk. He wore one garment for more than a year but later went naked and had no possessions—not even a bowl for obtaining alms or drinking water. He allowed insects to crawl on his body and bite him, bearing the pain with patience. People frequently harangued and hit him because of his uncouth and unsightly body, but he endured abusive language and physical injuries with equanimity. Meditating day and night, he lived in various places—workshops, cremation and burial grounds, and at the foot of trees. Trying to avoid all sinful activity, he especially avoided injuring any kind of life, thus developing the doctrine of ahimsa, or nonviolence. He fasted often and never ate anything that was expressly prepared for him. Although he wandered continuously during most of the year, Mahavira spent the rainy season in villages and towns. After 12 years of extreme asceticism, he attained kevala, the highest stage of perception.

Mahavira may be regarded as the founder of Jainism. According to tradition, he based his doctrines on the teachings of the 23rd Tirthankara, Parshvanatha, a teacher from Banaras (Varanasi, Uttar Pradesh) of the 7th century BCE, Mahavira systematized earlier Jain doctrines as well as Jainism's metaphysical, mythological, and cosmological beliefs. He also established the rules of religious life for Jain monks, nuns, and laity.

Mahavira taught that people can save their souls from the contamination of matter by living a life of extreme asceticism and by practicing nonviolence toward all living creatures. This advocacy of nonviolence encouraged his followers, monastic and lay, to become strong advocates of vegetarianism. Mahavira's followers were aided in their quest for salvation by the five mahavratas. Attributed to Mahavira (though they show connections with contemporary Brahmanical practice), these great vows were the renunciation of killing, of speaking untruths, of greed, of sexual pleasure, and of all attachments to living beings and nonliving things. Mahavira's predecessor, Parshvanatha, had preached only four vows.

Mahavira was given the title Jina, or "Conqueror" (conqueror of enemies such as attachment and greed), which subsequently became synonymous with Tirthankara. He died, according to tradition, in 527 BCE at Pava in Bihar State, leaving a group of followers who established Jainism. Through their practice of nonviolence, they have profoundly influenced Indian culture.

CONFUCIUS

(b. 551 BCE, Qufu, state of Lu [now in Shandong Province, China]—d. 479 BCE, Lu)

Confucius was China's most famous teacher, philosopher, and political theorist, whose ideas have influenced the civilization of East Asia.

Confucius's life, in contrast to his tremendous importance, seems starkly undramatic, or, as a Chinese expression has it, it seems "plain and real." The plainness and reality of Confucius's life, however, underlines that his humanity was not revealed truth but an expression of self-cultivation, of the ability of human effort to shape its own destiny. The faith in the possibility of ordinary human beings to become awe-inspiring sages and worthies is deeply rooted in the Confucian heritage, and the insistence that human beings are teachable, improvable, and perfectible through personal and communal endeavour is typically Confucian.

Although the facts about Confucius's life are scanty, they do establish a precise time frame and historical context. Confucius was born in the 22nd year of the reign of Duke Xiang of Lu (551 BCE). The traditional claim that he was born on the 27th day of the eighth lunar month has been questioned by historians, but September 28 is still widely observed in East Asia as Confucius's birthday. It is an official holiday, "Teachers' Day," in Taiwan.

Confucius was born in Qufu in the small feudal state of Lu, in what is now Shandong Province, which was noted for its preservation of the traditions of ritual and music of the Zhou civilization. His family name was Kong and his personal name Qiu, but he is referred to as either Kongzi or Kongfuzi (Master Kong) throughout Chinese history. The adjective "Confucian," derived from the Latinized Confucius, is not a meaningful term in Chinese, nor is the term Confucianism, which was coined in Europe as recently as the 18th century.

Confucius's ancestors were probably members of the aristocracy who had become virtual poverty-stricken commoners by the time of his birth. His father died when Confucius was only three years old. Instructed first by his mother, Confucius then distinguished himself as an indefatigable learner in his teens. He recalled toward the end of his life that at age 15 his heart was set upon learning. A historical account notes that, even though he was already known as an informed young scholar, he felt it appropriate to inquire about everything while visiting the Grand Temple.

Confucius had served in minor government posts managing stables and keeping books for granaries before he married a woman of similar background when he was 19. It is not known who Confucius's teachers were, but he made a conscientious effort to find the right masters to teach him, among other things, ritual and music. His mastery of the six arts—ritual, music, archery, charioteering, calligraphy, and arithmetic—and his familiarity with the classical traditions, notably poetry and history, enabled him to start a brilliant teaching career in his 30s.

Confucius is known as the first teacher in China who wanted to make education broadly available and who was instrumental in establishing the art of teaching as a vocation, indeed as a way of life. Before Confucius, aristocratic families had hired tutors to educate their sons in specific arts, and government officials had instructed their subordinates in the necessary techniques, but he was the first person to devote his whole life to learning and teaching for the purpose of transforming and improving society. He believed that all human beings could benefit from self-cultivation. He inaugurated a humanities program for potential leaders, opened the doors of education to all, and defined learning not merely as the acquisition of knowledge but also as character building.

For Confucius the primary function of education was to provide the proper way of training exemplary persons (*junzi*), a process that involved constant self-improvement and continuous social interaction. Although he emphatically noted that learning was "for the sake of the self" (the end of which was self-knowledge and self-realization), he found public service integral to true education. Confucius confronted learned hermits who challenged the validity of his desire to serve the world; he resisted the temptation to "herd with birds and animals," to live apart from the human community, and opted to try to transform the world from within. For decades Confucius tried to be actively involved in politics, wishing to put his humanist ideas into practice through governmental channels.

In his late 40s and early 50s Confucius served first as a magistrate, then as an assistant minister of public works, and eventually as minister of justice in the state of Lu. It is likely that he accompanied King Lu as his chief minister on one of the diplomatic missions. Confucius's political career was, however, short-lived. His loyalty to the king alienated him from the power holders of the time, the large Ji families, and his moral rectitude did not sit well with the king's inner circle, who enraptured the king with sensuous delight. At 56, when he realized that his superiors were uninterested in his policies, Confucius left the country in an attempt to find another feudal state to which he could render his service. Despite his political frustration he was accompanied by an expanding circle of students during this self-imposed exile of almost 12 years.

His reputation as a man of vision and mission spread. A guardian of a border post once characterized him as the "wooden tongue for a bell" of the age, sounding heaven's prophetic note to awaken the people (Analects, 3:24). Indeed, Confucius was perceived as the heroic conscience who knew realistically that he might not succeed but, fired by a righteous passion, continuously did the best he could. At the age of 67 he returned home to teach and to preserve his cherished classical traditions by writing and editing. He died in 479 BCE, at the age of 73. According to the *Records of the Grand Historian*, 72 of his students mastered the "six arts," and those who claimed to be his followers numbered 3,000.

BUDDHA

(b. c. 6th–4th century BCE, Lumbini, near Kapilavastu, Shakya republic, Kosala kingdom [now in Nepal]—died, Kusinara, Malla republic, Magadha kingdom [now Kasia, India])

Hundreds of years before Jesus was born—and at about the same time that Confucius was teaching the Chinese how to lead the good life—a prince named Siddhartha Gautama (or Gotama) became famous in India for his holiness and love for all creatures. He was called the Buddha, meaning "the Enlightened One," a title used by many groups in ancient India but associated now mainly with Gautama. Many persons believed in the Buddha's teachings while he lived. After his death, shrines called stupas were built in his honor, and his religion spread through a great part of Asia. By the early 21st century some 380 million people professed the Buddhist faith.

The life of the Buddha is known only from much later texts, and much of what is believed about him is legendary. The Buddha, according to tradition, was born to a noble family of the ruling class in Lumbini in what is now southwestern Nepal. His mother dreamed one night that a white elephant entered her womb, and 10 months later a child emerged from her right side. He was able to talk and walk from birth, and with each step he took, a lotus flower sprung up under his foot. He was raised in luxury by an adoring father, who sought to protect him from the sight and knowledge of evil and the ills of the world, including sickness and death. He married a beautiful princess at age 16 and enjoyed life in the numerous palaces his father had given him. One day, according to legend, he rode forth from the palace in his chariot after his father had cleared the route of all aged and sick people. By the roadside he saw an aged man who had escaped notice, and on later trips he saw a sick man and a corpse on a litter. Shocked by his first experience with old age, sickness, and death, the prince decided to seek a better way of living.

Soon he renounced the world and took up the life of self-denial, to the point of almost starving himself to death. After concluding that this was not the best way to gain insight into life's meanings, he decided to sit under the Bo tree, which Buddhists call the tree of wisdom, and meditate until he found the

Seated Buddha with attendants, carved ivory sculpture from Kashmir, c. 8th century CE.

answer. At first he was tempted by a demon, but he triumphed over him and continued to meditate. Finally, Siddhartha Gautama experienced a spiritual awakening, known as "the Enlightenment." Once he was awakened to the truth, he became the Buddha and devoted his life to sharing his teachings with others. Preaching at first to only five followers, he soon founded an order of monks. For 45 years he traveled throughout northern India teaching and giving private counseling. He died, or achieved Nirvana (as Buddhists believe), at the age of 80 after sharing a meal with a blacksmith. He was then cremated, and his relics were distributed to his followers and housed in stupas throughout India.

Buddha did not claim to be of divine origin, nor did he claim revelation from above. He meditated, but he prayed to no higher being. The Buddha accepted the belief, as did the religion of his time, that life was a continuous cycle of rebirth. Life was suffering, and his teachings offered a way out of suffering and rebirth.

In a sermon at Benares (now Varanasi, India), Buddha set forth his beliefs. There is a middle way of life between the extremes of self-indulgence and self-mortification. To pursue the middle way, one must recognize the Four Noble Truths. They may be briefly stated as follows: Human life is an existence of suffering. Human suffering is caused by desire for things that cannot satisfy the spirit. Suffering can be ended and man set free by renouncing these desires, which are rooted in ignorance. Man can free himself of desire by following the Noble Eightfold Path of right views, right aspirations, right speech, right behavior, right mode of livelihood, right efforts, right thoughts, and right contemplation.

In everyday life, the Eightfold Path requires that the individual do no harm to any creature and adopt a vegetarian diet. Expressly forbidden are theft, falsehood, unchastity, strong drink, and the taking of life. As a rule of conduct Buddha taught the Golden Rule. He believed in the statement that "all that we are is the result of what we have thought."

In February 1996 a team of United Nations–sponsored archaeologists announced that they had discovered the ancient birth chamber of Prince Siddhartha beneath the Mayadevi temple in Lumbini, more than 200 miles (350 kilometers) southwest of the Nepalese capital, Kathmandu. The discovery settled an international debate over whether Buddha was born in India or Nepal.

The archaeologists excavated 15 chambers more than 16 feet (4.9 meters) beneath the ancient temple. A key find was a commemorative stone placed atop a platform of seven layers of bricks dating to 249 BCE. According to ancient Buddhist literature, that was the year in which Emperor Asoka, the ruler credited with expanding Buddhism into East Asia, placed a stone on top of a pile of bricks at the birthplace of Prince Siddhartha. Archaeologists also discovered a memorial pillar built by Asoka at the site, a terra-cotta figure of Siddhartha and his wife, and silver and copper coins.

The United Nations and the government of Nepal announced plans to build a center for world peace at the Lumbini site. Officials expected that the temple would become a shrine for the more than 380 million Buddhists around the world.

ZHUANGZI

(b. c. 369 BCE, Meng [now Shangqiu, Henan Province], China—d. 286 BCE)

Zhuangzi was the most significant of China's early interpreters of Daoism, whose work (Zhuangzi) is considered one of the definitive texts of Daoism and is thought to be more comprehensive than the Daodejing, which is attributed to Laozi, the first philosopher of Daoism. Zhuangzi's teachings also exerted a great influence on the development of Chinese Buddhism and had considerable effect on Chinese landscape painting and poetry.

In spite of his importance, details of Zhuangzi's life, apart from the many anecdotes about him in the *Zhuangzi* itself, are unknown. The "Grand Historian" of the Han dynasty, Sima Qian (died c. 87 BCE), incorporated in his biographical sketch of Zhuangzi only the most meagre information. It indicates that Zhuangzi was a native of the state of Meng, that his personal name was Zhou, and that he was a minor official at Qiyuan in his home state. He lived during the reign of Prince Wei of Chu (died 327 BCE) and was therefore a contemporary of Mencius, an eminent Confucian scholar known as China's Second Sage. According to Sima Qian, Zhuangzi's teachings were drawn primarily from the sayings of Laozi, but his perspective was much broader. He used his literary and philosophical skills to refute the Confucians and Mohists (followers of Mozi, who advocated "concern for everyone").

Zhuangzi is best known through the book that bears his name, the *Zhuangzi*, also known as *Nanhua zhenjing* ("The Pure Classic of Nanhua"). At about the turn of the 4th century CE, Guo Xiang, the first and perhaps the best commentator on the *Zhuangzi*, established the work as a primary source for Daoist thought. It is composed of 33 chapters, and evidence suggests that there may have been as many as 53 chapters in copies of the book circulated in the 4th century. It is generally agreed that the first seven chapters, the "inner books," are for the most part from the hand of Zhuangzi himself, whereas the "outer books" (chapters 8–22) and the miscellany (chapters 23–33) are largely the product of his later followers. A vivid description of Zhuangzi's character comes from the anecdotes about him in the book's later chapters.

ASHOKA

(b. 304 BCE –d. 238? BCE, India)

Ashoka was the last major emperor in the Mauryan dynasty of India. His vigorous patronage of Buddhism during his reign (c. 265–238 BCE; also given as c. 273–232 BCE) furthered the expansion of that religion throughout India. Following his successful but bloody conquest of the Kalinga country on the east coast, Ashoka renounced armed conquest and adopted a policy that he called "conquest by dharma" (i.e., by principles of right life).

In order to gain wide publicity for his teachings and his work, Ashoka made them known by means of oral announcements and by engravings on rocks and pillars at suitable sites. These inscriptions—called the rock edicts and pillar edicts (e.g., the lion capital of the pillar found at Sarnath, which has become India's national emblem), mostly dated in various years of his reign—contain statements regarding his thoughts and actions and provide information on his life and acts. His utterances rang of frankness and sincerity.

According to his own accounts, Ashoka conquered the Kalinga country (modern Orissa state) in the eighth year of his reign. The sufferings that the war inflicted on the defeated people moved him to such remorse that he renounced armed conquests. It was at this time that he came in touch with Buddhism and adopted it. Under its influence and prompted by his own dynamic temperament, he resolved to live according to, and preach, the dharma and to serve his subjects and all humanity.

Ashoka repeatedly declared that he understood dharma to be the energetic practice of the sociomoral virtues of honesty, truthfulness, compassion, mercifulness, benevolence, nonviolence, considerate behaviour toward all, "little sin and many good deeds," nonextravagance, nonacquisitiveness, and noninjury to animals. He spoke of no particular mode of religious creed or worship, nor of any philosophical doctrines. He spoke of Buddhism only to his coreligionists and not to others.

Toward all religious sects he adopted a policy of respect and guaranteed them full freedom to live according to their own principles, but he also urged them to exert themselves for the "increase of their inner worthiness." Moreover, he exhorted them to respect the creeds of others, praise the good points of others, and refrain from vehement adverse criticism of the viewpoints of others.

To practice the dharma actively, Ashoka went out on periodic tours preaching the dharma to the rural people and relieving their sufferings. He ordered his high officials to do the same, in addition to attending to their normal duties; he exhorted administrative officers to be constantly aware of the joys and sorrows of the common folk and to be prompt and impartial in dispensing justice. A special class of high officers, designated "dharma ministers," was appointed to foster dharma work by the public, relieve sufferings wherever found, and look to the special needs of women, of people inhabiting outlying regions, of neighbouring peoples, and of various religious communities. It was ordered that matters concerning public welfare were to be reported to him at all times. The only glory he sought, he said, was for having led his people along the path of dharma. No doubts are left in the minds of readers of his inscriptions regarding his earnest zeal for serving his subjects. More success was attained in his work, he said, by reasoning with people than by issuing commands.

Among his works of public utility were the founding of hospitals for men and animals and the supplying of medicines, and the planting of roadside trees and groves, digging of wells, and construction of watering sheds and rest houses. Orders were also issued for curbing public laxities and preventing cruelty to animals. With the death of Ashoka, the Mauryan Empire disintegrated and his work was discontinued. His memory survives for what he attempted to achieve and the high ideals he held before himself.

Most enduring were Ashoka's services to Buddhism. He built a number of stupas (commemorative burial mounds) and monasteries and erected pillars on which he ordered inscribed his understanding of religious doctrines. He took strong measures to suppress schisms within the *sangha* (the Buddhist religious community) and prescribed a course of scriptural studies for adherents. The Sinhalese chronicle Mahavamsa says that when the order decided to send preaching missions abroad, Ashoka helped them enthusiastically and sent his own son and daughter as missionaries to Sri Lanka. It is as a result of Ashoka's patronage that Buddhism, which until then was a small sect confined to particular localities, spread throughout India and subsequently beyond the frontiers of the country.

A sample quotation that illustrates the spirit that guided Ashoka is:

All men are my children. As for my own children I desire that they may be provided with all the welfare and happiness of this world and of the next, so do I desire for all men as well.

JUDAS MACCABEUS

(b. ?–d. 161/160 BCE)

Judas Maccabeus was a Jewish guerrilla leader who defended his country from invasion by the Seleucid king Antiochus IV Epiphanes, preventing the imposition of Hellenism upon Judaea, and preserving the Jewish religion.

The son of Mattathias, an aged priest who took to the mountains in rebellion when Antiochus attempted to impose the Greek religion on the Jews, Judas took over the rebel leadership on his father's death and proved to be a military genius, overthrowing four Seleucid armies in quick succession and restoring the Temple of Jerusalem. This deed is celebrated in the Jewish festival of lights, Ḥanukka. On Antiochus's death in 164 BCE, the Seleucids offered the Jews freedom of worship, but Judas continued the war, hoping to free his nation politically as well as religiously. Although he himself was killed two years later, his younger brothers took over the fight, finally securing the independence of Judaea.

MARY

(flourished beginning of the Christian Era)

(b. c. 18 BCE–d. 43 CE)

Through the many centuries of church history, the mother of Jesus achieved a status second only to Jesus himself in the Roman Catholic, Eastern Orthodox, and other churches. She has been the focus of much debate and the subject of some of the greatest art in the Western world. Many of the finest medieval cathedrals are dedicated to her—including the Gothic masterpiece in Chartres, France.

In some denominations she has been venerated and worshiped, while in others she has been almost entirely ignored. It is believed that she has made appearances to the faithful throughout the history of Christianity. Probably the most famous was a vision perceived in 1917 by three children at Fatima, Portugal. The varying viewpoints regarding Mary are the result of strong doctrinal differences as well as of diverse interpretations of the New Testament. She has never ceased to play a role in the religious, cultural, and social life of the West. Often ignored is the influence she has had on the status of women.

The only reliable written accounts are in the first five books of the New Testament—the Gospels and the Book of Acts. Of her ancestry, background, childhood, and later life, there is no written testimony in the Bible itself. Luke's Gospel introduces her as a young girl living in Nazareth, a town well north of Jerusalem. She is engaged to Joseph, a local carpenter. She is confronted by an angel who tells her she has been chosen to bear an infant who will become the savior of Israel. Both Luke and Matthew tell of the birth of Jesus in detail.

Neither Mark nor John included these stories in their Gospels. The focus in all four books is on Jesus himself. Mary makes a number of appearances, occasionally accompanied by men who are said to be brothers of Jesus. During these episodes she is accorded no special honor by Jesus or his followers. At the end of his life she is in Jerusalem for the crucifixion, and she is mentioned in the Book of Acts as a member of the early church in Jerusalem. But it is only at the beginning and end of his life that she plays prominent roles. It is very likely that she understood no more about him and his work than did his other followers during his lifetime.

In his letters St. Paul makes only one vague reference to her when he uses the phrase "born of woman" to describe Jesus. The term itself was intended to establish that Jesus was fully human, in contrast to the teaching of some that he did not have a completely human life. Of Mary's later life nothing is known. There is a tradition, probably from the 2nd century, that she went to live in Ephesus in Asia Minor. A cult devoted to her is supposed to have emerged there. This story may have arisen as an attempt to downplay the significance of the Roman goddess Diana, or Greek Artemis, whose great temple stood there.

As Mary came to play a pivotal role in the worship life of the churches, several teachings about her emerged. Among these are the doctrines of the virgin birth, her perpetual virginity, the title Mother of God, the Immaculate Conception, and the Assumption into heaven.

The doctrine that Jesus was born of a virgin is loosely based on the Gospels of Luke and Matthew, but the term virgin birth is not used in either place. As a teaching it arose in the 2nd century in a book called the Protoevangelium of St. James. Gradually the doctrine came to be accepted by all the churches.

From the fact that she was chosen by God to be the mother of Jesus, it was deduced that Mary was herself a pure and sinless human being. It was further assumed that she remained a virgin throughout her life and had no more children. This, of course, is contradicted by the New Testament accounts. Defenders of the teaching say that the brothers of Jesus are really sons of Joseph by a previous marriage or are perhaps cousins.

As a faultless human being, Mary too had to have been born without sin. The theologian Thomas Aquinas taught that all original sin was extinguished within her before she was born. The theologian Duns Scotus asserted that she was free of sin from the moment of conception. Hence arose the doctrine of the Immaculate Conception, which became a dogma in the Roman Catholic Church in 1854.

Mary's exalted position also earned her the titles Mother of God and Coredemptrix, suggesting that she played an active role in the redemption of mankind along with her son. The Mother of God title was applied early in church history, based on the notion that Jesus was fully God as well as human. This was established as a doctrine in the 4th century. In the Eastern churches this doctrine played a major devotional role and became a favorite subject for icon painters. During the Reformation era it was accepted by both Catholic and Protestant scholars, though Mary's role in Protestant theology has declined markedly since then.

The Assumption is the most recent dogma to be promulgated about Mary. Most Roman Catholics had come to believe that Mary was taken up to heaven bodily. By the 1860s many were petitioning that this belief be stated as a dogma—something that must be believed. The church was at first reluctant to do so because there is no evidence for such a teaching either in the New Testament or in early church history. In 1950 Pope Pius XII finally confirmed the dogma, leaving open the question as to whether she had died first.

JESUS

(b. c. 6–4 BCE, Bethlehem—d. c. 30 CE, Jerusalem)

Jesus Christ was a religious leader who is revered in Christianity, one of the world's major religions. He is regarded by most Christians as the Incarnation of God.

Ancient Jews usually had only one name, and, when greater specificity was needed, it was customary to add the father's name or the place of origin. Thus, in his lifetime Jesus was called Jesus son of Joseph (Luke 4:22; John 1:45, 6:42), Jesus of Nazareth (Acts 10:38), or Jesus the Nazarene (Mark 1:24; Luke 24:19). After his death he came to be called Jesus Christ. Christ was not originally a name but a title derived from the Greek word *christos*, which translates the Hebrew term *meshiah* (Messiah), meaning "the anointed one." This title indicates that Jesus's followers believed him to be the anointed son of King David, whom some Jews expected to restore the fortunes of Israel. Passages such as Acts of the Apostles 2:36 show that some early Christian writers knew that Christ was properly a title, but in many passages of the New Testament, including those in the letters of the Apostle Paul, the name and title are combined and used together as Jesus's name: Jesus Christ or Christ Jesus (Romans 1:1; 3:24). Paul sometimes simply used Christ as Jesus's name (e.g., Romans 5:6).

Although born in Bethlehem, according to Matthew and Luke, Jesus was a Galilean from Nazareth, a village near Sepphoris, one of the two major cities of Galilee (Tiberias was the other). He was born to Joseph and Mary sometime between 6 BCE and shortly before the death of Herod the Great (Matthew 2; Luke 1:5) in 4 BCE. According to Matthew and Luke, however, Joseph was only legally his father. They report that Mary was a virgin when Jesus was conceived and that she "was found to be with child from the Holy Spirit" (Matthew 1:18; cf. Luke 1:35). Joseph is said to have been a carpenter (Matthew 13:55)—that is, a craftsman who worked with his hands—and, according to Mark 6:3, Jesus also became a carpenter.

Luke (2:41–52) states that Jesus as a child was precociously learned, but there is no other evidence of the nature of his childhood or early life. As a young adult, he went to be baptized by the prophet John the Baptist and shortly thereafter became an itinerant preacher and healer (Mark 1:2–28). In his mid-30s Jesus had a short public career, lasting perhaps less than one year, during which he attracted considerable attention. Sometime between 29 and 33 CE — possibly 30 CE — he went to observe Passover in Jerusalem, where his entrance, according to the Gospels, was triumphant and infused with eschatological significance. While there he was arrested, tried, and executed. His disciples became convinced that he still lived and had appeared to them. They converted others to belief in him, which eventually led to a new religion, Christianity.

The only substantial sources for the life and message of Jesus are the Gospels of the New Testament, the earliest of which was Mark (written 60–80 CE), followed by Matthew, Luke, and John (75–90 CE). Some additional evidence can be found in the letters of Paul, which were written beginning in 50 CE and are the earliest surviving Christian texts. There are, however, other sources that may have further information. Noncanonical sources, especially the apocryphal gospels, contain many sayings attributed to Jesus, as well as stories about him that are occasionally held to be "authentic." Among these apocrypha is the Gospel of Judas, a gnostic text of the 2nd century CE that portrays Judas as an important collaborator of Jesus and not his betrayer. Another important text, the mid-2nd-century-CE Gospel of Thomas, has attracted much attention. A "sayings" gospel (114 sayings attributed to Jesus, without narrative), it is grounded in gnosticism, the philosophical and religious movement of the 2nd century CE that stressed the redemptive power of esoteric knowledge acquired by divine revelation. For Thomas, salvation consists of self-knowledge, and baptism results in restoration to the primordial state — man and woman in one person, like Adam before the creation of Eve (saying 23). Spiritual reversion to that state meant that nakedness need not result in shame. One passage (saying 37) allows it to be suspected that the early Christian followers of the Gospel of Thomas took off their garments and trampled on them as part of their baptismal initiation. There are a few connections between this worldview and that of Paul and the Gospel According to John, but the overall theology of the Gospel of Thomas is so far removed from the teaching of Jesus as found in the Gospels of Matthew, Mark, and Luke—in which Jewish eschatology is central—that it is not considered a major source for the study of Jesus. It is, of course, possible or even likely that individual sayings in Thomas or other apocryphal gospels originated with Jesus, but it is unlikely that noncanonical sources can contribute much to the portrait of the historical Jesus. As in the case of the Gospel of Thomas, the traditions found in other apocryphal gospels are often completely unlike the evidence of the canonical gospels and are embedded in documents that are generally believed to be unreliable.

There are a few references to Jesus in 1st-century Roman and Jewish sources. Documents indicate that within a few years of Jesus's death, Romans were aware that someone named Chrestus (a slight misspelling of Christus) had been responsible for disturbances in the Jewish community in Rome (Suetonius, *The Life of the Deified Claudius* 25.4). Twenty years later, according to Tacitus, Christians in Rome were prominent enough to be persecuted by Nero, and it was known that they were devoted to Christus, whom Pilate had executed (*Annals* 15.44). This knowledge of Jesus, however, was dependent on familiarity with early Christianity and does not provide independent evidence about Jesus. Josephus wrote a paragraph about Jesus (*The Antiquities of the Jews* 18.63ff.)—as he did about Theudas, the Egyptian, and other charismatic leaders (*History of the Jewish War* 2.258–263; *The Antiquities of the Jews* 20.97–99, 167–172)—but it has been heavily revised by Christian scribes, and Josephus's original remarks cannot be discerned.

The letters of Paul contain reliable but meagre evidence. Their main theme, that Jesus was crucified and raised from the dead, is especially prominent in 1 Corinthians 15, where Paul evokes an early tradition about Jesus's death and subsequent appearances to his followers. The Crucifixion and Resurrection were accepted by all first-generation Christians. Paul also quotes a few of Jesus's sayings: the prohibition of divorce and remarriage (1 Corinthians 7:10–11), the words over the bread and cup at Jesus's Last Supper (1 Corinthians 11:23–25), and a prediction of the imminent arrival of the Saviour from heaven (1 Thessalonians 4:15–17).

Fuller information about Jesus is found in the Gospels of the New Testament, though those are not of equal value in reconstructing his life and teaching. The Gospels of Matthew, Mark, and Luke agree so closely with one another that they can be studied together in parallel columns in a work called a synopsis and are hence called the Synoptic Gospels. John, however, is so different that it cannot be reconciled with the Synoptics except in very general ways (e.g., Jesus lived in Palestine, taught, healed, was crucified and raised). In the Synoptics Jesus's public career appears to have lasted less than one year, since only one Passover is mentioned, but in John three Passovers occur, implying a ministry of more than two years. In all four Gospels Jesus performs miracles, especially healings, but, while exorcisms are prevalent in the Synoptics, there are none in John. The greatest differences, though, appear in the methods and content of Jesus's teaching. In the Synoptic Gospels he speaks about the kingdom of God in short aphorisms and parables, making use of similes and figures of speech, many drawn from agricultural and village life. He seldom refers to himself, and, when asked for a "sign" to prove his authority, he refuses (Mark 8:11–12). In John, on the other hand, Jesus employs long metaphorical discourses, in which he himself is the main subject. His miracles are described as "signs" that support the authenticity of his claims.

Scholars have unanimously chosen the Synoptic Gospels' version of Jesus's teaching. The verdict on the miracles is the same, though less firmly held: in all probability Jesus was known as an exorcist, which resulted in the charge that he cast out demons by the prince of demons (Mark 3:22–27). The choice between the narrative outline of the Synoptics and that of John is less clear. Besides presenting a longer ministry than do the other Gospels, John also describes several trips to Jerusalem. Only one is mentioned in the Synoptics. Both outlines are plausible, but a ministry of more than two years leaves more questions unanswered than does one of a few months. It is generally accepted that Jesus and his disciples were itinerant, that they traveled around Galilee and its immediate environs and that Jesus taught and healed in various towns and villages as well as in the countryside and on the shore of the Sea of Galilee. But where did they spend their winters? Who supported them? None of the Gospels explains how they lived (though Luke 8:1–3 alludes to some female supporters), but the omission is even more glaring in John, where the longer ministry presumes the need for winter quarters, though none are mentioned. That and other considerations are not decisive, but the brief career of the Synoptic Gospels is slightly to be preferred.

The Synoptic Gospels, then, are the primary sources for knowledge of the historical Jesus. They are not, however, the equivalent of an academic biography of a recent historical figure. Instead, the Synoptic Gospels are theological documents that provide information the authors regarded as necessary for the religious development of the Christian communities in which they worked. The details of Jesus's daily life are almost entirely lacking, as are such important features as his education, travel, and other developmental experiences. The characters on the whole are "flat": emotions, motives, and personalities are seldom mentioned. There are nevertheless a few exceptions that show how little is actually known: Peter wavers (Matthew 14:28–31; Mark 14:66–72), James and John ask for preferential treatment in the coming kingdom (Mark 10:35–40), and Pilate anguishes over the decision to execute Jesus (Matthew 27:15–23; Luke 23:2–25). On the other hand, the Pharisees and scribes periodically challenge Jesus and then disappear, with little indication of what, from their point of view, they hoped to accomplish. Even Jesus is a rather flat character in the Gospels. He is sometimes angry and sometimes compassionate (Mark 3:5; 6:34, respectively), but one can say little more. This is a frustrating aspect of the Gospels. The situation is different with regard to Paul, whose letters are extant and self-revelatory. The force of his personality is in the letters, but the force of Jesus's personality must be found somewhere behind the Gospels.

The Gospels comprise brief self-contained passages, or pericopes (from the Greek word *perikopē* meaning "cut around"), relating to Jesus. Further study reveals that the authors of the Synoptic Gospels moved the pericopes around, altering the contexts to suit their own editorial policies—for example, by arranging the pericopes according to subject matter. In chapters 8 and 9, Matthew collects 10 healing pericopes, with a few other passages interspersed. Mark and Luke contain most of those passages, but their arrangements are different. Table 1 delineates the Synoptics' accounts of 10 of Jesus's healings. Matthew put all those healings in one place, whereas Mark and Luke scattered them but in different ways. Since the authors of the Gospels rearranged the material to suit their own needs, it must be assumed that earlier Christian teachers had also organized stories about Jesus didactically. That means that the sequence of events in Jesus's ministry is unknown.

Moreover, the Evangelists and other early Christian teachers also shaped the material about Jesus. During the course of transmission, the factual narrative elements that surrounded each saying or event were stripped away, leaving only a central unit, which was applied to various situations, with the addition of new introductions and conclusions. For example, both Matthew and Luke relate the Parable of the Lost Sheep. In Matthew 18:12–14, the parable is told to the disciples, and the meaning is that they, like the shepherd, should go in search of the lost. In Luke 15:4–7 the same story is directed at the Pharisees, this time to instruct them not to grumble because Jesus has attracted repentant sinners. Both applications of the parable were useful homiletically and were therefore preserved. The context in which Jesus originally used the parable, however, is unknown. Another example is the saying "love your enemies" (Matthew 5:44). Homiletically, it may be applied to numerous circumstances, which makes it very useful for sermons and teaching. Historically, however, it is not known to whom Jesus referred when he spoke those words. The lack of firm knowledge of original context makes the precise interpretation of individual passages difficult.

Further, not all the sayings and deeds in the Synoptic Gospels are reports of things that Jesus actually said and did. Believing that Jesus still lived in heaven, the early Christians spoke to him in prayer and sometimes he answered (2 Corinthians 12:8–9; cf. 1 Corinthians 2:13). Those early Christians did not distinguish between "the historical Jesus" and "the heavenly Lord" as firmly as most modern people do, and some sayings heard in prayer almost certainly ended up in the Gospels as sayings uttered by Jesus during his lifetime.

Since both the original context of Jesus's sayings and deeds and those passages in the Gospels that go back to the historical Jesus are unknown, there are substantial difficulties in attempting to reconstruct the Jesus of history. Of these two difficulties, the lack of immediate context is the more serious. It must be admitted that, on many points, precision and nuance in describing the teaching and ministry of Jesus cannot be achieved.

There are, however, tests of authenticity that make it possible to acquire good general information about Jesus's teachings. One of the most important of these is "multiple attestation": a passage that appears in two or more independent sources is likely to be authentic. A prime example is the prohibition of divorce, which appears in the letters of Paul and in two different forms in the Synoptic Gospels. The short form, which is focused on remarriage after divorce, is found in Matthew 5:31–32 and Luke 16:18. The long form, which is more absolute in prohibiting divorce, appears in Matthew 19:1–12 and Mark 10:1–12. Paul's version (1 Corinthians 7:10–11) agrees most closely with the short form. Because of that excellent attestation, it is almost indisputable that Jesus opposed divorce and especially remarriage after divorce, though study of the five passages does not reveal precisely what he said.

A second test is "against the grain of the Gospels": a passage that seems to be contrary to one of the main themes or views expressed in one or more Gospels is likely to be authentic because the early Christians were not likely to have created material with which they disagreed. Matthew's depiction of John the Baptist is a good example. The author apparently found it to be embarrassing that Jesus received John's baptism of repentance (why would Jesus have needed it?). Thus, he has John protest against the baptism and claim that Jesus should instead baptize him (Matthew 3:13–17; this objection is not in Mark or Luke). Those verses in Matthew assume that John recognized Jesus as being greater than he, but Matthew later shows John, in prison, sending a message to ask Jesus whether he was "the one who is to come" (Matthew 11:2–6). Those passages make it virtually certain that John baptized Jesus and highly probable that John asked Jesus who he was. John's protest against baptizing Jesus appears to be Matthew's creation. In keeping those passages while, in effect, arguing against them, Matthew validates the authenticity of the tradition that John baptized Jesus and later enquired about his true identity.

These are only a few examples of tests that may confirm the authenticity of passages in the Gospels. In many cases, however, the criteria do not apply: many passages neither meet nor fail the tests. Grouping passages into categories—probable, improbable, possible but unconfirmed—is a useful exercise but does not go very far toward determining a realistic portrayal of Jesus as a historical figure. More is needed than just the minute study of the Gospels, though that is an essential task.

Good historical information about Jesus can be acquired by establishing the overall context of his public ministry. As noted earlier, he began his career by being baptized by John, an eschatological prophet, and an understanding of eschatology is pivotal to interpreting Jesus's world. Although eschatology is the doctrine of last things, the Jews who anticipated future redemption did not expect the end of the world. Instead, they thought that God would intervene in human history and make the world perfect: that is, the Jews would live in the Holy Land free of foreign domination and in peace and prosperity. Many Jews, including John, expected final judgment to precede this golden age, and he taught that people should repent in view of its imminence (Matthew 3:1–12; Luke 3:3–9). Since Jesus accepted John's baptism, he must have agreed with this message, at least in part. After Jesus's death and resurrection, his followers believed that he would soon return to bring in the kingdom of God. The clearest expression of this belief is offered by Paul, whose earliest letter indicates that the Lord will return before most of the people then alive die (1 Thessalonians 4:13–18). If Jesus began his career by being baptized by an eschatological prophet and if after his Crucifixion his followers expected him to return to save them (1 Thessalonians 1:9–10; 1 Corinthians 15:20–28), it is highly probable that he himself shared the basic views of Jewish eschatology.

Many aspects of Jesus's career support the view that he expected divine intervention. One of the most common beliefs of Jewish eschatology was that God would restore the Twelve Tribes of Israel, including the Ten Lost Tribes. That Jesus shared this view is indicated by his call of 12 disciples, who apparently represented the 12 tribes (Matthew 19:28). Moreover, he proclaimed the arrival of the kingdom of God; he predicted the destruction of the Temple (Mark 13:2) and possibly its rebuilding "without hands" (Mark 14:58); he entered Jerusalem on a donkey, symbolizing his kingship (Mark 11:4–8; Matthew 21:1–11; see Zechariah 9:9 for the symbol); and he had a final meal with his disciples in which he said that he would "drink no more of the fruit of the vine until that day when I drink it in the new kingdom of God" (Mark 14:25). It is no surprise that after his death his disciples formed a small community that expected Jesus to return and inaugurate a kingdom in which the world would be transformed.

In this light, Jesus can be seen as an eschatological prophet, grouped historically in the same general category as John the Baptist and a few other 1st-century Jewish prophets, such as Theudas. Like John, Jesus believed in the coming judgment, but he stressed inclusion more than condemnation and welcomed "customs officers and sinners" in the coming kingdom of God (Matthew 11:18–19; 21:31–32). Moreover, his teaching was multifaceted and rich and was not limited to eschatological expectation.

A prophet and teacher of ethics, Jesus was also a healer and miracle worker. In the 1st century, healers and miracle workers were fairly well known, though not precisely common, and were not considered to be superhuman beings. Jesus himself granted that others were capable of performing miracles, such as exorcisms, regardless of whether they followed him (Matthew 12:27; Mark 9:38–41; 6:7). Thus, the significance of this very important aspect of his life is frequently misunderstood. In Jesus's time, it was accepted that people could heal and perform nature miracles, such as causing rain. The question was, by what power, or spirit, they did so. Some of Jesus's opponents accused him of casting out demons by the prince of demons (Mark 3:19–22; Matthew 12:24; Luke 11:15). He countered that he did so by the spirit of God (Matthew 12:28; Luke 11:20). Obviously, many people disagreed, but this was the issue in Jesus's lifetime—not whether he, like a few others, could perform miracles, but by what power he did so. In his own day, miracles were proof neither of divinity nor of messiahship, and, at most, they might be used to validate an individual's message or way of life.

In about the year 30 CE, Jesus and his disciples went to Jerusalem from Galilee to observe Passover. Presumably they went a week early, as did tens of thousands of other Jews (perhaps as many as 200,000 or 300,000), in order to be cleansed of "corpse-impurity," in accordance with Numbers 9:10–12 and 19:1–22. The Gospels do not mention purification, but they do place Jesus near the Temple in the days preceding Passover. He entered Jerusalem on a donkey, perhaps intending to recall Zechariah 9:9, which Matthew (21:5) quotes: "your king is coming to you, humble, and mounted on a donkey." This touched off a demonstration by his followers, who hailed Jesus as either "Son of David" (Matthew 21:9) or as "the one who comes in the name of the Lord" (Mark

11:9). Matthew speaks of "crowds," which suggests that many people were involved, but the demonstration was probably fairly small. Jerusalem at Passover was dangerous; it was well known to both Caiaphas, who governed the city, and Pilate, the prefect to whom the high priest was responsible, that the festivals were likely times for uprisings. Pilate's troops patrolled the roofs of the porticoes of the Temple. A large demonstration would probably have led to Jesus's immediate arrest, but, because he lived for several more days, it is likely that the crowd was relatively small.

Jesus spent some time teaching and debating (Mark 12) and also told his disciples that the Temple would be destroyed (Mark 13:1–2). On one of the days of purification prior to the Passover sacrifice and meal, he performed his most dramatic symbolic action. He entered the part of the temple precincts where worshipers exchanged coins to pay the annual temple tax of two drachmas or bought pigeons to sacrifice for inadvertent transgressions of the law and as purificatory offerings after childbirth. Jesus turned over some of the tables (Mark 11:15–17), which led "the chief priests and the scribes" ("and the principal men of the people," Luke adds) to plan to have him executed (Mark 11:18; Luke 19:47; cf. Mark 14:1–2).

Later, the disciples found a room for the Passover meal, and one of them bought an animal and sacrificed it in the Temple (Mark 14:12–16; verse 16 states simply, "they prepared the passover"). Judas Iscariot, however, one of the 12, betrayed Jesus to the authorities. At the meal, Jesus blessed the bread and wine, designating the bread "my body" and the wine "my blood of the covenant" (Mark 14:22–25) or "the new covenant in my blood" (Luke 22:20 and 1 Corinthians 11:25). He also stated that he would not drink wine again until he drank it with the disciples in the kingdom (Matthew 26:29).

After supper, Jesus took his disciples to the Mount of Olives to pray. While he was there, Judas led armed men sent by the chief priests to arrest him (Mark 14:43–52). They took Jesus to Caiaphas, who had gathered some of his councillors (called collectively the Sanhedrin). Jesus was first accused of threatening to destroy the Temple, but this charge was not substantiated. Caiaphas then asked him if he was "the Christ, the Son of God." According to Mark (14:61–62), Jesus said "yes" and then predicted the arrival of the Son of Man. According to Matthew (26:63–64), he said, "You say so, but [emphasis added] I tell you that you will see the Son of Man," apparently implying the answer was no. According to Luke he was more ambiguous: "If I tell you, you will not believe" and "You say that I am" (22:67–70). (Some scholars believe that the New International Version misrepresents Jesus's answer in Matthew and Luke.)

Whatever the answer, Caiaphas evidently had already decided that Jesus had to die. He cried "blasphemy" and rent his own garments, a dramatic sign of mourning that the Hebrew Bible prohibits the high priest from making (Leviticus 21:10). The gesture was effective, and the councillors agreed that Jesus should be sent to Pilate with the recommendation to execute him.

It is doubtful that the titles Messiah and Son of God were actually the issue because there was no set meaning for either in 1st-century Judaism. As Mark, reprised by Matthew and Luke, presents the scene, when the attempt to have Jesus executed for threatening the Temple failed, Caiaphas simply declared whatever Jesus said (about which we must remain uncertain) to be blasphemy. This may be what convinced the council to recommend Jesus's execution. It appears, however, that the charges against Jesus that Caiaphas transmitted to Pilate (Mark 15:1–2, 26) may have included the accusation that Jesus claimed to be "king of the Jews."

Although Pilate did not care about the fine points of Jewish law or Jesus's alleged blasphemy, most likely he saw Jesus as a potential troublemaker and therefore ordered his execution. The Gospels of Matthew, Luke, and John ascribe a rather good character to Pilate and show him as troubled over the decision but yielding to Jewish insistence (Matthew 27:11–26; Luke 21:1–25; John 18:28–40). In Luke, for example, Pilate states three times that he finds no fault with Jesus. This passage suggests that the early church, faced with making its way in the Roman Empire, did not wish its leader to be thought of as being truly guilty in Roman eyes. From other evidence Pilate is known to have been callous, cruel, and given to wanton executions (Philo, "On the Embassy to Gaius," 300–302). He was finally dismissed from office for executing a group of Samaritans (Josephus, *Antiquities of the Jews*, 18.85–89), and he probably sent Jesus to his death without anguishing over the decision.

Crucified as would-be "king of the Jews" (Mark 15:26 and parallels Matthew 27:37; Luke 23:38; John 19:19), Jesus also was taunted on the cross as the one who would destroy and rebuild the Temple (Mark 15:29). These two charges help to explain the decision to execute him. Jesus's minor assault on the Temple and prediction of its destruction seem to be what led to his arrest. His own thinking was almost certainly that God would destroy the Temple as part of the new kingdom, perhaps rebuilding it himself (Mark 14:58). The Temple Scroll from Qumran has a similar expectation. Caiaphas and his advisers probably understood Jesus well enough: they knew that he was a prophet, not a demolition expert, and that his disciples could not damage the Temple seriously even if they were allowed to attack its walls with picks and sledges. But someone who spoke about the Temple's destruction, and who turned over tables in its precincts, was clearly dangerous. These were inflammatory acts in a city that, at festival time, was prone to uprisings that could lead to the deaths of many thousands of Jews. Caiaphas probably had the thought that John 11:50 attributes to him, that "it is better to have one man die for the people than to have the whole nation destroyed." The high priest, under Roman rule, was responsible for keeping the peace, and he and his advisers acted accordingly.

The accusation that Jesus claimed to be "king of the Jews" was also sufficient to account for his execution. There is no direct evidence that Jesus ever said, "I am the king," but his preaching on "the kingdom of God" was inflammatory. This phrase could have been interpreted several ways, but it certainly did not mean that Rome would continue to govern Judaea. Many people resented Roman rule, and Rome was quick to dispatch those who became too vocal in their opposition. Nevertheless, Pilate did not think that Jesus and his followers constituted a military threat. Had he thought so, he would have had the disciples, too, executed, either at the time or when they returned to Jerusalem to take up their new mission. Instead, the prefect limited his actions to their charismatic leader and turned Jesus over to his soldiers for execution. They took him and two thieves outside Jerusalem and crucified them.

Although Caiaphas did not think that Jesus could actually destroy the Temple, and Pilate did not believe that he could organize a serious revolt, inflammatory speech was a problem. Moreover, Jesus had a following, the city was packed with pilgrims who were celebrating the exodus from Egypt and Israel's liberation from foreign bondage, and Jesus had committed a small act of violence in the sacred precincts. He was dangerous, and his execution is perfectly understandable in this historical context; that is, he was executed for being what he was, an eschatological prophet. Caiaphas and his councillors fulfilled their mandate to keep the peace and suppress any signs of an uprising. Pilate presumably acted from similar motives. It is unlikely that the responsible parties lost much sleep over their decision; they were doing their duty.

Jesus's proclamation of the kingdom and his apparent threats against the Temple were based on his view that the kingdom was at hand and that he and his disciples would soon feast in it. It is possible that even to the end he expected divine intervention because among his last words was the cry "My God, my God, why have you forsaken me?" (Mark 15:34).

What happened next changed history in a way quite different from what Jesus seems to have anticipated. Some of his followers claimed to have seen him after his death. The details are uncertain since the sources disagree on who saw him and where he was seen (the final sections of Matthew, Luke, and John; the beginning of Acts; and the list in Paul's First Letter to the Corinthians, 15:5–8). According to Matthew, an angel showed the empty tomb to Mary Magdalene and "the other Mary" and instructed them to tell the disciples to go to Galilee. While still in Jerusalem, the two Marys saw Jesus, who told them the same thing, and he appeared once more, to the disciples in Galilee. Matthew's account is implied in Mark 14:28 and 16:7, though the Gospel of Mark does not have a resurrection story, ending instead with the empty tomb (Mark 16:8; translations print scribal additions in brackets). According to Luke, however, while the disciples remained in Jerusalem, the women (Mary Magdalene; Joanna; Mary, the mother of James; and "the other women") found the empty tomb. "Two men in dazzling clothes" told them that Jesus had been raised. Later, Jesus appeared to two followers on the road to Emmaus (near Jerusalem), then to Peter, and later to the disciples. John (now including chapter 21, usually thought to be an appendix) mentions sightings in Galilee and Jerusalem. Acts provides a more extensive series of appearances than Luke, though written by the same author, but like it places all of these in or near Jerusalem. Paul's list of people to whom Jesus appeared does not agree very closely with the other accounts (1 Corinthians 15:5–8).

Because of the uncertain evidence it is hard to say what really happened. Two points are important: the sources describe the resurrected Jesus as neither a resuscitated corpse, a badly wounded man staggering around, nor as a ghost. According to Luke, the first two disciples to see Jesus walked with him for several hours without recognizing him (24:13–32). Luke also reports that Jesus could disappear and reappear at will (24:31, 36). For Paul, the bodies of Christian believers will be transformed to be like the Lord's, and the resurrection body will not be "flesh and blood" (1 Corinthians 15:42–53). According to these two authors, Jesus was substantially transformed, but he was not a ghost. Luke says this explicitly (24:37–39), and Paul insists on using the word "body" as part of the term "spiritual body" rather than "spirit" or "ghost." Luke and Paul do not agree entirely since Luke attributes "flesh and bones" to the risen Jesus (24:39). Luke's account nevertheless requires a transformation. The authors, in other words, were trying to explain something for which they did not have a precise vocabulary, as Paul's term "spiritual body" makes clear.

It is difficult to accuse these sources, or the first believers, of deliberate fraud. A plot to foster belief in the Resurrection would probably have resulted in a more consistent story. Instead, there seems to have been a competition: "I saw him," "so did I," "the women saw him first," "no, I did; they didn't see him at all," and so on. Moreover, some of the witnesses of the Resurrection would give their lives for their belief. This also makes fraud unlikely.

The uncertainties are substantial, but, given the accounts in these sources, certainty is unobtainable. We may say of the disciples' experiences of the Resurrection approximately what the sources allow us to say of the life and message of Jesus: we have fairly good general knowledge, though many details are uncertain or dubious.

ZHANG DAOLING

(b. 34 CE, Pei, Jiangxi, China—d. 156, Hanzhong)

Zhang Daoling was the founder and first patriarch of the Tianshidao ("Way of the Celestial Masters") movement within Daoism.

Zhang settled in the Sichuan area and there studied Daoism sometime during the reign of Shundi (125–144) of the Dong (Eastern) Han dynasty. Zhang claimed to have received a revelation from the great sage Laozi and began to prophesy the coming of a time called Great Peace (Taiping). According to tradition, he composed the Xiang'er commentary to the Daodejing to propagate his movement. He attracted to the movement many followers among both the Chinese and the indigenous ethnic groups in Sichuan. Like other Daoists of his day, Zhang promised physical immortality and longevity to his followers, but unlike the others, he emphasized the importance of religious organization. Consequently, he founded the Way of the Celestial Masters, popularly known as Five Pecks of Rice (Wudoumi) because it required its members as well as its patients to contribute five pecks of rice a year, presumably for the upkeep of the organization.

What made Zhang's movement particularly attractive to the common people was its faith-healing method. Illness, it taught, was a result of sinful mindedness, which could be most effectively cured by making confession to a priest; purification formed the solid foundation of physical health. Probably in imitation of the Han imperial throne, the patriarchate of the movement was made hereditary. It passed from Zhang to his son Zhang Heng and then to his distinguished grandson Zhang Lu, collectively known as the Three Zhangs. Zhang Lu even succeeded in establishing a Daoist theocratic state in Hanzhong commandery (modern Sichuan and part of Shaanxi) toward the end of the Han dynasty (c. 188–215). The basic text the movement used for religious instruction was the Daodejing, accompanied by the Xiang'er.

AKIBA BEN JOSEPH

(b. 40 CE—d. c. 135, Caesarea, Palestine [now in Israel])

Akiba ben Joseph was a Jewish sage and a principal founder of rabbinic Judaism. He introduced a new method of interpreting Jewish oral law (Halakha), thereby laying the foundation of what was to become the Mishna, the first postbiblical written code of Jewish law.

The subject of numerous popular legends, Akiba is said to have been an illiterate shepherd who began to study after the age of 40. His devoted wife, Rachel, supported him both morally and materially during this arduous period of late learning (12 years, according to one account). His principal teachers were the great masters of the Law, Eliezer ben Hyrcanus and Joshua ben Hananiah. Akiba established his academy in Bene Beraq (near present-day Tel Aviv–Yafo), and the leading sages of the following generation, especially Meïr and Simeon ben Yoḥai, were his disciples.

Akiba perfected the method of biblical interpretation called Midrash, whereby legal, sacral, and ethical tenets that had been sanctioned by Jewish oral tradition were viewed as being implied in Scripture. Thus, Scripture, in addition to its overt meaning, is understood as replete with implied teaching; it is, in fact, all encompassing. The "Written Law" of Scripture and the "Oral Law" of tradition are ultimately one. Many midrashic works of the 2nd century originated in Akiba's school. In addition, he collected the oral traditions that regulated the conduct of Jewish personal, social, and religious life and arranged them systematically. (Akiba has been called the father of the Mishna.) His apprehension of Scripture was opposed by the contemporary exegete Rabbi Ishmael ben Elisha, who taught that "the Torah speaks in the language of men" and should not be forced to yield special meanings but instead should be interpreted exclusively by means of set, logical rules of interpretation.

Akiba's importance lies both in his achievements as a rabbinic scholar and in the impact of his personality on his time. He was strict in matters of law ("No pity in judgment!"—i.e., compassion is irrelevant in establishing what the law is or means), but he opposed the death penalty. He respected the role of the woman in life and attributed the redemption of the Israelites from Egyptian bondage to the meritoriousness of the women of that generation. He was modest in his personal life, and he was known for his concern for the poor.

As judge he addressed litigating parties: "Know before whom you are standing. You are standing before him whose word created the world, not before Akiba ben Joseph."

His lectures were on legal subjects, scriptural exegesis, and religious thought. For him the central teaching of Judaism resided in the commandment "love your neighbour as yourself." God's love for man is expressed in that he created man in his image. Man has freedom of will ("Everything is foreseen, yet freedom of choice is given"); his deeds determine his fate, yet his true reward will be granted only in the world to come. In the present life there is much suffering, but "suffering is precious" and man should praise God for it. The people of Israel, who in a special sense are "God's children," have the task to "proclaim the glory of God to all the nations of the world." Akiba interpreted the Song of Solomon as a dialogue of love between Israel and God. For the sake of this love Israel withdraws from the affairs of the world. In these teachings—partly in answer to early Christian tenets—Akiba laid the basis for an ideology of Israel in dispersion among the nations of the world.

About the year 95, Akiba and other sages journeyed to Rome. Arriving at the seaport Puteoli they beheld the power and grandeur of the empire. While his companions wept, remembering the victory of Rome over Judaea some two decades ago, Akiba remained calm. If God is so kind to the wicked Romans, he explained, he will, in the end, be even kinder to Israel. He was equally calm when he visited the ruins of the Jerusalem Temple, destroyed by the Romans in the year 70. The prophecies of doom have come true, he commented; now we may anticipate the fulfillment of the prophecies of reconstruction.

Scholarly opinion is divided on the extent of Akiba's participation in an ill-fated rebellion against Rome (132–135) led by Bar Kokhba (originally Simeon ben Koziba). Some consider Akiba to have been the spiritual force behind the uprising. Others take note of the Talmudic report that Akiba considered Bar Kokhba to be the promised messianic king but see no evidence of further action on his part. Akiba was, it is true, apprehended by the Romans, imprisoned in Caesarea, and finally martyred (c. 135), but his offense is recorded as having been his continued public teaching rather than revolutionary activity. He accepted the agony of martyrdom serenely (he was flayed alive, according to tradition), grateful for the opportunity to fulfill the commandment to "love God...with all your life," which he always interpreted to mean "even when he takes your life." His last words were, "the Lord is one," the final words of the Jewish confession of faith ("Hear, O Israel! The Lord is our God, the Lord is one").

NAGARJUNA

(Lived 2nd century CE)

Nagarjuna was an Indian Buddhist philosopher who articulated the doctrine of emptiness (*shunyata*) and is traditionally regarded as the founder of the Madhyamika ("Middle Way") school, an important tradition of Mahayana Buddhist philosophy.

Very little can be said concerning his life; scholars generally place him in South India during the 2nd century CE. Traditional accounts state that he lived 400 years after the Buddha passed into nirvana (c. 5th–4th century BCE). Some biographies also state, however, that he lived for 600 years, apparently identifying him with a second Nagarjuna known for his Tantric (esoteric) writings. Two of the works attributed to Nagarjuna are verses of advice to a king, which suggests that he achieved some fame during his lifetime. Other sources indicate that he also served as abbot of a monastery and that he was the teacher of Aryadeva, the author of important Madhyamika texts. Numerous commentaries on Nagarjuna's works were composed in India, China, and Tibet.

Although he is best known in the West for his writings on emptiness, especially as set forth in his most famous work, the *Madhyamika-shastra* ("Treatise on the Middle Way," also known as the *Mulamadhyamakakarika*, "Fundamental Verses on the Middle Way"), Nagarjuna wrote many other works on a wide range of topics (even when questions of attribution are taken into account). It is only from a broad assessment of these works that an adequate understanding of his thought can be gained.

Nagarjuna wrote as a Buddhist monk and as a proponent of the Mahayana (Sanskrit: "Greater Vehicle") school, which emphasized the idea of the bodhisattva, or one who seeks to become a buddha; in several of his works he defended the Mahayana sutras as the authentic word of the Buddha. He compiled an anthology, entitled the *Sutrasamuccaya* ("Compendium of Sutras"), consisting of passages from 68 sutras, most of which were Mahayana texts. Nagarjuna is particularly associated with the *Prajnaparamita* ("Perfection of Wisdom") sutras in this corpus. According to legend, he retrieved from the bottom of the sea a perfection-of-wisdom sutra that the Buddha had entrusted to the king of the nagas (water deities) for safekeeping. Nagarjuna also composed hymns of praise to the Buddha and expositions of Buddhist ethical practice.

Despite his monastic background, Nagarjuna addressed his works to a variety of audiences. His philosophical texts were sometimes directed against logicians of non-Buddhist schools, but most often they offered critiques of the doctrines and assumptions of the non-Mahayana Buddhist schools, especially the Sarvastivada (literally, "Asserting Everything That Exists"). Nagarjuna's overriding theme, however, is the bodhisattva's path to buddhahood and the merit and wisdom that the bodhisattva must accumulate in order to achieve enlightenment. By wisdom, Nagarjuna meant the perfection of wisdom, declared in the sutras to be the knowledge of emptiness. Nagarjuna is credited with transforming the sutras' poetic and sometimes paradoxical declarations on emptiness into a philosophical system.

MANI

(b. April 14, 216, southern Babylonia—d. 274?, Gundeshapur)

Mani was an Iranian founder of the Manichaean religion, a church advocating a dualistic doctrine that viewed the world as a fusion of spirit and matter, the original contrary principles of good and evil, respectively.

Before Mani's birth, his father, Patek, a native of Hamadan, had joined a religious community practicing baptism and abstinence. Through his mother Mani was related to the Parthian royal family (overthrown in 224). Information about his life appears to derive from his own writings and the traditions of his church. He grew up at his birthplace, speaking a form of eastern Aramaic. Twice, as a boy and young man, he saw in vision an angel, the "Twin," who, the second time, called him to preach a new religion.

He traveled to India (probably Sind and Turan) and made converts. Favourably received on his return by the newly crowned Persian king, Shāpūr I, he was permitted to preach his religion in the Persian empire during that long reign. There is little information about Mani's life in those years. He probably traveled widely in the western parts of the empire, but later traditions that he visited the northeast seem unsound. Under the reign of the Persian king Bahrām I, however, he was attacked by Zoroastrian priests and was imprisoned by the king at Gundeshapur (Belapet), where he died after undergoing a trial that lasted 26 days.

EUSEBIUS OF CAESAREA

(flourished 4th century, Caesarea Palestinae, Palestine)

Eusebius of Caesarea was a bishop, exegete, polemicist, and historian whose account of the first centuries of Christianity, in his *Ecclesiastical History*, is a landmark in Christian historiography.

Eusebius was baptized and ordained at Caesarea, where he was taught by the learned presbyter Pamphilus, to whom he was bound by ties of respect and affection and from whom he derived the name Eusebius Pamphili (the son or servant of Pamphilus). Pamphilus came to be persecuted for his beliefs by the Romans and died in martyrdom in 310. Eusebius may himself have been imprisoned by the Roman authorities at Caesarea, and he was taunted many years later with having escaped by performing some act of submission.

The work of the scholars of the Christian school at Caesarea extended into all fields of Christian writing. Eusebius himself wrote voluminously as apologist, chronographer, historian, exegete, and controversialist, but his vast erudition is not matched by clarity of thought or attractiveness of presentation. His fame rests on his *Ecclesiastical History*, which he probably began to write during the Roman persecutions and revised several times between 312 and 324. In this work Eusebius produced what may be called, at best, a fully documented history of the Christian church, and, at worst, collections of passages from his sources. In the *Ecclesiastical History* Eusebius constantly quotes or paraphrases his sources, and he thus preserved portions of earlier works that are no longer extant. He had already compiled his *Chronicle*, which was an outline of world history, and he carried this annalistic method over into his *Ecclesiastical History*, constantly interrupting his narrative of the church's history to note the accession of Roman emperors and of the bishops of the four great sees (Alexandria, Antioch, Jerusalem, and Rome). He expanded his work in successive editions to cover events to 324, the year before the Council of Nicaea. Eusebius, however, was not a great historian. His treatment of heresy, for example, is inadequate, and he knew next to nothing about the Western church. His historical works are really apologetic, showing by facts how the church had vindicated itself against heretics and heathens.

Eusebius became bishop of Caesarea (in Palestine) about 313. When about 318 the theological views of Arius, a priest of Alexandria, became the subject of controversy because he taught the subordination of the Son to the Father, Eusebius was soon involved. Expelled from Alexandria for heresy, Arius sought and found sympathy at Caesarea, and, in fact, he proclaimed Eusebius as one of his supporters. Eusebius did not fully support either Arius or Alexander, bishop of Alexandria from 313 to 328, whose views appeared to tend toward Sabellianism (a heresy that taught that God was manifested in progressive modes). Eusebius wrote to Alexander, claiming that Arius had been misrepresented, and he also urged Arius to return to communion with his bishop. But events were moving fast, and at a strongly anti-Arian synod at Antioch, about January 325, Eusebius and two of his allies, Theodotus of Laodicea and Narcissus of Neronias in Cilicia, were provisionally excommunicated for Arian views. When the Council of Nicaea, called by the Roman emperor Constantine I, met later in the year, Eusebius had to explain himself and was exonerated with the explicit approval of the emperor.

In the years following the Council of Nicaea, the emperor was bent on achieving unity within the church, and so the supporters of the Nicene Creed in its extreme form soon found themselves forced into the position of dissidents. Eusebius took part in the expulsion of Athanasius of

Alexandria (335), Marcellus of Ancyra (c. 336), and Eustathius of Antioch (c. 337). Eusebius remained in the emperor's favour, and, after Constantine's death in 337, he wrote his *Life of Constantine*, a panegyric that possesses some historical value chiefly because of its use of primary sources. Throughout his life Eusebius also wrote apologetic works, commentaries on the Bible, and works explaining the parallels and discrepancies in the Gospels.

AUGUSTINE

(b. 354 CE–d. 430 CE)

The bishop of Hippo in Roman Africa for 35 years, St. Augustine lived during the decline of Roman civilization on that continent. Considered the greatest of the Fathers of the Church in the West, he helped form Christian theology.

Augustine was born Aurelius Augustinus on Nov. 13, 354, at Tagaste in the Roman province of Numidia (now Souk-Ahras in Algeria). Although his mother, St. Monica, was a devout Christian, he was not baptized in infancy. His father, Patricius, a wealthy landowner, was a pagan.

In his *Confessions* Augustine wrote seven chapters about an incident in his early life—stealing pears from a neighbor's tree. This sin troubled him for the rest of his life. He also confessed to immoral behavior at the University of Carthage, where he was sent at the age of 16.

Augustine remained in Carthage, teaching rhetoric, until he was 29. Then he went to Rome, taking with him his mistress and his son, Adeodatus. His religion at this time was Manichaeism, which combined Christianity with Zoroastrian elements.

By 386 Augustine was teaching in Milan, where his mother joined him. He came under the influence of the

St. Augustine, fresco by Sandro Botticelli, 1480; in the church of Ognissanti, Florence.

city's great bishop, St. Ambrose, who baptized Augustine and Adeodatus on the following Easter.

From this time Augustine lived as an ascetic. He returned to Africa and spent three years with friends on his family's estate. He was ordained a priest and five years later, in 396, was consecrated a bishop. He spent the remainder of his life in Hippo (now Annaba, Algeria) with his clergy, encouraging the formation of religious communities. Augustine, who was ill when the Vandals besieged Hippo, died on Aug. 28, 430, before the town was taken.

Augustine's most widely read book is *Confessions*, a vivid account of his early life and religious development. *The City of God* was written after 410, when Rome fell to the barbarians. The aim of this book was to restore confidence in the Christian church, which Augustine said would take the place of the earthly city of Rome. During the Middle Ages the book gave strong support to the theory that the church was above the state. Augustine's writings on communal life form the Rule of St. Augustine, the basis of many religious orders.

BODHIDHARMA

(flourished 6th century CE)

B odhidharma was a Buddhist monk who, according to tradition, is credited with establishing the Zen branch of Mahayana Buddhism.

The accounts of Bodhidharma's life are largely legendary, and historical sources are practically nonexistent. Two very brief contemporary accounts disagree on his age (one claiming that he was 150 years old, the other depicting him as much younger) and nationality (one identifies him as Persian, the other as South Indian). The first biography of Bodhidharma was a brief text written by the Chinese monk Daoxuan (flourished 7th century) about a century after

Bodhidharma's death. As his legend grew, Bodhidharma was credited with the teaching that meditation was a return to the Buddha's precepts. He was also credited with aiding the monks of Shaolin Monastery—famous for their prowess in the martial arts—in meditation and training. During the Tang dynasty (618–907), he came to be regarded as the first patriarch of the tradition that was subsequently known as Chan in China, Zen in Japan, Sŏn in Korea, and Thien in Vietnam. Those names correspond to the pronunciation of the Sanskrit word *dhyana* ("meditation") in Chinese, Japanese, Korean, and Vietnamese, respectively. Bodhidharma was also considered to be the 28th Indian patriarch in a direct line of transmission from the Buddha.

Most traditional accounts state that Bodhidharma was a South Indian dhyana master, possibly a Brahman, who traveled to China perhaps in the late 5th century. About 520 he was granted an interview with the Nan (Southern) Liang emperor Wudi, who was noted for his good works. According to a famous story about their meeting, the emperor inquired how much merit (positive karma) he had accrued by building Buddhist monasteries and temples. To the emperor's dismay, Bodhidharma stated that good works performed with the intention of accumulating merit were without value, as they would result in favourable rebirths but would not bring about enlightenment. Another story states that, soon after meeting the emperor, Bodhidharma went to a monastery in Luoyang, where he spent nine years staring at a cave wall in intense concentration. Still another states that, in a fit of anger after repeatedly falling asleep while attempting to practice meditation, he cut off his eyelids. (This is one reason why he was often portrayed in art with an intense wide-eyed stare.) Upon touching the ground, the first tea plant sprang up from that spot. The first two of these legends are like others that seem intended to offer instruction in religious truths or in the importance of concentration in religious practice. The third provided a folkloric basis for the traditional practice among Zen monks of drinking strong tea in order to stay awake during meditation. It also provided an account of the introduction of tea into East Asia.

MUHAMMAD

(b. 570, Mecca, Arabia [now in Saudi Arabia]—d. June 8, 632, Medina)

Muhammad was the founder of the religion of Islam and is accepted by Muslims throughout the world as the last of the prophets of God.

The sources for the study of Muhammad are multifarious and include, first and foremost, the Qurʾān, the sacred scripture of Islam. Although the Qurʾān is considered by Muslims to be the word of God and not of Muhammad, it nevertheless reveals the most essential aspects associated with Muhammad. There are also the sayings of Muhammad himself (Hadith) and accounts of his actions (Sunnah). Furthermore, there are biographies (sīrah) of him going back to the works of Ibn Isḥāq (c. 704–767) in the 9th-century recensions of Ibn Hishām and Yūnus ibn Bukayr. Works of sacred history by later writers such as al-Ṭabarī and al-Thaʿālibī also contain extensive biographies of Muhammad. Then there are the accounts of the *maghāzī* ("battles") that determined the fate of the early Islamic community. The most important of these works is the *Kitāb al-maghāzī of al-Wāqidī* (747–823). The *Kitāb al-ṭabaqāt al-kabīr* of Ibn Saʿd (died 844/845) is another important source on the life of Muhammad, his companions, and later figures in Islamic history. Finally, there are oral traditions. Although usually discounted by positivist historians, oral tradition plays a major role in the Islamic understanding of

Muhammad, just as it does in the Christian understanding of Jesus Christ or the Jewish understanding of Moses and the other ancient prophets of Israel.

Beyond these there are later Western works, many of which, from the 18th century onward, distanced themselves from the polemical histories of earlier Christian authors. These more historically oriented treatments, which generally reject the prophethood of Muhammad, are coloured by the Western philosophical and theological framework of their authors. Many of these studies reflect much historical research, and most pay more attention to human, social, economic, and political factors than to religious, theological, and spiritual matters. It was not until the latter part of the 20th century that Western authors combined rigorous scholarship as understood in the modern West with empathy toward the subject at hand and, especially, awareness of the religious and spiritual realities involved in the study of the life of the founder of a major world religion.

The most common name of Muhammad of Islam, Muhammad ("the Glorified One"), is part of the daily call to prayer (*adhān*); following the attestation to the oneness of God, the believer proclaims, "Verily, I bear witness that Muhammad is the Messenger of God" (*Ashhadu anna Muḥammadan rasūl Allāh*). When this name is uttered among Muslims, it is always followed by the phrase *ṣalla Allāhu 'alayhi wa sallam* ("may God's blessings and peace be upon him"), just as, whenever Muslims mention the name of other prophets such as Abraham, Moses, or Jesus, they recite the words *'alayhi al-salām* ("upon him be [God's] peace"). Muhammad also became widely known in Europe by diverse forms of the name such as Mahon, Mahomés, Mahun, Mahum, and Mahumet (all French), Machmet (German), and Maúmet (Old Icelandic). Moreover, Muhammad is the most popular male name in the Islamic world either by itself or in combination with other names such as ʿAlī and Ḥusayn.

Muhammad, however, has many other names, including "sacred names," which Muslims believe were given to him by God and by which he is called in various contexts. Muslim tradition counts 99 names for Muhammad. Among the most often used and also central to the understanding of his nature is Aḥmad ("the Most Glorified"), which is considered an inner and celestial name for Muhammad. Over the centuries Muslim authorities have believed that, when Christ spoke of the coming reign of the Paraclete, he was referring to Aḥmad. Also of great importance are the names that identify Muhammad as the Prophet, including Nabī ("Prophet") and Rasūl Allāh ("the Messenger of God"). Other names of the Prophet are Ṭaha ("the Pure Purifier and Guide"), Yāsīn ("the Perfect Man"), Muṣṭafā ("the One Chosen"), ʿAbd Allāh ("the Perfect Servant of God"), Ḥabīb Allāh ("the Beloved of God"), Dhikr Allāh ("the Remembrance of God"), Amīn ("the Trusted One"), Sirāj ("the Torch Lighting the True Path"), Munīr ("the Illuminator of the Universe"), Hudā ("the Guide to the Truth"), Ghiyāth ("the Helper"), and Niʿmat Allāh ("the Gift of God"). These and his many other names play a major role in daily Muslim piety and in the practice of Sufism. An understanding of their meaning is essential to gaining any serious knowledge of the Islamic view of Muhammad or what some have called Islamic prophetology.

Both before the rise of Islam and during the Islamic period, Arab tribes paid great attention to genealogy and guarded their knowledge of it with meticulous care. In fact, during Islamic history a whole science of genealogy (ʿilm al-ansāb) developed that is of much historical significance. In the pre-Islamic period, however, this knowledge remained unwritten, and for that very reason it has not been taken seriously by Western historians relying only on written records.

For Muslims, however, the genealogy of Muhammad has always been certain. They trace his ancestry to Ismāʿīl (Ishmael) and hence to the prophet Abraham. This fact was accepted even by medieval European opponents of Islam but has been questioned by modern historians.

According to traditional Islamic sources, Muhammad was born in Mecca in "the Year of the Elephant," which corresponds to the year 570 CE, the date modern Western scholars cite as at least his approximate birth date. A single event gave the Year of the Elephant its name when Abrahah, the king of Abyssinia, sent an overwhelming force to Mecca to destroy the Kaʿbah, the sanctuary Muslims believe to have been built by Adam and reconstructed by Abraham and which Abrahah viewed as a rival to his newly constructed temple in Sanaa in Yemen. According to tradition, the elephant that marched at the head of Abrahah's army knelt as it approached Mecca, refusing to go farther. Soon the sky blackened with birds that pelted the army with pebbles, driving them off in disarray. Thus, the sanctuary that Muslims consider an earthly reflection of the celestial temple was saved, though at the time it served Arab tribes who (with the exception of the *ḥanīfs*, or primordialists) disregarded Abrahamic monotheism.

Soon after this momentous event in the history of Arabia, Muhammad was born in Mecca. His father, ʿAbd Allāh, and his mother, Āminah, belonged to the family of the Banū Hāshim, a branch of the powerful Quraysh, the ruling tribe of Mecca, that also guarded its most sacred shrine, the Kaʿbah. Because ʿAbd Allāh died before Muhammad's birth, Āminah placed all her hopes in the newborn child. Without a father, Muhammad experienced many hardships even though his grandfather ʿAbd al-Muṭṭalib was a leader in the Meccan community. The emphasis in Islamic society on generosity to orphans is related to the childhood experiences of Muhammad as well as to his subsequent love for orphans and the Qur'ānic injunctions concerning their treatment.

In order for Muhammad to master Arabic in its pure form and become well acquainted with Arab traditions, Āminah sent him as a baby into the desert, as was the custom of all great Arab families at that time. In the desert, it was believed, one learned the qualities of self-discipline, nobility, and freedom. A sojourn in the desert also offered escape from the domination of time and the corruption of the city. Moreover, it provided the opportunity to become a better speaker through exposure to the eloquent Arabic spoken by the Bedouins. In this way the bond with the desert and its purity and sobriety was renewed for city dwellers in every generation. Āminah chose a poor woman named Halīmah from the tribe of Banū Sa'd, a branch of the Hawāzin, to suckle and nurture her son. And so the young Muhammad spent several years in the desert.

It was also at this time that, according to tradition, two angels appeared to Muhammad in the guise of men, opened his breast, and purified his heart with snow. This episode, which exemplifies the Islamic belief that God purified his prophet and protected him from sin, was also described by Muhammad: "There came unto me two men, clothed in white, with a gold basin full of snow. Then they laid upon me, and, splitting open my breast, they brought forth my heart. This likewise they split open and took from it a black clot which they cast away. Then they washed my heart and my breast with the snow" (Martin Lings, *Muhammad: His Life, Based on the Earliest Sources*, 1991). Muhammad then repeated the verse, found in the Hadith, "Satan toucheth every son of Adam the day his mother beareth him, save only Mary and her son." Amazed by this event and also noticing a mole on Muhammad's back (later identified in the traditional sources as the sign of prophecy), Halīmah and her husband, Hārith, took the boy back to Mecca.

Muhammad's mother died when he was six years old. Now completely orphaned, he was brought up by his grandfather ʿAbd al-Muṭṭalib, who also died two years later. He was then placed in the care of Abū Ṭālib, Muhammad's uncle and the father of ʿAlī, Muhammad's cousin. Later in life Muhammad would repay this kindness by taking ʿAlī into his household and giving his daughter Fāṭimah to him in marriage.

It is believed that Muhammad grew into a young man of unusual physical beauty as well as generosity of character. His sense of fairness and justice were so revered that the people of Mecca often went to him for arbitration and knew him as al-Amīn, "the Trusted One." His striking appearance is the subject of countless poems in various Islamic languages. Muhammad, according to ʿAlī,

> was neither tall nor lanky nor short and stocky, but of medium height. His hair was neither crispy curled nor straight but moderately wavy. He was not overweight and his face was not plump. He had a round face. His complexion was white tinged with redness. He had big black eyes with long lashes. His brows were heavy and his shoulders broad. He had soft skin, with fine hair covering the line from mid chest to navel. The palms of his hands and the soles of his feet were firmly padded. He walked with a firm gait, as if striding downhill. On his back between his shoulders lay the Seal of Prophethood [a mole], for he was the last of the prophets. (Tosun Bayrak al-Jerrahi al-Halveti, *The Name & the Named: The Divine Attributes of God*, 2000)

Islamic sources indicate that others recognized the mole as the sign of prophethood, including the Christian monk Baḥīrā, who met Muhammad when the Prophet joined Abū Ṭālib on a caravan trip to Syria.

When he was 25 years old, Muhammad received a marriage proposal from a wealthy Meccan woman, Khadījah bint Khuwaylid, whose affairs he was conducting. Despite the fact that she was 15 years older than he, Muhammad accepted the proposal, and he did not take another wife until after her death (though polygyny was permitted and common). She bore him two sons, both of whom died young. It is from the first son, Qāsim, that one of the names of the Prophet, Abū᾿ al-Qāsim ("the Father of Qāsim"), derives. She also bore him four daughters, Zaynab, Ruqayyah, Umm Kulthūm, and Fāṭimah. The youngest, Fāṭimah, who is called the second Mary, had the greatest impact on history of all his children. Shī῾ite imams and sayyids, or sharifs, are thought to be descendants of Muhammad, from the lineage of Fāṭimah and ῾Alī. Khadījah herself is considered one of the foremost female saints in Islam and, along with Fāṭimah, plays a very important role in Islamic piety and in eschatological events connected with the souls of women.

By age 35, Muhammad had become a very respected figure in Mecca and had taken ῾Alī into his household. When he was asked, according to Islamic tradition, to arbitrate a dispute concerning which tribe should place the holy black stone in the corner of the newly built Ka῾bah, Muhammad resolved the conflict by putting his cloak on the ground with the stone in the middle and having a representative of each tribe lift a corner of it until the stone reached the appropriate height to be set in the wall. His reputation stemmed, in part, from his deep religiosity and attention to prayer. He often would leave the city and retire to the desert for prayer and meditation. Moreover, before the advent of his prophecy, he received visions that he described as being like "the breaking of the light of dawn." It was during one of these periods of retreat, when he was 40 years old and meditating in a cave called al-Ḥirā' in the Mountain of Light (Jabal al-Nūr) near Mecca, that Muhammad experienced the presence of the archangel Gabriel and the process of the Qur'ānic revelation began.

In the month of Ramadan, in the year 610, Gabriel, in the form of a man, appeared to Muhammad, asked him to "recite" (*iqra'*), then overwhelmed him with a very strong embrace. Muhammad told the stranger that he was not a reciter. But the angel repeated his demand and embraced him three more times, before the verses of the Qur'ān, beginning with "Recite in the Name of thy Lord who created," were revealed. Although the command *iqra'* is sometimes translated as "read," "recite" is a more appropriate translation because, according to traditional Islamic sources, the Prophet was *ummī* ("unlettered"), meaning that his soul was unsullied by human knowledge and virginal before it received the divine Word. Many Western scholars and some modern Muslim commentators have provided other connotations for the word *ummī*, but "unlettered" has been the traditionally accepted meaning.

In any case, Muhammad fled the cave thinking that he had become possessed by the jinn, or demons. When he heard a voice saying, "Thou art the messenger of God and I am Gabriel," Muhammad ran down the mountain. Gazing upward, he saw the man who had spoken to him in his real form, an angel so immense that in whatever direction the Prophet looked the celestial figure covered the sky, which had turned green, the official colour of Islam to this day. Muhammad returned home, and, when the effect of the great awe in his soul abated, he told Khadījah what had happened. She believed his account and sent for her blind cousin Waraqah, a Christian who possessed much religious wisdom. Having heard the account, Waraqah also confirmed the fact that Muhammad had been chosen as God's prophet, and shortly afterward Muhammad received a second revelation. As the Prophet said later, the revelation would either come through the words of the archangel or be directly revealed to him in his heart. The revelation also was accompanied by the sound of bell-like reverberations. According to Islamic tradition, this was the beginning of the process of the revelation of the Qurʾān that lasted some 23 years and ended shortly before the Prophet's death.

Muhammad first preached his message to the members of his family, then to a few friends, and finally, three years after the advent of the revelation, to the public at large. The first to accept Muhammad's call to become Muslims were Khadījah; ʿAlī; Zayd ibn al-Ḥārith, who was like a son to the Prophet; and Abū Bakr, a venerable member of the Meccan community who was a close friend of the Prophet. This small group was the centre from which Islam grew in ever-wider circles. Besides his family and friends, a number of prominent Meccans embraced Islam. However, most influential figures and families rejected his call, especially those prominent in trade. Even within his family there were skeptics. Although Muhammad gained the support of many of the Banū Hāshim, his uncle Abū Lahab, a major leader of the Quraysh, remained adamantly opposed to Islam and Muhammad's mission. These naysayers feared that the new religion, based on the oneness of God and unequivocally opposed to idolatry, would destroy the favoured position of the Kaʿbah as the centre of the religious cults of various Arab tribes and hence jeopardize the commerce that accompanied the pilgrimage to Mecca to worship idols kept in or on the Kaʿbah.

As Muhammad's message spread, opposition to him grew and was led by ʿAmr ibn Hishām, dubbed Abū Jahl ("Father of Ignorance") by the early Muslims. Abū Jahl even had some early converts tortured, which resulted in the death of one of them named Summayyah. Muhammad himself, unharmed because of the protection of his family and especially his uncle Abū Ṭālib, then gave permission to a number of early disciples to migrate temporarily to Abyssinia, where the country's monarch, the *negus*, received them with kindness and generosity. They joined Muhammad later in Medina.

Meanwhile in Mecca, life for Muhammad and the early Muslims was becoming ever more difficult and dangerous as the result of extreme pressure exerted upon them by the Quraysh rulers of the city. Even the conversions of leaders of the Meccan community, such as ʿUmar al-Khaṭṭāb and ʿUthmān ibn ʿAffān, did not diminish the severe difficulties encountered by Muhammad in his later years in Mecca.

In 619 Muhammad was greatly saddened by the death of two people who were especially close to him, Khadījah and his uncle Abū Ṭālib. Not only was Khadījah his devoted wife of 25 years and the mother of his children, but she was also his friend and counselor. Only after her death did Muhammad marry other women, mostly as a means of creating alliances with various families and tribes. The exception was the daughter of Abū Bakr, ʿĀʾishah, who was betrothed to the Prophet when she was very young and in whose arms he would die in Medina. Later in the year the death of Abū Ṭālib, Muhammad's protector, created a much more difficult situation for him and for the young Islamic community in Mecca. These deaths, combined with Muhammad's lack of success in propagating the message of Islam in the city of Ṭāʾif, severely tested his determination and resolve.

As if by heavenly compensation, during this extremely difficult time Muhammad underwent the supreme spiritual experience of his life. On one of his nightly visits to the Kaʿbah, he fell asleep in the Ḥijr, an uncovered sanctuary attached to the north wall of the Kaʿbah, and experienced the Nocturnal Ascent (Isrā᾽ or Mi῾rāj), which is mentioned in the Qur᾽ān, numerous Hadith, and nearly every work of Islamic sacred history. It has also been described and elaborated on in countless later mystical and philosophical writings. According to traditional accounts, among which there are certain minor variations, Muhammad was taken by the archangel Gabriel on the winged steed Burāq to Jerusalem. From the rock upon which Abraham offered to sacrifice his son (now the site of the Dome of the Rock, one of Islam's earliest and greatest mosques), they ascended through all the higher states of being to the Divine Presence itself. At one point Gabriel explained that he could go no farther because, were he to do so, his wings would be burned; that is, Muhammad had reached a state higher than that of the archangels. Muhammad is said to have received the supreme treasury of knowledge while he stood and then prostrated himself before the divine throne. God also revealed to him the final form and number of the Islamic daily prayers. In addition, it is said that, while going through the higher states of being symbolized by the heavenly spheres, Muhammad met earlier great prophets such as Moses and Jesus.

Traditional Muslims believe that the Mi῾rāj of the Prophet was not only spiritual but also corporeal in the same way that Christ's Ascension was accomplished in both body and spirit, according to traditional Christian belief. Modern Western scholars usually consider Muhammad's experience to be an inner vision or dream, while some modernized Muslims, responding to secularist and rationalistic objections, claim that the Mi῾rāj was only spiritual. The Mi῾rāj is the prototype of spiritual realization in Islam and signifies the final integration of the spiritual, psychic, and physical elements of the human state. Because of its central spiritual importance, the Mi῾rāj has been the source of many major literary and metaphysical works in both prose and poetry, and figures as different as Ibn Sīnā (Avicenna) and Ibn al-ʿArabī have written of its inner meaning. The idea of a journey through the levels of being, symbolized by the celestial spheres, to the presence of God, which marks the peak of the Miʿrāj, even reached Europe and, as some have argued, may have been instrumental in the structure of *The Divine Comedy*, by Dante. The Miʿrāj is also one of the reasons why Muslims hold Jerusalem sacred.

The idea of spreading the message of Islam beyond Mecca grew in Muhammad's mind despite the setback in Ṭāʾif. In or around 621 a delegation from Yathrib, a city north of Mecca, contacted Muhammad and, having heard of his sense of justice and power of leadership, invited him to go to their city and become their leader. At that time Yathrib suffered from constant struggle between its two leading tribes, the ʿAws and the Khazraj, with a sizable Jewish community constituting the third important social group of the city. After some deliberation by Muhammad, a preliminary meeting was held in Al-ʿAqabah (a place in Mina, on the outskirts of Mecca), and during the pilgrimage season of 622 a formal agreement was made with the people of Yathrib, according to which Muhammad and his followers would be protected by the people of that city. Upon finalizing the agreement, Muhammad ordered his followers to leave Mecca in small groups, so as not to attract attention, and to await him in Yathrib.

Finally, he departed one evening with Abū Bakr for Yathrib, using an indirect route after commanding ʿAlī to sleep in the Prophet's bed. The Quraysh, who had decided to get rid of the Prophet once and for all, attacked the house but found ʿAlī in his place. They then set out to find the Prophet. According to the traditional Islamic version, rejected by most modern Western historians, Muhammad and Abū Bakr hid in a cave that was then camouflaged by spiders, which spun webs over its mouth, and birds, which placed their nests in front of the cave. Once the search party arrived at the mouth of the cave, they decided not to go in because the unbroken cobwebs and undisturbed nests seemed to indicate that no one could be inside. This story, mentioned in chapter 9 of the Qur'ān, is of great symbolic importance and is also a popular part of Islamic piety and Sufi literature.

On September 25, 622, Muhammad completed the Hijrah ("migration"; Latin: Hegira) and reached Yathrib, which became known as Madīnat al-Nabī ("City of the Prophet"), or Medina. This momentous event led to the establishment of Islam as a religious and social order and became the starting point for the Islamic calendar. The caliph 'Umar I was the first to use this dating system and established the first day of the lunar month of Muharram, which corresponds to July 16, 622, as the beginning of the Islamic calendar.

Muhammad arrived in Qubā', on the outskirts of Medina, where he ordered the first mosque of Islam to be built. The people of the city came in large numbers to greet him, and each family wanted to take him to its own quarters. Therefore, he said that his camel, Qaṣwrā', should be allowed to go where it willed, and where it stopped, he would stay. A mosque, known later as the Mosque of the Prophet (Masjid al-Nabī), was built in the courtyard next to the house where the camel stopped and Muhammad lived. Muhammad's tomb is in the mosque.

When Muhammad first settled in Medina, his most trusted followers were those who had migrated from Mecca—some before him and some, including 'Alī, shortly after. Soon, however, many Medinans embraced Islam, so the early Islamic community came to consist of the emigrants (*al-muhājirūn*) and the Medinan helpers (*al-anṣār*). A few Medinan families and some prominent figures such as ʿAbd Allāh ibn Ubayy held back, but gradually all the Arabs of Medina embraced Islam. Nevertheless, tribal divisions remained, along with a continued Jewish presence that included wealthy tribes that enjoyed the support of Jewish communities farther north, especially in Khaybar. Muhammad hoped that they would embrace Islam and accept him as a prophet, but that happened in only a few cases. On the contrary, as Muhammad integrated the Medinan community—the muhājirūn and the anṣār and the ʿAws and Khazraj tribes—into an Islamic society, the enmity between Medina's Jewish community and the newly founded Islamic order grew.

During the second year of the Hijrah, Muhammad drew up the Constitution of Medina, defining relations between the various groups in the first Islamic community. Later generations of Islamic political thinkers have paid much attention to the constitution, for Muslims believe that Muhammad created the ideal Islamic society in Medina, providing a model for all later generations. It was a society in which the integration of tribal groups and various social and economic classes was based on social justice. According to Islamic belief, that same year the direction of daily prayers, or the *qiblah*, was changed by divine order from Jerusalem to Mecca, which marked the clear crystallization of Islam as a distinct monotheistic religion. Jerusalem has continued to be revered as the first direction of the prayers chosen by God for Muslims, and, according to Islamic eschatological teachings, the first qiblah will become one with the qiblah at Mecca at the end of time.

It was also in the year 622 that the message of Islam was explicitly defined as a return to the pure monotheism of Abraham, or the primordial monotheism (*al-dīn al-ḥanīf*). Some in the West have called the second year of the Hijrah the period of the establishment of a theocracy led by

Muhammad. But what in fact occurred was the establishment of a nomocracy under Divine Law, with Muhammad as the executor. In any case, from that time until his death, Muhammad not only continued to be the channel for the revelation of the Qur'ān but also ruled the community of Muslims. He was also the judge and supreme interpreter of the law of Medinan society.

The enmity between the Quraysh and Muhammad remained very strong, in part because of the persecution, aggression, and confiscation of property the Muslims suffered at the hands of the Quraysh. On several occasions warriors from Medina intercepted caravans from Mecca going to or coming from Syria, but Muhammad did not want to fight a battle against the Meccans until they marched against the nascent Medinan community and threatened the very future of Islam. At this time the following Qur'ānic verse was revealed: "Permission to fight is granted to those against whom war is made, because they have been wronged, and God indeed has the power to help them. They are those who have been driven out of their homes unjustly only because they affirmed: Our Lord is God" (22:39–40). Muslims saw this verse as a declaration of war by God against the idolatrous Quraysh. In 624 an army of 1,000 assembled by the Quraysh marched against Medina and met a much smaller force of 313 Muslims at a place called Badr on the 17th day of the month of Ramadan. Although the number of those involved was small, this event is seen by Muslims as the most momentous battle of Islamic history, and many later crucial battles were named after it. Muhammad promised all those who were killed at Badr the death of a martyr and direct entry into paradise. Although heavily outnumbered, the Muslims achieved a remarkable victory in which, however, nine of the Companions of the Prophet (al-ṣaḥābah), the close associates of Muhammad and the faithful who were associated directly with him, were killed. Muslims believe that the battle was won with the help of the angels, and to this day the whole episode remains etched deeply in the historical consciousness of Muslims. Although seemingly an insignificant foray in a faraway desert between a few fighters, the battle changed world history.

The Quraysh, however, did not give up their quest to destroy the nascent Islamic community. With that goal in mind, in 624–625 they dispatched an army of 3,000 men under the leader of Mecca, Abū Sufyān. Muhammad led his forces to the side of a mountain near Medina called Uḥud, and battle ensued. The Muslims had some success early in the engagement, but Khālid ibn al-Walīd, a leading Meccan general and later one of the outstanding military figures of early Islamic history, charged Muhammad's left flank after the Muslims on guard deserted their posts to join in the looting of the Quraysh camp. Many of Muhammad's followers then fled, thinking that the Prophet had fallen. In fact, although wounded, he was led to safety through a ravine. Meanwhile, the Quraysh did not pursue their victory. A number of eminent Muslims, including Muhammad's valiant uncle Ḥamzah, however, lost their lives in the struggle. The Jews of Medina, who allegedly plotted with the Quraysh, rejoiced in Muhammad's defeat, and one of their tribes, the Banū Naḍīr, was therefore seized and banished by Muhammad to Khaybar.

The Jews of Medina then urged the Quraysh to take over Medina in 626–627. To this end the Quraysh helped raise an army of 10,000 men, which marched on Medina. Salmān al-Fārsī, the first Persian convert to Islam whom Muhammad had adopted as a member of his household, suggested that the Muslims dig a ditch around the city to protect it, a technique known to the Persians but not to the Arabs at that time. The Meccan army arrived and, unable to cross the ditch, laid siege to the city but without success. The invading army gradually began to disperse, leaving the Muslims victorious in the Battle of the Ditch (al-Khandaq).

When it was discovered that members of the Jewish tribe Qurayẓah had been complicit with the enemy during the Battle of the Ditch, Muhammad turned against them. The Qurayẓah men were separated from the tribe's women and children and ordered by the Muslim general Saʿd ibn Muʿādh to be put to death; the women and children were to be enslaved. This tragic episode cast a shadow upon the relations between the two communities for many centuries, even though the Jews, a "People of the Book" (that is, like Christians and Zoroastrians, as well as Muslims, possessors of a divinely revealed scripture), generally enjoyed the protection of their lives, property, and religion under Islamic rule and fared better in the Muslim world than in the West. Moreover, Muslims believe that the Prophet did not order the execution of the Jews of Medina, but many Western historians believe that he must have been, at the very least, informed of it.

The Islamic community had become more solidly established by 628, and in that year Muhammad decided to make the ʿumrah ("lesser pilgrimage") to the Kaʿbah. He set out for Mecca with a large entourage and many animals meant for sacrifice, but an armed Meccan contingent blocked his way. Because he had intended to perform a religious rite, he did not want to battle the Meccans at that time. So he camped at a site known as Al-Ḥudaybiyah and sent ʿUthmān to Mecca to negotiate a peaceful visit. When ʿUthmān was delayed, Muhammad assembled his followers and had them make a pact of allegiance (al-bayʿah) to follow him under all conditions unto death, an act of great significance for later Islamic history and Sufi belief and practice. ʿUthmān finally returned with Quraysh leaders who proposed as a compromise that Muhammad return to Medina but make a peaceful pilgrimage to Mecca the next year. In addition, a 10-year truce was signed with the Meccans.

In 628–629 Muhammad's first conquest was made when the Muslims captured Khaybar in a battle in which the valour of ʿAlī played an important role. The Jews and Christians of Khaybar were allowed to live in peace, protected by the Muslims, but they were required to pay a religious tax called the jizʿyah. This became the model for the later treatment of People of the Book in Islamic history.

It was also at this time that Muhammad, according to Islamic sources, sent letters inviting various leaders to accept Islam, including Muqawqis, the governor of Alexandria; the negus of Abyssinia; Heraclius, the emperor of Byzantium; and Khosrow II, the king of Persia. There are several letters kept in various libraries today that some claim to be Muhammad's original invitations, although many Western scholars have doubted their authenticity. Few, however, doubt that he sent the letters, although a number of Western scholars believe that they were addressed to the surrogates of these rulers. In any case, he emphasized in these letters that there should be no compulsion for People of the Book—Jews, Christians, or Zoroastrians—to accept Islam.

In 628–629 Muhammad finally made a pilgrimage to Mecca and reconciled members of his family and also of many of his followers. It was also during this pilgrimage that a number of eminent Meccans—including two later major military and political figures, Khālid ibn Walīd and ʿAmr ibn al-ʿĀṣ—accepted Islam and that Muhammad's uncle al-ʿAbbās, then the head of the Banū Hāshim family, is said to have secretly become a Muslim.

Meanwhile, Islam continued to spread throughout Arabia, although military expeditions to the north were not successful. In one battle at Muʾtah in Byzantine territory, Zayd ibn Ḥārith, the adopted son of the Prophet, and Jaʿfar ibn Abī Ṭalib, the brother of ʿAlī, were killed. Still, many northern tribes embraced Islam.

In 628–629 the Quraysh broke the pact agreed upon at Al-Ḥudaybiyah, freeing Muhammad to march on Mecca, which he did with a large group of the *ansār*, the *muhājirūn*, and Bedouins. The Quraysh pleaded for amnesty, which was granted. After many years of hardship and exile, Muhammad entered Mecca triumphantly and directed his followers not to take revenge for the persecution many of them had endured. He went directly to the Kaʿbah, where he ordered ʿAlī and Bilāl, the Abyssinian caller to prayer (*al-muʾadhdhin*), to remove all the idols and restore the original purity of the Kaʿbah, which Muslims believe was built by Abraham as the house of the one God. All the Meccans then embraced Islam.

The Islamization of Arabia, however, was not as yet complete. The Hawāzin tribe rose against Muhammad, and the city of Ṭāʾif, which had treated him so harshly during his Meccan years, still followed idolatrous practices. Muhammad's army defeated the Hawāzin but could not capture Ṭāʾif, which surrendered of its own volition a year later.

In 630–631 embassies from all over the Arabian Peninsula arrived in Medina to accept Islam, and by that time most of Arabia, save for the north, had united under the religion's banner. Muhammad, therefore, marched with a large army north to Tabūk but did not engage the enemy. Nevertheless, the Jews and Christians of the region submitted to his authority, whereupon Muhammad again guaranteed their personal safety and freedom to practice their religion as he did for the Zoroastrians of eastern Arabia. At that time too the pagan Arab tribes in the north, as well as in other regions, embraced Islam. By 631 Muhammad had brought to a close "the age of ignorance" (*al-jāhiliyyah*), as Muslims called the pre-Islamic epoch in Arabia. He united the Arabs for the first time in history under the banner of Islam and broke the hold of tribal bonds as the ultimate links between an Arab and the society around him. Although tribal relations were not fully destroyed, they were now transcended by a more powerful bond based on religion.

Finally, in 632, Muhammad made the first Islamic pilgrimage to Mecca (*al-ḥajj*), which remains the model to this day for the millions of Muslims who make the hajj each year. This event marked the peak of Muhammad's earthly life. At that time he delivered his celebrated farewell sermon, and the last verse of the Qur'ān was revealed, completing the sacred text: "This day have I perfected for you your religion and fulfilled My favour unto you, and it hath been My good pleasure to choose Islam for you as your religion" (5:3). On the way back from Mecca, he and his entourage stopped at a pond called Ghadīr Khumm where, according to both Sunni and Shī'ite sources, he appointed 'Alī as the executor of his last will and as his *walī*, a term that means "friend" or "saint" and also describes a person who possesses authority. This major event is seen by Sunni Muslims as signifying a personal and family matter, while Shī'ites believe that at this time 'Alī received the formal investiture to succeed the Prophet.

Late in the spring of 632 Muhammad, who had been considering another expedition to the north, suddenly fell ill and, according to tradition, died three days later on June 8, 632. His legacy included the establishment of a new order that would transform and affect much of the world from the Atlantic to the China Sea, from France to India. According to Islamic norms that he established, his body was washed by his family, especially by 'Alī, and buried in his house adjacent to the mosque of Medina. His tomb remains the holiest place in Islam after the Ka'bah; it is visited by millions of pilgrims annually.

XUANZANG

(b. 602, Goushi, Luozhou, now Yanshi, Henan Province, China—d. 664, Chang'an, now Xi'an, China)

Xuanzang was a Buddhist monk and Chinese pilgrim to India who translated the sacred scriptures of Buddhism from Sanskrit into Chinese and founded in China the Buddhist Consciousness Only school. His fame rests mainly on the volume and diversity of his translations of the Buddhist sutras and on the record of his travels in Central Asia and India, which, with its wealth of detailed and precise data, has been of inestimable value to historians and archaeologists.

Born into a family in which there had been scholars for generations, Xuanzang received a classical Confucian education in his youth, but under the influence of an older brother he became interested in the Buddhist scriptures and was soon converted to Buddhism. With his brother he traveled to Chang'an and then to Sichuan to escape the political turmoil that gripped China at that time. While in Sichuan, Xuanzang began studying Buddhist philosophy but was soon troubled by numerous discrepancies and contradictions in the texts. Not finding any solution from his Chinese masters, he decided to go to India to study at the fountainhead of Buddhism. Being unable to obtain a travel permit, he left Chang'an by stealth in 629. On his journey he traveled north of the Takla Makan Desert, passing through such oasis centres as Turfan, Karashar, Kucha, Tashkent, and Samarkand, then beyond the Iron Gates into Bactria, across the Hindu Kush (mountains) into Kapisha, Gandhara, and Kashmir in northwest India. From there he sailed down the Ganges River to Mathura, then on to the holy land of Buddhism in the eastern reaches of the Ganges, where he arrived in 633.

In India, Xuanzang visited all the sacred sites connected with the life of the Buddha, and he journeyed along the east and west coasts of the subcontinent. The major portion of his time, however, was spent at the Nalanda monastery, the great Buddhist centre of learning, where he perfected his knowledge of Sanskrit, Buddhist philosophy, and Indian thought. While he was in India, Xuanzang's reputation as a scholar became so great that even the powerful king Harsha, ruler of North India, wanted to meet and honour him. Thanks largely to that king's patronage, Xuanzang's return trip to China, begun in 643, was greatly facilitated.

Xuanzang returned to Chang'an, the Tang capital, in 645, after an absence of 16 years. He was accorded a tumultuous welcome at the capital, and a few days later he was received in audience by the emperor, who was so enthralled by his accounts of foreign lands that he offered the Buddhist monk a ministerial post. Xuanzang, however, preferred to serve his religion, so he respectfully declined the imperial offer.

Xuanzang spent the remainder of his life translating the Buddhist scriptures, numbering 657 items packed in 520 cases, that he brought back from India. He was able to translate only a small portion of this huge volume, about 75 items in 1,335 chapters, but his translations included some of the most important Mahayana scriptures.

Xuanzang's main interest centred on the philosophy of the Yogacara (Vijnanavada) school, and he and his disciple Kuiji (632–682) were responsible for the formation of the Weishi (Consciousness Only school) in China. Its doctrine was set forth in Xuanzang's *Chengweishilun* ("Treatise on the Establishment of the Doctrine of Consciousness Only"), a translation of the essential

Yogacara writings, and in Kuijhi's commentary. The main thesis of this school is that the whole world is but a representation of the mind. While Xuanzang and Kuiji lived, the school achieved some degree of eminence and popularity, but with the passing of the two masters the school rapidly declined. Before this happened, however, a Japanese monk named Dōshō arrived in China in 653 to study under Xuanzang, and, after he had completed his study, he returned to Japan to introduce the doctrines of the Ideation Only school in that country. During the 7th and 8th centuries, this school, called Hossō by the Japanese, became the most influential of all the Buddhist schools in Japan.

In addition to his translations, Xuanzang composed the *Datang-Xiyu-Ji* ("Records of the Western Regions of the Great Tang Dynasty"), the great record of the various countries passed through during his journey. Out of veneration for this intrepid and devout Buddhist monk and pilgrim, the Tang emperor canceled all audiences for three days after Xuanzang's death.

Two studies of Xuanzang are Arthur Waley's *The Real Tripitaka*, pp. 11–130 (1952), a popular biography written in a lively and interesting style and the more complete biography by René Grousset, *Sur les traces du Bouddha* (1929; In the Footsteps of the Buddha), which discusses the life of the Chinese pilgrim against the background of Tang history and Buddhist philosophy.

SHANKARA

(b. 700?, Kaladi village?, India—d. 750?, Kedarnath)

Shankara was a philosopher and theologian and the most renowned exponent of the Advaita Vedanta school of philosophy, from whose doctrines the main currents of modern Indian thought are derived. He wrote commentaries on the Brahma-sutra, the principal Upanishads, and the Bhagavadgita, affirming his belief in one eternal unchanging reality (*brahman*) and the illusion of plurality and differentiation.

There are at least 11 works that profess to be biographies of Shankara. All were composed several centuries after the time of Shankara and are filled with legendary stories and incredible anecdotes, some of which are mutually conflicting. Today there are no materials with which to reconstruct his life with certainty. His date of birth is naturally a controversial problem. It was once customary to assign him the birth and death dates 788–820, but the dates 700–750, grounded in modern scholarship, are more acceptable.

According to one tradition, Shankara was born into a pious Nambudiri Brahman family in a quiet village called Kaladi on the Periyar (Purna) River, Kerala, southern India. He is said to have lost his father, Shivaguru, early in his life. He renounced the world and became a *sannyasin* (ascetic) against his mother's will. He studied under Govinda, who was a pupil of Gaudapada. Nothing certain is known about Govinda, but Gaudapada is notable as the author of an important Vedanta work, Mandukya-karika, in which the influence of Mahayana Buddhism—a form of Buddhism aiming at the salvation of all beings and tending toward non-dualistic or monistic thought—is evident and even extreme, especially in its last chapter.

A tradition says that Shiva, one of the principal gods in Hinduism, was Shankara's family deity and that he was, by birth, a Shakta, or worshipper of Shakti, the consort of Shiva and female personification of divine energy. Later he came to be regarded as a worshipper of Shiva or even an incarnation of Shiva himself. His doctrine, however, is far removed from Shaivism and Shaktism. It is ascertained from his works that he had some faith in, or was favourable to, Vaishnavism, the worship of the god Vishnu. It is highly possible that he was familiar with Yoga (one of the classical systems of Indian philosophy, as well as a technique to achieve salvation). One study has suggested that in the beginning he was an adherent of Yoga and later became an Advaitin (Nondualist).

Biographers narrate that Shankara first went to Kashi (Varanasi), a city celebrated for learning and spirituality, and then traveled all over India, holding discussions with philosophers of different creeds. His heated debate with Mandana Mishra, a philosopher of the Mimamsa (Investigation) school, whose wife served as an umpire, is perhaps the most interesting episode in his biography and may reflect a historical fact—that is, keen conflict between Shankara, who regarded the knowledge of brahman as the only means to final release, and followers of the Mimamsa school, which emphasized the performance of ordained duty and the Vedic rituals.

Shankara was active in a politically chaotic age. He would not teach his doctrine to city dwellers. The power of Buddhism was still strong in the cities, though already declining, and Jainism, a nontheistic ascetic faith, prevailed among the merchants and manufacturers. Popular Hinduism occupied the minds of ordinary people, while city dwellers pursued ease and pleasure. There were also epicureans in cities. It was difficult for Shankara to communicate Vedanta philosophy to these people. Consequently, Shankara propagated his teachings chiefly to sannyasins and intellectuals in the villages, and he gradually won the respect of Brahmans and feudal lords. He enthusiastically endeavoured to restore the orthodox Brahmanical tradition without paying attention to the bhakti (devotional) movement, which had made a deep impression on ordinary Hindus in his age.

It is very likely that Shankara had many pupils, but only four are known (from their writings): Padmapada, Sureshvara, Totaka (or Trotaka), and Hastamalaka. Shankara is said to have founded four monasteries, at Shringeri (south), Puri (east), Dvaraka (west), and Badarinatha (north), probably following the Buddhist monastery (*vihara*) system. Their foundation was one of the most significant factors in the development of his teachings into the leading philosophy of India.

More than 300 works—commentative, expository, and poetical—written in the Sanskrit language, are attributed to him. Most of them, however, cannot be regarded as authentic. The *Brahma-sutra-bhashya*, his masterpiece, is a commentary on the Brahma-sutra, which is a fundamental text of the Vedanta school. The commentaries on the principal Upanishads that are attributed to Shankara are certainly all genuine, with the possible exception of the commentary on the Shvetashvatara Upanishad. The commentary on the Mandukya-karika was also composed by Shankara himself. It is very probable that he is the author of the *Yoga-sutra-bhashya-vivarana,* the exposition of Vyasa's commentary on the *Yoga-sutra*, a fundamental text of the Yoga school. The *Upadeshasahasri*, which is a good introduction to Shankara's philosophy, is the only noncommentative work that is certainly authentic.

Shankara's style of writing is lucid and profound. Penetrating insight and analytical skill characterize his works. His approach to truth is psychological and religious rather than logical; for that reason, he is perhaps best considered to be a prominent religious teacher rather than a philosopher in the modern sense. His works reveal that he not only was versed in the orthodox Brahmanical traditions but also was well acquainted with Mahayana Buddhism. He is often criticized as a "Buddhist in disguise" by his opponents because of the similarity between his doctrine and Buddhism. Despite this criticism, it should be noted that he made full use of his knowledge of Buddhism to attack Buddhist doctrines severely or to transmute them into his own Vedantic nondualism, and he tried with great effort to "vedanticize" the

Vedanta philosophy, which had been made extremely Buddhistic by his predecessors. The basic structure of his philosophy is more akin to Samkhya, a philosophic system of nontheistic dualism, and the Yoga school than to Buddhism. It is said that Shankara died at Kedarnatha in the Himalayas. The Advaita Vedanta school founded by him has always been preeminent in the learned circles of India.

RAMANUJA

(b. c. 1017, Shriperumbudur, India—d. 1137, Shrirangam)

Ramanuja was a South Indian Brahman theologian and philosopher, the single most influential thinker of devotional Hinduism. After a long pilgrimage, Ramanuja settled in Shrirangam, where he organized temple worship and founded centres to disseminate his doctrine of devotion to the god Vishnu and his consort Shri (Lakshmi). He provided an intellectual basis for the practice of bhakti (devotional worship) in three major commentaries: the Vedartha-samgraha (on the Vedas, the earliest scriptures of Hinduism), the Shri-bhashya (on the Brahma-sutras), and the Bhagavadgita-bhashya (on the Bhagavadgita).

Information on the life of Ramanuja consists only of the accounts given in the legendary biographies about him, in which a pious imagination has embroidered historical details. According to tradition, he was born in southern India, in what is now Tamil Nadu (formerly Madras) state. He showed early signs of theological acumen and was sent to Kanchi (Kanchipuram) for schooling, under the teacher Yadavaprakasha, who was a follower of the monistic (Advaita) system of the Vedanta of Shankara, the famous 8th-century philosopher. Ramanuja's profoundly religious nature was soon at odds with a doctrine that offered no room for a personal god. After falling out with his teacher he had a vision of the god Vishnu and his consort Shri and instituted a daily worship ritual at the place where he beheld them.

He became a temple priest at the Varadaraja temple at Kanchi, where he began to expound the doctrine that the goal of those who aspire to final release (*moksha*) from transmigration is not the impersonal brahman but rather brahman as identified with the personal god Vishnu. In Kanchi, as well as Shrirangam, where he was to become associated with the Ranganatha temple, he developed the teaching that the worship of a personal god and the soul's union with him is an essential part of the doctrines of the Upanishads (speculative commentaries on the Vedas) on which the system of Vedanta is built; therefore, the teachings of the Vaishnavas and Bhagavatas (worshippers and ardent devotees of Vishnu) are not heterodox. In this he continued the teachings of Yamuna (Yamunacharya; 10th century), his predecessor at Shrirangam, to whom he was related on his mother's side. He set forth this doctrine in his three major commentaries.

Like many Hindu thinkers, he made an extended pilgrimage, circumambulating India from Rameswaram (part of Adam's Bridge), along the west coast to Badrinath, the source of the holy river Ganges, and returning along the east coast. Tradition has it that later he suffered from the zeal of King Kulottunga of the Chola dynasty, who adhered to the god Shiva, and withdrew to Mysore, in the west. There he converted numbers of Jains, as well as King Bittideva of the Hoyshala dynasty; this led to the founding in 1099 of the town Milukote (Melcote, present Karnataka State) and the dedication of a temple to Shelva Pillai (Sanskrit, Sampatkumara, the name of a form of Vishnu). He returned after 20 years to Shrirangam, where he organized the temple worship, and, reputedly, he founded 74 centres to disseminate his doctrine. After a life of 120 years, according to the tradition, he passed away in 1137.

Ramanuja's chief contribution to philosophy was his insistence that discursive thought is necessary in humanity's search for the ultimate verities, that the phenomenal world is real and provides real knowledge, and that the exigencies of daily life are not detrimental or even contrary to the life of the spirit. In this emphasis he is the antithesis of Shankara, of whom he was sharply critical and whose interpretation of the scriptures he disputed. Like other adherents of the Vedanta system, Ramanuja accepted that any Vedanta system must base itself on the three "points of departure," namely, the Upanishads, the Brahma-sutras (brief exposition of the major tenets of the Upanishads), and the Bhagavadgita, the colloquy of the deity Krishna and his friend Arjuna. He wrote no commentary on any single Upanishad but explained in detail the method of understanding the Upanishads in his first major work, the *Vedartha-samgraha* ("Summary of the Meaning of the Veda"). Much of this was incorporated in his commentary on the Brahma-sutras, the *Shri-bhashya*, which presents his fully developed views. His commentary on the Bhagavadgita, the *Bhagavadgita-bhashya*, dates from a later age.

Although Ramanuja's contribution to Vedanta thought was highly significant, his influence on the course of Hinduism as a religion has been even greater. By allowing the urge for devotional worship (bhakti) into his doctrine of salvation, he aligned the popular religion with the pursuits of philosophy and gave bhakti an intellectual basis. Ever since, bhakti has remained the major force in the religions of Hinduism. His emphasis on the necessity of religious worship as a means of salvation continued in a more systematic context the devotional effusions of the Alvars, the 7th–10th century poet-mystics of southern India, whose verse became incorporated into temple worship. This bhakti devotionalism, guided by Ramanuja, made its way into northern India, where its influence on religious thought and practice has been profound.

Ramanuja's worldview accepts the ontological reality of three distinct orders: matter, soul, and God. Like Shankara and earlier Vedanta, he admits that there is nonduality (*advaita*), an ultimate identity of the three orders, but this nonduality for him is asserted of God, who is modified (*vishishta*; literally "qualified") by the orders of matter and soul; hence, his doctrine is known as Vishishtadvaita ("qualified nonduality") as opposed to the unqualified nonduality of Shankara. Central to his organic conception of the universe is the analogy of body and soul: just as the body modifies the soul, has no separate existence from it, and yet is different from it, just so the orders of matter and soul constitute God's "body," modifying it, yet having no separate existence from it. The goal of the human soul, therefore, is to serve God just as the body serves the soul. Anything different from God is but a shesha of him, a spilling from the plenitude of his being. All the phenomenal world is a manifestation of the glory of God (*vibhuti*), and to detract from its reality is to detract from his glory. Ramanuja transformed the practice of ritual action into the practice of divine worship and the way of meditation into a continuous loving pondering of God's qualities, both in turn subservient to bhakti, the fully realized devotion that finds God. Thus, release is not merely a shedding of the bonds of transmigration but a positive quest for the contemplation of God, who is pictured as enthroned in his heaven, called Vaikuntha, with his consort and attendants.

Ramanuja's doctrine, which was passed on and augmented by later generations, still identifies a caste of Brahmans in southern India, the Shrivaishnavas. They became divided into two subcastes, the northern, or Vadakalai, and the southern, or Tenkalai. At issue between the two schools is the question of God's grace. According to the Vadakalai, who in this seem to follow Ramanuja's intention more closely, God's grace is certainly active in man's quest for him but does not supplant the necessity of man's acting toward God. The Tenkalai, on the other hand, hold that God's grace is paramount and that the only gesture needed from man is his total submission to God (*prapatti*).

The site of Ramanuja's birthplace in Shriperumbudur is now commemorated by a temple and an active Vishishtadvaita school. The doctrines he promulgated still inspire a lively intellectual tradition, and the religious practices he emphasized are still carried on in the two most important Vaishnava centres in southern India, the Ranganatha temple in Shrirangam, Tamil Nadu, and the Venkateshvara temple in Tirupati, Andhra Pradesh.

RASHI

(b. 1040, Troyes, Champagne—d. July 13, 1105, Troyes)

Rashi was a renowned medieval French commentator on the Bible and the Talmud (the authoritative Jewish compendium of law, lore, and commentary). Rashi combined the two basic methods of interpretation, literal and nonliteral, in his influential Bible commentary. His commentary on the Talmud was a landmark in Talmudic exegesis, and his work still serves among Jews as the most substantive introduction to biblical and postbiblical Judaism. Rashi also composed some penitential hymns (*selihot*), which revolve around twin themes: the harsh reality of exile and the comforting belief in redemption.

Shlomo (Solomon) Yitzhaqi (son of Isaac) studied in the schools of Worms and Mainz, the old Rhenish centres of Jewish learning, where he absorbed the methods, teachings, and traditions associated with Rabbi Gershom ben Judah (c. 960–1028/1040), called the Light of the Exile because of his preeminence as the first great scholar of northern European Judaism. Rashi then transferred his scholarly legacy to the valley of the Seine (c. 1065), where he was the de facto but unofficial head of the small Jewish community (about 100–200 people) in Troyes.

Rashi's Bible commentary illustrates vividly the coexistence and, to some extent, the successful reconciliation of the two basic methods of interpretation: the literal and the nonliteral. Rashi seeks the literal meaning, deftly using rules of grammar and syntax and carefully analyzing both text and context, but does not hesitate to mount Midrashic explanations, utilizing allegory, parable, and symbolism, upon the underlying literal interpretation. As a result, some of his successors are critical of his searching literalism and deviation from traditional Midrashic exegesis, while others find his excessive fondness for nonliteral homilies uncongenial. Yet it is precisely the versatility and mixture, the blend of creative eclecticism and originality, that account for the genius, the animation, and the unrivaled popularity of his commentary, which, symbolically, was the first book printed in Hebrew (1475). The commentary had a significant influence on Christian Bible study from the 12th-century Victorines to the Franciscan scholar Nicholas of Lyra (c. 1270–1349), who, in turn, was a major source of Martin Luther's Bible work. Its influence continues in contemporary exegesis and revised translations. Rashi's customary use of a vernacular gloss to clarify the exact meaning of an obscure or technical term—there are more than 3,000 of them in his works—also makes his commentary an important source for the study of Old French.

Rashi's commentary on the Talmud, based on the collective achievements of the previous generations of

Franco-German scholars, reflects its genesis in the oral classroom instruction that Rashi gave in Troyes for several decades. The commentary, sometimes referred to as *kuntros* (literally, "notebook"), resembles a living tutor; it explains the text in its entirety, guides the student in methodological and substantive matters, resolves linguistic difficulties, and indicates the normative conclusions of the discussion. Unlike Maimonides's commentary on the Mishna (the authoritative compendium of Jewish Oral Law), which may be read independently of the underlying text, Rashi's commentary is interwoven with the underlying text. Indeed, text and commentary form a unified mosaic.

Rashi's work was literally epochal, and the agreement of subsequent scholars that the basic needs of text commentary had been fulfilled stimulated the rise of a new school of writers known as *tosafists*, who composed *tosafot* (glosses), refining, criticizing, expanding, or qualifying Rashi's interpretations and conclusions. Skillfully and honestly combining stricture and supplement, they were able to perpetuate and augment the achievement of the great Rashi.

SAINT HILDEGARD

(b. 1098, Böckelheim, West Franconia [Germany]—d. Sept. 17, 1179, Rupertsberg, near Bingen; canonized May 10, 2012; feast day Sept. 17)

S aint Hildegard was a German abbess, visionary mystic, and composer. Hildegard was born of noble parents and was educated at the Benedictine cloister Disibodenberg by Jutta, an anchorite and sister of the count of Spanheim. Hildegard was 15 years old when she began wearing the Benedictine habit and pursuing a religious life. She succeeded Jutta as prioress in 1136. Having experienced visions since she was a child, at age 43 she consulted her confessor, who in turn reported the matter to the archbishop of Mainz. A committee of theologians subsequently confirmed the authenticity of Hildegard's visions, and a monk was appointed to help her record them in writing. The finished work, *Scivias* (1141–52), consists of 26 visions that are prophetic and apocalyptic in form and in their treatment of such topics as the church, the relationship between God and man, and redemption. About 1147 Hildegard left Disibodenberg with several nuns to found a new convent at Rupertsberg, where she continued to exercise the gift of prophecy and to record her visions in writing.

A talented poet and composer, Hildegard collected 77 of her lyric poems, each with a musical setting composed by her, in *Symphonia armonie celestium revelationum*. Her numerous other writings include lives of saints; two treatises on medicine and natural history, reflecting a quality of scientific observation rare at that period; and extensive correspondence, in which are to be found further prophecies and allegorical treatises. She also for amusement contrived her own language. She traveled widely throughout Germany, evangelizing to large groups of people about her visions and religious insights.

Her earliest biographer proclaimed her a saint, and miracles were reported during her life and at her tomb. However, she was not formally canonized until 2012, when Pope Benedict XVI declared her to be a saint through the process of "equivalent canonization," a papal proclamation of canonization based on a standing tradition of popular veneration. Later that year Benedict proclaimed Hildegard a doctor of the church.

As one of the few prominent women in medieval church history, Hildegard became the subject of increasing interest in the latter half of the 20th century. Her writings were widely translated into English; several recordings of her music were made available; and works of fiction, including Barbara Lachman's *The Journal of Hildegard of Bingen* (1993) and Joan Ohanneson's *Scarlet Music: A Life of Hildegard of Bingen* (1997), were published.

IBN ABĪ ʿAṢRŪN

(b. February 1099/1100, Ḥadīthah, Baghdad Caliphate [now in Iraq]—d. October/November 1189, Damascus [now in Syria])

Ibn Abī ʿAṣrūn was a scholar who became a leading Shāfiʿī (one of the four schools of Islamic law) theologian and the chief judicial officer of the Ayyūbid caliphate.

After completing his theological training, Ibn Abī ʿAṣrūn held various religious and judicial posts in Iraq. In 1154 he was invited to Damascus by its ruler; he taught religious subjects there and became the administrator of the *waqfs* (religious endowments). He held numerous other judicial appointments in Syria, Iraq, and Turkey until in 1177/78 the famous Saladin, the Ayyūbid sultan, appointed him as the Shāfiʿī qāḍī ("judge") of Syria, the highest judicial appointment in the realm.

Ibn Abī ʿAṣrūn had to retire because of blindness in 1179/80. During his lifetime six madrasas (religious colleges) were built in his honour. He wrote a number of works on religious subjects, none of which is extant.

ZHU XI

(b. Oct. 18, 1130, Youxi, Fujian Province, China—d. April 23, 1200, China)

Zhu Xi was a Chinese philosopher whose synthesis of neo-Confucian thought long dominated Chinese intellectual life.

Zhu Xi was the son of a local official. He was educated in the Confucian tradition by his father and passed the highest civil service examination at the age of 18, when the average age for such an accomplishment was 35. Zhu Xi's first official position (1151–58) was as a registrar in Tongan, Fujian. There he proceeded to reform the management of taxation and police, improve the library and the standards of the local school, and draw up a code of proper formal conduct and ritual, none being previously available. Before proceeding to Tongan, Zhu Xi called on Li Tong, a thinker in the tradition of Song Confucianism who decisively influenced his future thinking. He visited Li again in 1158 and spent several months studying with him in 1160. Li was one of the ablest followers of the 11th-century neo-Confucians who had created a new metaphysical system to compete with Buddhist and Daoist philosophy and regain the Confucian intellectual ascendancy lost for nearly a millennium. Under his influence, Zhu's allegiance turned definitely to Confucianism at this time.

After his assignment at Tongan ended, Zhu Xi did not accept another official appointment until 1179. He did, however, continue to express his political views in memorandums addressed to the emperor. Though Zhu Xi also remained involved in public affairs, his persistent refusal to accept a substantive public office reflected his dissatisfaction with the men in power and their policies, his spurning of factional politics, and his preference for the life of a teacher and scholar, which was made possible by his receipt of a series of government sinecures.

These years were productive in thought and scholarship, as indicated both by his formal writings and by his correspondence with friends and scholars of diverse views. In 1175, for instance, he held a famous philosophical debate with the philosopher Lu Jiuyuan (Lu Xiangshan) at which neither man was able to prevail. In contrast to Lu's insistence on the exclusive value of inwardness, Zhu Xi emphasized the value of inquiry and study, including book learning. Consistent with this view was Zhu Xi's own prolific literary output. In a number of works, including a compilation of the works of the Cheng brothers and studies of Zhou Dunyi (1017–73) and Zhang Zai (1020–77), he expressed his esteem for these four philosophers, whose ideas he incorporated and synthesized into his own thought. According to Zhu Xi, these thinkers had restored the transmission of the Confucian Way (dao), a process that had been lost after the death of Mencius. In 1175 Zhu Xi and his friend Lu Ziqian (1137–81) compiled passages from the works of the four to form their famous anthology, *Jinsi Lu* ("Reflections on Things at Hand"). Zhu Xi's philosophical ideas also found expression during this period in his enormously influential commentaries on the *Lunyu* (known in English as the *Analects of Confucius*) and on the *Mencius*, both completed in 1177.

Zhu Xi also took a keen interest in history and directed a reworking and condensation of Sima Guang's history, the *Zizhi tongjian* ("Comprehensive Mirror for Aid in Government"), so that it would illustrate moral principles in government. The resulting work, known as the *Tongjian gangmu* ("Outline and Digest of the General Mirror"), basically completed in 1172, was not only widely read throughout eastern Asia but also served as the basis for the first comprehensive history of China published in Europe, J.-A.-M. Moyriac de Mailla's *Histoire générale de la Chine* (1777–85).

While serving as prefect (1179–81) in Nankang, Jiangsi, Zhu Xi used the opportunity to rehabilitate the White Deer Grotto Academy, which had been founded in the 9th century and had flourished in the 10th century but had later fallen to ruin. The prestige restored to it by

Zhu was to last through eight centuries. Academies such as this provided an invaluable institutional basis for the neo-Confucian movement.

In 1188 Zhu Xi wrote a major memorandum in which he restated his conviction that the emperor's character was the basis for the well-being of the realm. *Daxue* (*Great Learning*), a text on moral government, asserted that by cultivating his mind the emperor set off a chain reaction leading to the moral transformation of the entire world. In 1189 Zhu Xi wrote an important commentary on this text, and he continued to work on *Daxue* for the rest of his life. Similarly, in 1189 he wrote a commentary on *Zhongyong* (known in the West as the "Doctrine of the Mean"). It was largely because of the influence of Zhu Xi that these two texts came to be accepted along with the *Analects* and *Mencius* as the Four Books basic to the Confucian educational curriculum.

On several occasions during his later career Zhu was invited to the imperial court and seemed destined for more influential positions, but his invariably frank and forceful opinions and his uncompromising attacks on corruption and political expediency each time brought his dismissal or his transfer to a new post conveniently distant from the capital. On the last of these occasions, near the end of his life, his enemies retaliated with virulent accusations concerning his views and conduct, and he was barred from political activity. He was still in political disgrace when he died in 1200. Zhu Xi's reputation was rehabilitated soon after his death, however, and posthumous honours for him followed in 1209 and 1230, culminating in the placement of his tablet in the Confucian Temple in 1241. In later centuries, rulers more authoritarian than those he had criticized, discreetly forgetting his political and intellectual nonconformity, made his philosophic system the sole orthodox creed, which it remained until the end of the 19th century.

MOSES MAIMONIDES

(b. March 30, 1135, Córdoba [Spain]—d. Dec. 13, 1204, Egypt)

Moses Maimonides was a Jewish philosopher, jurist, and physician, the foremost intellectual figure of medieval Judaism. His first major work, begun at age 23 and completed 10 years later, was a commentary on the Mishna, the collected Jewish oral laws. A monumental code of Jewish law followed, *The Guide for the Perplexed*, and numerous other works, many of major importance. His contributions in religion, philosophy, and medicine have influenced Jewish and non-Jewish scholars alike.

Maimonides was born into a distinguished family in Córdoba (Cordova), Spain. The young Moses studied with his learned father, Maimon, and other masters and at an early age astonished his teachers with his remarkable depth and versatility. Before Moses reached his 13th birthday, his peaceful world was suddenly disturbed by the ravages of war and persecution.

As part of Islamic Spain, Córdoba had accorded its citizens full religious freedom. But now the Islamic Mediterranean world was shaken by a revolutionary and fanatical Islamic sect, the Almohads (Arabic: al-Muwaḥḥidūn, "the Unitarians"), who captured Córdoba in 1148, leaving the Jewish community faced with the grim alternative of submitting to Islam or leaving the city. The Maimons temporized by practicing their Judaism in the privacy of their homes, while disguising their ways in public as far as possible to appear like Muslims. They remained in Córdoba for some 11 years, and Maimonides continued his education in Judaic studies as well as in the scientific disciplines in vogue at the time.

When the double life proved too irksome to maintain in

Córdoba, the Maimon family finally left the city about 1159 to settle in Fez, Morocco. Although it was also under Almohad rule, Fez was presumably more promising than Córdoba because there the Maimons would be strangers, and their disguise would be more likely to go undetected. Moses continued his studies in his favourite subjects, rabbinics and Greek philosophy, and added medicine to them. Fez proved to be no more than a short respite, however. In 1165 Rabbi Judah ibn Shoshan, with whom Moses had studied, was arrested as a practicing Jew and was found guilty and then executed. This was a sign to the Maimon family to move again, this time to Palestine, which was in a depressed economic state and could not offer them the basis of a livelihood. After a few months they moved again, now to Egypt, settling in Fostat, near Cairo. There Jews were free to practice their faith openly, though any Jew who had once submitted to Islam courted death if he relapsed to Judaism. Moses himself was once accused of being a renegade Muslim, but he was able to prove that he had never really adopted the faith of Islam and so was exonerated.

Though Egypt was a haven from harassment and persecution, Moses was soon assailed by personal problems. His father died shortly after the family's arrival in Egypt. His younger brother, David, a prosperous jewelry merchant on whom Moses leaned for support, died in a shipwreck, taking the entire family fortune with him, and Moses was left as the sole support of his family. He could not turn to the rabbinate because in those days the rabbinate was conceived of as a public service that did not offer its practitioners any remuneration. Pressed by economic necessity, Moses took advantage of his medical studies and became a practicing physician. His fame as a physician spread rapidly, and he soon became the court physician to the sultan Saladin, the famous Muslim military leader, and to his son al-Afḍal. He also continued a private practice and lectured before his fellow physicians at the state hospital. At the same time he became the leading member of the Jewish community, teaching in public and helping his people with various personal and communal problems.

Maimonides married late in life and was the father of a son, Abraham, who was to make his mark in his own right in the world of Jewish scholarship.

SAINT FRANCIS OF ASSISI

(b. 1182, Assisi, Italy–d. 1226, Assisi)

The founder of the Franciscan order, St. Francis was born at Assisi, in central Italy, in 1182. He was baptized Giovanni. His father, Pietro Bernardone, was a wealthy cloth merchant.

Francis had little education. He spent much of his youth seeking fun in parties with friends. In 1202, after a year as a prisoner of war and a serious illness, Francis tired of worldly pleasure. He sold his property and gave the money to the church.

The young man began to tend the poor and the sick, even caring for lepers. When his father disinherited him, Francis supported himself by repairing chapels around Assisi. At last, throwing aside even his shoes, he lived in absolute poverty.

Soon he began to attract followers. In ragged gray gowns, barefoot, and without money, the "begging brothers" went forth two by two to spread the gospel of service and poverty.

Members of the brotherhood were sent to preach in France, Germany, Hungary, Spain, and England. When an 18-year-old girl named Clare left her home to follow his teachings, Francis formed a separate order for women known as the Franciscan Nuns or the Poor Clares.

Saint Francis of Assisi, detail of a fresco by Cimabue, late 13th century; in the lower church of San Francesco, Assisi, Italy.

For the rest of his life "little brother Francis," as he called himself, continued his religious labors. He made long journeys to many parts of the world.

He called all creatures his brothers and sisters. It is said that Francis was so kind to animals that wild rabbits ran to him for protection. A famous story tells how he preached to birds, telling them to be thankful to God, their creator. Francis was also a poet, writing many simple and beautiful lines.

In 1224, during a 40-day fast on a mountain, Francis had a vision and received the "stigmata"—the marks of the nails and the spear of Jesus' passion—on his own body. Francis died on Oct. 3, 1226, at Assisi. Two years later he was canonized, or declared a saint, by Pope Gregory IX.

Twenty years after the death of St. Francis his order had grown so large that 9,000 religious houses had been built. The Franciscan friars at one time numbered more than 100,000. Differences about the rules brought divisions of the order. In missionary work, in caring for the poor, in education, and in other good works, the Franciscan order is still active.

DŌGEN

(b. Jan. 19, 1200, Kyōto, Japan—d. Sept. 22, 1253, Kyōto)

Dōgen was a leading Japanese Buddhist during the Kamakura period (1192–1333), who introduced Zen to Japan in the form of the Sōtō school (Chinese: Ts'ao-tung). A creative personality, he combined meditative practice and philosophical speculation.

Dōgen was born into a family of the court nobility and was orphaned at the age of seven. He was ordained a monk at 13 and studied the holy scriptures of Buddhism on Mount Hiei, the centre of Tendai Buddhism, without, however, fully satisfying his spiritual aspirations. Between

1223 and 1227 he studied Zen meditation in China and gained enlightenment under the Zen master Ju-ching. Back in Japan again, he lived at various temples and worked for the spread of Zen practice. He spent his last years at Eihei Temple, which he had founded on a hill in present-day Fukui. His first literary work, *Fukan zazen gi* (1227; "General Teachings for the Promotion of Zazen"), contains a brief introduction to the Zen practice. He wrote a number of other instructive works as well. His chief work, *Shōbōgenzō* (1231–53; "Treasury of the True Dharma Eye"), containing 95 chapters and written over a period of more than 20 years, consists of his elaboration of Buddhist principles. Dōgen taught *shikan taza*, "*zazen* only," *zazen* signifying the Zen practice of meditation in the cross-legged (lotus) position. He stressed the identity of practice and enlightenment.

RŪMĪ

(b. c. Sept. 30, 1207, Balkh [now in Afghanistan] — d. Dec. 17, 1273)

Rūmī was the greatest Sufi mystic and poet in the Persian language, famous for his lyrics and for his didactic epic *Masnavī-yi Ma'navī* ("Spiritual Couplets"), which widely influenced mystical thought and literature throughout the Muslim world. After his death, his disciples were organized as the Mawlawīyah order.

Jalāl al-Dīn's father, Bahā' al-Dīn Walad, was a noted mystical theologian, author, and teacher. Because of either a dispute with the ruler or the threat of the approaching Mongols, Bahā' al-Dīn and his family left their native town in about 1218. According to a legend, in Nīshāpūr, Iran, the family met Farīd al-Dīn 'Aṭṭār, a Persian mystical poet, who blessed young Jalāl al-Dīn. After a pilgrimage to Mecca and journeys through the Middle East, Bahā' al-Dīn and his family reached Anatolia (Rūm, hence the surname Rūmī), a region that enjoyed peace and prosperity under the rule of the Turkish Seljuq dynasty. After a short stay at Laranda (Karaman), where Jalāl al-Dīn's mother died and his first son was born, they were called to the capital, Konya, in 1228. Here, Bahāʾ al-Dīn Walad taught at one of the numerous madrasahs (religious schools); after his death in 1231 he was succeeded in this capacity by his son.

A year later, Burhān al-Dīn Muḥaqqiq, one of Bahāʾ al-Dīn's former disciples, arrived in Konya and acquainted Jalāl al-Dīn more deeply with some mystical theories that had developed in Iran. Burhān al-Dīn, who contributed considerably to Jalāl al-Dīn's spiritual formation, left Konya about 1240. Jalāl al-Dīn is said to have undertaken one or two journeys to Syria (unless his contacts with Syrian Sufi circles were already established before his family reached Anatolia); there he may have met Ibn al-ʿArabī, the leading Islamic theosophist whose interpreter and stepson, Ṣadr al-Dīn al-Qunawī, was Jalāl al-Dīn's colleague and friend in Konya.

The decisive moment in Rūmī's life occurred on Nov. 30, 1244, when in the streets of Konya he met the wandering dervish—holy man—Shams al-Dīn (Sun of Religion) of Tabrīz, whom he may have first encountered in Syria. Shams al-Dīn cannot be connected with any of the traditional mystical fraternities; his overwhelming personality, however, revealed to Jalāl al-Dīn the mysteries of divine majesty and beauty. For months the two mystics lived closely together, and Rūmī neglected his disciples and family so that his scandalized entourage forced Shams to leave the town in February 1246. Jalāl al-Dīn was heartbroken; his eldest son, Sulṭān Walad, eventually brought Shams back from Syria. The family, however, could not tolerate the close relation of Jalāl al-Dīn with his beloved, and one night in 1247 Shams disappeared forever. In the

20th century it was established that Shams was indeed murdered, not without the knowledge of Rūmī's sons, who hurriedly buried him close to a well that is still extant in Konya.

This experience of love, longing, and loss turned Rūmī into a poet. His poems—ghazals (about 30,000 verses) and a large number of *robā 'īyāt* ("quatrains")—reflect the different stages of his love, until, as his son writes, "he found Shams in himself, radiant like the moon." The complete identification of lover and beloved is expressed by his inserting the name of Shams instead of his own pen name at the end of most of his lyrical poems. The *Dīvān-e Shams* ("The Collected Poetry of Shams") is a true translation of his experiences into poetry; its language, however, never becomes lost in lofty spiritual heights or nebulous speculation. The fresh language, propelled by its strong rhythms, sometimes assumes forms close to popular verses. There would seem to be cause for the belief, expressed by chroniclers, that much of this poetry was composed in a state of ecstasy, induced by the music of the flute or the drum, the hammering of the goldsmiths, or the sound of the water mill in Meram, where Rūmī used to go with his disciples to enjoy nature. He found in nature the reflection of the radiant beauty of the Sun of Religion and felt flowers and birds partaking in his love. He often accompanied his verses by a whirling dance, and many of his poems were composed to be sung in Sufi musical gatherings.

A few years after Shams al-Dīn's death, Rūmī experienced a similar rapture in his acquaintance with an illiterate goldsmith, Ṣalāḥ al-Dīn Zarkūb. It is said that one day, hearing the sound of a hammer in front of Ṣalāḥ al-Dīn's shop in the bazaar of Konya, Rūmī began his dance. The shop owner had long been one of Rūmī's closest and most loyal disciples, and his daughter became the wife of Rūmī's eldest son. This love again inspired Rūmī to write poetry. After Ṣalāḥ al-Dīn's death, Ḥusām al-Dīn Chelebi became his spiritual love and deputy. Rūmī's main work, the *Masnavī-yi Ma'navī*, was composed under his influence. Ḥusām al-Dīn had asked him to follow the model of the poets 'Aṭṭār and Sanā'i, who had laid down mystical teachings in long poems, interspersed with anecdotes, fables, stories, proverbs, and allegories. Their works were widely read by the mystics and by Rūmī's disciples. Rūmī followed Ḥusām al-Dīn's advice and composed nearly 26,000 couplets of the *Masnavī* during the following years. It is said that he would recite his verses even in the bath or on the roads, accompanied by Ḥusām al-Dīn, who wrote them down. The *Masnavī*, which shows all the different aspects of Sufism in the 13th century, often carries the reader away with loose associations of thought, so that one understands what subjects the master had in mind at a particular stage of his life. The work reflects the experience of divine love; both Ṣalāḥ al-Dīn and Ḥusām al-Dīn were, for Rūmī, renewed manifestations of Shams al-Dīn, the all-embracing light. He called Ḥusām al-Dīn, therefore, Ḍiyā' al-Ḥaqq ("Light of the Truth"); *ḍiyā'* is the Arabic term for sunlight.

Rūmī lived for a short while after completing the *Masnavī*. He always remained a respected member of Konya society, and his company was sought by the leading officials as well as by Christian monks. His burial procession, according to one of Rūmī's contemporaries, was attended by a vast crowd of people of many faiths and nationalities. His mausoleum, the Green Dome, is today a museum in Konya; it is still a place of pilgrimage, primarily for Turkish Muslims.

Ḥusām al-Dīn was Rūmī's successor and was in turn succeeded by Sulṭān Walad, who organized the loose fraternity of Rūmī's disciples into the Mawlawīyah, known in the West as the Whirling Dervishes because of the mystical dance that constitutes their principal ritual. Sultān Walad's poetical accounts of his father's life are the most important source of knowledge of Rūmī's spiritual development.

Besides his poetry, Rūmī left a small collection of occasional talks as they were noted down by his friends; in the collection, known as *Fīhi mā fīhi* ("There Is in It What Is in It"), the main ideas of his poetry recur. There also exist sermons and a collection of letters (*Maktūbāt*) directed to different persons. It is impossible to systematize his ideas, which at times contradict each other, and changes in the use of symbols often puzzle the reader. His poetry is a most human expression of mystical experiences, in which readers can find their own favourite ideas and feelings—from enthusiastic flights into the heavens to matter-of-fact descriptions of daily life.

Rūmī's use of Persian and Arabic in his poetry, in addition to some Turkish and less Greek, has resulted in his being claimed variously for Turkish literature and Persian literature, a reflection of the strength of his influence in Iran and Turkey. The influence of his writings in the Indian subcontinent is also substantial. By the end of the 20th century, his popularity had become a global phenomenon, with his poetry achieving a wide circulation in western Europe and the United States.

NICHIREN

(b. March 30, 1222, Kominato, Japan—d. Nov. 14, 1282, Ikegami)

The most controversial and troublesome figure in the history of Japanese Buddhism is the monk Nichiren. He devoted his life to a search for true Buddhist doctrine, and when he found it he persistently demanded that all other Buddhist sects be banished and his accepted as the national religion.

Nichiren was born on March 30, 1222, in Kominato, Japan. At age 11 he entered the monastery of Kiyosumi-dera. For years he visited other monasteries and read all the Buddhist texts in his search for the correct doctrine. In 1253 he determined that the Lotus Sutra, one of the religion's ancient scriptures, presented the true interpretation of the Buddha's teachings. When he proclaimed this decision he was persecuted by both his fellow monks and the government. He spent his last years studying and teaching. He died in Ikegami on Nov. 14, 1282. He has had a pronounced influence on today's Buddhist sects.

SAINT THOMAS AQUINAS

(b. 1224/25, Roccasecca, near Aquino, Terra di Lavoro, Kingdom of Sicily [Italy]—d. March 7, 1274, Fossanova, near Terracina, Latium, Papal States)

The Roman Catholic Church regards St. Thomas Aquinas as its greatest theologian and philosopher. Pope John XXII canonized him in 1323, and Pius V declared him a doctor of the church in 1567. Leo XIII made him patron of Roman Catholic schools in 1880.

Thomas Aquinas, or Thomas of Aquino, was born in about 1225 in the castle of Roccasecca, near Naples, Italy. His father was the count of Aquino. The boy received his early education at the abbey of Monte Cassino before attending the University of Naples. While at the university Thomas came under the influence of the Dominicans, an order of mendicant preaching friars. In spite of the opposition of his family, he joined the order. His brothers captured him and imprisoned him at Roccasecca. After two years he escaped.

St. Thomas Aquinas, painting attributed to Sandro Botticelli, 15th century.

The Dominicans then sent Thomas to Cologne to study with Albertus Magnus, the most learned man of the time. In 1252 Thomas was in Paris, France, composing his Commentaries on the Books of Sentences of Peter the Lombard. He was later admitted as master of theology at the University of Paris.

In 1259 the pope called Thomas to Rome, Italy. He spent the rest of his life lecturing and preaching in the service of his order, chiefly in Italian cities and in Paris. He died on March 7, 1274, while traveling to a church council at Lyons, France.

A revival of learning had begun in Western Europe toward the end of the 11th century. By the 13th century many universities had been founded. They were linked to the church, and the chief subjects taught were theology and the liberal arts. The teachers were called Schoolmen or Scholastics. Thomas was recognized in his lifetime as the greatest of the Schoolmen and was known as the "angelic doctor."

The Schoolmen accepted Christian doctrines as beyond dispute, but they also studied the ancient Greek philosophers. Until the 13th century they relied on Plato as interpreted by St. Augustine of Hippo. Aristotle's treatises on logic were also admitted into the schools, but his other works, which were known in their Arabic translations, were forbidden because of their pantheistic tendencies. Albertus Magnus introduced Thomas to the works of Aristotle, which were beginning to be translated from the original Greek. Thomas set himself the task of harmonizing Aristotle's teachings with Christian doctrine.

Thomas held that there are two sources of knowledge: revelation (theology) and reason (philosophy). He held that revelation is a divine source of knowledge and that revealed truths must be believed even when they cannot be fully understood. His literary output was enormous. At times he dictated to several scribes on different subjects. His chief works are *Summa Contra Gentiles* and *Summa Theologiae*, which form the classical systematization of Roman Catholic theology.

JOHN WYCLIFFE

(b. *c.*1330, Yorkshire, England—died Dec. 31, 1384, Lutterworth, Leicestershire)

The "morning star of the Reformation" was John Wycliffe, English priest and reformer of the late Middle Ages. His teachings had a great effect on Jan Hus and, through Hus, on Martin Luther.

Wycliffe was born about 1330 in Yorkshire, England. He was a student and later a teacher at Oxford University. In 1374 he became rector of Lutterworth in Leicestershire. Wycliffe opposed the pope's claim to the right to tax and to appoint men to church offices without asking the king. In 1377 he was brought to trial before the archbishop of Canterbury and the bishop of London, but a crowd of his London supporters came to his rescue.

The pope issued papal decrees against him, and his teachings were condemned at Oxford. He continued to preach fearlessly, however, and he wrote many Latin treatises to support his attacks on the beliefs and practices of the church. To help those who could read to understand the Bible, Wycliffe's followers made the first full English translation.

Wycliffe had the support of the nobles as long as he denounced rich churchmen, but he began to teach that lordship and property were held only by God's grace and were forfeited if the owners fell into mortal sin. These teachings helped bring on the Peasants' Revolt in 1381 and lost Wycliffe the support of the nobles. In 1384 Wycliffe died in his parish of Lutterworth.

JAN HUS

(b. *c.* 1370, Husinec, Bohemia [now in Czech Republic]—died July 6, 1415, Konstanz [Germany])

A forerunner of the Reformation, Jan Hus of Bohemia was burned at the stake as a heretic rather than recant his religious views and his criticisms of the clergy. Hus founded the Moravian church.

Jan Hus was born in the Bohemian village of Husinec in about 1369. He studied for the priesthood at the University of Prague. After graduation he lectured there on philosophy and for a time served as rector of the university. Hus and his fellow scholars wrote in Latin as did all learned men throughout Europe, but Hus also wrote in his native Bohemian, or Czech, helping to establish Bohemian as a literary language. He also preached in Bohemian, winning the trust of the people and a devoted following.

As a young priest Hus was drawn to the writings of the English priest and reformer John Wycliffe, who denounced evil practices of the church. Hus carried on Wycliffe's protests, and as a result he gained many enemies. Hus disagreed with some of Wycliffe's beliefs. He did not reject the church's doctrine of transubstantiation, for example. When he opposed the burning of Wycliffe's books, however, he was charged with heresy and was forbidden to preach or to teach.

This was the time of the Great Western Schism in the church (1378–1417), caused by rival claims to the papacy. One of the antipopes, John XXIII, proclaimed a crusade and promised indulgences to volunteers. Hus attacked this procedure. His followers burned the pope's decree.

The church excommunicated Hus, laying an interdict on any place that sheltered him. Friends defied the interdict and hid Hus in the countryside. During this period Hus spent his time writing.

In 1415 the Council of Constance met to heal the Great Schism and to discuss reform. Called by the council, Hus was given safe-conduct by the German king Sigismund. While Hus was at Constance, however, Sigismund repudiated his pledge. Arrested and thrown into prison, Hus was called before the council and accused of beliefs that he had never held. He refused to take back things he had not said and was put to death on July 6, 1415. He is the national hero and saint of Bohemia.

SAINT JOAN OF ARC

(b. *c.* 1412, Domrémy, Bar, France—died May 30, 1431, Rouen)

One of the most romantic figures in European war history was Joan of Arc, a peasant girl who saved the kingdom of France from English domination. She has also been called the Maid of Orléans and the Maid of France. When she was only 17 years old, Joan inspired a French army to break the English siege of the French city of Orléans and to win other important victories.

Joan of Arc (in French Jeanne d'Arc) was born in the village of Domrémy, in the Meuse River valley, probably in 1412. She was the daughter of a wealthy tenant farmer. From her mother she learned how to spin, sew, and cook, and also to love and serve God. She spent much of her time praying in church.

For almost 100 years France and much of Europe had been fighting in what became known as the Hundred Years' War. The English occupied much of northern France and the Duke of Burgundy was their ally. Because the impoverished French king, Charles VII, had not yet been crowned, he was still called the Dauphin. Reims, where the coronation ceremonies for French kings had been held for 1,000 years, was in enemy hands. The valley where Joan lived was constantly overrun by armies and guerrilla bands.

Joan was only about 13 when she first saw a heavenly vision. She later claimed that St. Michael had told her to be a good girl, to obey her mother, and to go to church often. For some time, however, she told no one of the visions. When St. Catherine and St. Margaret commanded her to journey to the Dauphin in order to inspire his armies to clear the way to Reims for the coronation, she told her parents and others. Her father refused to let her go.

Joan's visions continued to command her. Her friends, who believed that she was truly inspired, secured boy's clothing and a horse for her. Several rode with her on the long trip to the Dauphin's court at Chinon. Perhaps as a test, the Dauphin made one of his courtiers pretend to be the king. Joan, however, went directly to the true king and greeted him. The Dauphin and his councillors were not entirely convinced of her mission, however. Months of doubt and indecision followed while she was questioned.

Slowly an army was gathered. The Dauphin equipped Joan with armor, attendants, and horses. A special banner

Joan of Arc riding into battle, miniature from the manuscript Les Vies des femmes célèbres by Antoine Du Four, about 1505; in the Dobrée Museum, Nantes, France.

was made for Joan to carry into battle. On one side were the words "Jesus Maria" and a figure of God, seated on clouds and holding a glove. The other side had a figure of the Virgin and a shield, with two angels supporting the arms of France.

When the army at last moved toward Orléans, Joan was not its commander, but her presence inspired the soldiers with confidence. At Orléans, after Joan disapproved of the plans made for entering the besieged city, her own plan was adopted. From the city she led a series of sallies that so harassed and discouraged the English that they withdrew. In one of the skirmishes Joan was wounded.

On May 8, 1429, the victory was celebrated by the first festival of Orléans. The army entered Reims on July 16. The next day the Dauphin was crowned king as Joan stood by with her banner.

A decision was made to attack Paris, but the new monarch's hesitation and indecision prevented Joan's soldiers from concerted attack. Nevertheless, Compiègne and other nearby towns were taken. A French attack on a Paris salient was driven back and Joan was again wounded. Charles VII disbanded his army for the winter and retired southward. Through the cold months Joan chafed at royal delay.

In the spring she returned to Compiègne, now besieged by forces of the Duke of Burgundy. On May 23, 1430, Joan, on a sortie into the Burgundian lines, was separated from her soldiers and captured.

As a prisoner at Beaurevoir, she attempted to escape, but was injured in the leap from the donjon tower. Later she was sold to the English, who vowed that she would be executed. They removed her to Rouen, where she was held in chains.

Although the English wanted Joan's death, they desired her to be sentenced by an ecclesiastical court. The Burgundian-controlled University of Paris provided the charges of heresy and witchcraft. It also provided some of the members of the court. Other members came from areas under English occupation. Chief of the court was the bishop of Beauvais.

Joan was handed over to this bishop on January 3, 1431. The sittings began on February 21 and continued intermittently for months. Joan's appeal to be sent before the pope for judgment was denied. On May 23 she was condemned to be burned unless she recanted. She had been held for many months in chains, threatened with torture, and harassed by thousands of questions. In spite of all this, she had maintained her shy innocence, often confounding her oppressors with simple, unaffected answers to tricky questions. St. Catherine and St. Margaret, she said, still counseled her.

Faced with death in the flames, she recanted, but many historians think she did not understand what was meant in the statement of recantation. As a result of her submission, her punishment was commuted from death to life imprisonment. This leniency enraged the English, however, and it was not long before she was accused of relapsing from her submission. On May 30, 1431, when she was only 19 years old, Joan was turned over to civil authority and burned to death at the stake.

Charles VII had made no effort to save Joan. Some 25 years later he did aid her family to appeal the case to the pope, and in 1456 a papal court annulled the judgment of 1431. On May 16, 1920, Joan of Arc was canonized a saint by the Roman Catholic Church.

NANAK

(b. April 15, 1469, Rai Bhoi di Talvandi [now Nankana Sahib, Pak.], near Lahore, India—d. 1539, Kartarpur, Punjab)

Nanak was an Indian spiritual teacher who was the first guru of the Sikhs, a monotheistic religious group that combines Hindu and Muslim influences. His teachings, expressed through devotional hymns, many of which still survive, stressed salvation from rebirth through meditation on the divine name. Among modern Sikhs he enjoys a particular affection as their founder and as the supreme master of Punjabi devotional hymnody.

What little information there is about Nanak's life has been handed down mainly through legend and tradition. There is no doubt that he was born in 1469 in the village of Rai Bhoi di Talvandi. His father was a member of a sub-caste of the mercantile Khatri caste. The relatively high social rank of the Khatris distinguishes Nanak from other Indian religious reformers of the period and may have helped promote the initial growth of his following. He married the daughter of a Khatri, who bore him two sons.

For several years Nanak worked in a granary until his religious vocation drew him away from both family and employment, and, in the tradition of Indian religious mendicants, he embarked on a lengthy journey, probably traveling to the Muslim and Hindu religious centres of India, and perhaps even to places beyond India's borders. Neither the actual route nor the places he visited can be positively identified.

References found in four of his hymns suggest that Nanak was present at attacks Babur (an invading Mughal ruler) launched on Saidpur and Lahore, so it seems safe to conclude that by 1520 he had returned from his travels and was living in the Punjab.

The remaining years of his life were spent in Kartarpur, another village of central Punjab. Tradition holds that the village was actually built by a wealthy admirer to honour Nanak. It was presumably during this final period that the foundations of the new Sikh community were laid. By this time it must be assumed that Nanak was recognized as a guru, an inspired teacher of religious truth, and that, in accordance with the custom of India, disciples who accepted him as their guru gathered around him in Kartarpur. Some probably remained as permanent residents of the village; many more made periodic visits to obtain his blessing. All of them listened to the teachings expressed there in numerous devotional hymns

Guru Nanak.

intended for communal singing, many of which survive to this day.

The actual year of Nanak's death is disputed, tradition being divided between 1538 and 1539. Of these two possibilities, the latter appears to be the more likely. One of his disciples, Angad, was chosen by Nanak as his spiritual successor, and following Nanak's death he assumed the leadership of the young Sikh community as Guru Angad.

In view of the size of the following that Nanak attracted, numerous anecdotes concerning the deeds of the Guru began to circulate within the community soon after his death. Many of these were borrowed from the current Hindu and Muslim traditions, and others were suggested by Nanak's own works. These anecdotes were called *sakhis*, or "testimonies," and the anthologies into which they were gathered in rough chronological order are known as *Janam-sakhis*. The interest of the narrators and compilers of the Janam-sakhis has largely concentrated on the childhood of Nanak and above all on his travels. Among the earlier traditions are tales of visits he is supposed to have made to Baghdad and Mecca. Ceylon is a later addition, and later still the Guru is said to have traveled as far east as China and as far west as Rome. Today the Janam-sakhis offer a substantial corpus of hagiographical material, and the more important of these collections continue to be the basis of "biographies" of Nanak.

Nanak's message can be briefly summarized as a doctrine of salvation through disciplined meditation on the divine name. Salvation is understood in terms of escape from the transmigratory round of death and rebirth to a mystical union with God. The divine name signifies the total manifestation of God, a single Being, immanent both in the created world and within the human spirit. Meditation must be strictly inward, and all external aids such as idols, temples, mosques, scriptures, and set prayers are explicitly rejected. The Muslim influence is relatively slight; the influence of Hindu mystical and devotional beliefs is much more apparent. Always, though, the coherence and beauty of Nanak's own expression dominates early Sikh theology.

SIR THOMAS MORE

(b. Feb. 7, 1478, London, England—died July 6, 1535, London)

One of the most respected figures in English history, Thomas More was a statesman, scholar, and author. He was noted for his wit and also for his devotion to his religion. More was executed as a traitor for his refusal to acknowledge King Henry VIII's supremacy over the church. The story of More's life and death became familiar to many through Robert Bolt's play, *A Man for All Seasons*, first performed in 1960.

Thomas More was born in London on Feb. 7, 1478. His father was Sir John More, a prominent barrister. While in his early teens, young More entered the household of Cardinal Morton as a page. Later he attended Canterbury Hall, Oxford. The great Dutch scholar Desiderius Erasmus became his close friend. More, Erasmus, and John Colet, the distinguished dean of London's St. Paul's Cathedral, were leaders of a group of scholars and religious reformers. This group, which became known as the Oxford Reformers, did much to promote the Renaissance in England. More entered the profession of law, in which he gained distinction. His religious piety led him to fast, pray, and do penance. For a time he hoped to enter the priesthood. Throughout his life More's deep religious convictions dominated his actions.

He married Jane Colte in 1505, and they had four children. Shortly after More's first wife died in 1511, he married Alice Middleton, a widow with one daughter.

More became a member of Parliament. He was disliked by Henry VII, whom he opposed on financial matters. The accession of Henry VIII brought More to a high place at court. On Cardinal Wolsey's fall from power in 1529, More was made lord chancellor—the first time that the office had been held by a layman.

When Henry VIII divorced Catherine of Aragon, More as a loyal churchman resigned his office on the plea of ill health. He refused to acknowledge Henry's claim to be head of the English church. For this defiance the king had More—together with Bishop Fisher and others—committed to the Tower on a charge of treason. He was beheaded on Tower Hill on July 6, 1535. This was made his festival day when he was canonized by Pope Pius XI in 1935, 400 years later.

More is famous not only as a statesman and religious martyr but also as an author. *A Dialogue of Comfort Against Tribulation*, written in 1534 while he was in prison, shows his faith and his calm courage. Perhaps his best-known work is his *Utopia* (1516). *Utopia*, which is Greek for "nowhere," is the name of an imaginary island with a happy society, free from all cares, anxieties, and miseries.

MARTIN LUTHER

(b. Nov. 10, 1483, Eisleben, Saxony [Germany]—died Feb. 18, 1546, Eisleben)

The Protestant Reformation in Germany was inaugurated by Martin Luther in 1517. It was his intent to reform the medieval Roman Catholic Church, but the firm resistance of the church to Luther's challenge led

Martin Luther, oil on panel by Lucas Cranach, 1529; in the Uffizi, Florence.

instead to permanent divisions in the structure of Western Christianity.

Luther was born in Eisleben in the province of Saxony on Nov. 10, 1483, to Hans and Margaret Ziegler Luther. Shortly thereafter the family moved to Mansfeld, where Hans worked as a miner. The young Luther studied at Magdeburg and Eisenach before attending the University of Erfurt. In 1505, at the urging of his father, he began to study law; but within the year he decided to abandon law and enter the religious life by becoming an Augustinian monk. Later in life, Luther credited this sudden decision to having been caught in a thunderstorm and dashed to the ground by a bolt of lightning. In his fear, he renounced the world and entered the Augustinian monastery at Erfurt in July 1505. Luther became an outstanding theologian and Biblical scholar. He earned his doctorate in theology in 1512 and became professor of Biblical literature at Wittenberg University.

The seriousness with which Luther took his religious vocation led him into a severe personal crisis: how, he wondered, is it possible to reconcile the demands of God's law with human inability to live up to the law? He found his answer in the New Testament book of Romans: God had, in the obedience of Jesus, reconciled humanity to Himself. What was required of mankind, therefore, was not strict adherence to law or the fulfillment of religious obligations, but a response of faith that accepted what God had done. Such faith would lead to an obedience based on love, not fear.

This belief of Luther's led him into his first major confrontation with the Catholic church in 1517. Pope Leo X, in order to raise money for the building of St. Peter's Basilica in Rome, offered indulgences for sale to the people. These offered partial remission of the penalty for sins to those who made donations of money. Luther strongly objected to this practice.

On Oct. 31, 1517, Luther nailed to the door of the church in Wittenberg a list of 95 theses, or propositions. They denied the right of the pope to forgive sins by the sale of indulgences, among other challenges. The theses were widely circulated in Germany and caused a great controversy.

The pope ordered Luther to appear before Cardinal Cajetan in Augsburg. The cardinal demanded that Luther retract all he had said. Luther refused to do this unless it could be proved to him from the Bible that he was wrong.

Early in 1521 the pope issued a Bull of Excommunication against Luther and ordered Emperor Charles V to execute it. Instead, the emperor called a "diet," or council, at Worms and summoned Luther for examination. The diet demanded that Luther recant, but he refused and was outlawed.

With the help of his friend the elector of Saxony, Luther hid in the castle of Wartburg, near Eisenach. There he remained in disguise. During his time at Wartburg he began to translate the New Testament into German.

Finally the emperor's preoccupation with the war he was waging with France made it safe for Luther to return to his work at Wittenberg. While Luther was in conceal-ment some of his followers had carried the reform movement further than he had intended. On Luther's return he tried to correct these excesses but was not suc-cessful. In 1524 many of the German peasants used his teachings as a reason for revolting.

In 1525 Luther married a former nun, Katharina von Bora. This emphasized his rejection of monasticism and celibacy for the clergy. The remainder of Luther's life was spent in writing, preaching, and organizing the reformed church in Saxony. He replaced the Latin service of the mass with a service in the German language and wrote many hymns that are still in use, notably the famous "Ein feste Burg ist unser Gott" (A Mighty Fortress Is Our God). Luther died on Feb. 18, 1546, at Eisleben, his birthplace.

HULDRYCH ZWINGLI

(b. Jan. 1, 1484, Wildhaus in the Toggenburg, Sankt Gallen, Switz.—d. Oct. 11, 1531, near Kappel)

Huldrych Zwingli was the most important reformer in the Swiss Protestant Reformation and the only major reformer of the 16th century whose movement did not evolve into a church. Like Martin Luther, he accepted the supreme authority of the Scriptures, but he applied it more rigorously and comprehensively to all doctrines and practices.

Zwingli was the son of a free peasant who was a village magistrate. His mother, Margaret Meili, was the sister of the abbot of Fischingen in Thurgau, and his uncle Bartholomäus Zwingli was priest of Wildhaus and later dean of Wesen. Huldrych went to school at Wesen, then Basel (1494), and Bern (1496), where his master, Heinrich Wölflin, inspired in him an enthusiasm for the classics and a love of music. The Dominicans were interested in his musical gifts and almost enticed him to enter a convent. But his father and uncle dissuaded him, and, instead, he moved on to university studies at Vienna (1498) and then Basel (1502), where he was graduated in 1504.

Supported by teaching, he read theology and was deeply influenced by the lectures of the teacher and Reformer Thomas Wyttenbach. Ordained to the priesthood, he went, in 1506, to Glarus, where he proved a good pastor, encouraged education, commenced studying Greek and even Hebrew, and read widely in the Church Fathers. He was sympathetic toward the Renaissance movement and valued his correspondence with Erasmus. Service as chaplain with the Swiss Army led him to oppose the mercenary system. His stand provoked hostility at Glarus, and in 1516 he moved to a new charge at Einsiedeln, where he enjoyed both wide opportunities for preaching to the many pilgrims and fine facilities for study at the convent. Zwingli afterwards dated his evangelical understanding of the Scriptures from the period of transition to Einsiedeln. The difficulties at Glarus gave to this development a more than academic significance.

Zwingli at once began to preach his new convictions. Apart from topical criticism of abuses, he did not at first attack traditional positions, being content to expound the regular Gospel passages. A minor indulgence crisis arose in 1518, but Zwingli's witty castigation of the abuse found ecclesiastical favour and, finally, a titular honour by the papacy, from which he also drew a chaplaincy pension.

In 1518, despite much opposition, he was appointed people's priest at the Grossmünster (Great Minster) at Zürich. The post gave him little income or official influence but great scope for preaching. He commenced a series of expositions of the New Testament enlivened by topical application. Serious plague in 1519 found him faithful in his ministry, and his own illness and recovery, followed by his brother's death in 1520, deepened the spiritual and theological elements in his thinking and teaching that had hitherto been overshadowed to some degree by the humanistic. In 1520 he secured permission from the city's governing council to preach the "true divine scriptures," and the resulting sermons helped to stir revolts against fasting and clerical celibacy that initiated the Swiss Reformation (1522). In pursuance of his view of the supremacy of Scripture, Zwingli preached his now famous sermons at the Oetenbach convent and, despite local opposition to many of his ideas, he secured fresh authorization from his bishop to continue preaching. A tract *On Meats* and a printed version of the Oetenbach addresses, *The Clarity and Certainty of the Word of God*, appeared in 1522.

The year 1523 was crucial in the Zürich Reformation. In preparation for a disputation with the vicar general of Constance (Konstanz), arranged for January in the town hall of Zürich, Zwingli published his challenging 67 Artikel. His main contentions were adopted by most priests in the district and, in consequence, the celibacy of clergy came to be flouted, liturgical reform was begun, and a plan for the reform of the Grossmünster was drafted. A key part of this program was the reconstitution of the cathedral school as both a grammar school and a theological seminary to train Reformed pastors. The question of removing the images from the churches provoked a second disputation in October, in which Zwingli and his most intimate friend and fellow Reformer Leo Jud carried the day. Successive steps taken during 1524 and 1525 included the removal of images, the suppression of organs, the dissolution of religious houses, the replacement of the mass by a simple Communion service, the reform of the baptismal office, the introduction of prophesyings or Bible readings, the reorganization of the ministry, and the preparation of a native version of the Bible (the Zürcher Bibel appeared in 1529). Zwingli fostered the movement not only by his preaching and influence on the council but also by his various writings — e.g., *On Education, On Baptism, On the Lord's Supper*, and especially the comprehensive *Commentary on True and False Religion* (1525). He was publicly married to Anna Reinhard on April 2, 1524.

From the city of Zürich the movement quickly spread not only to the canton of Zürich but to neighbouring cantons as well. Aided by the learned Roman Catholic theologian Johann Eck, the five forest cantons of Luzern,

Zug, Schwyz, Uri, and Unterwalden resisted the new trend, but important centres like Basel and Bern declared for Zwingli. Zwingli himself, assisted by his fellow Swiss Reformer Heinrich Bullinger, took part in a disputation at Bern (1528) that formally introduced the principles of the Reformation to that city. The main theses he put forth were (1) that the church is born of the Word of God and has Christ alone as its head; (2) that its laws are binding only insofar as they agree with the Scripture; (3) that Christ alone is man's righteousness; (4) that the Holy Scripture does not teach Christ's corporeal presence in the bread and wine at the Lord's Supper; (5) that the mass is a gross affront to the sacrifice and death of Christ; (6) that there is no biblical foundation for the mediation or intercession of the dead, for purgatory, or for images and pictures; and (7) that marriage is lawful to all. With the friendly cantons of Basel and Bern, Zürich negotiated a Christian Civic Alliance (or League) based on the treaty by which Basel had been received into the Swiss confederacy but also including a common profession of faith.

From 1525 Zwingli's work was hampered by disagreements, both within Switzerland and with the Lutherans outside. In Zürich itself an extremist group quickly became dissatisfied with the Zwinglian program, desiring the abolition of tithes, a severance of the state connection, the creation of a pure or gathered church of true believers (those who have experienced a conversion according to the moral beliefs and precepts of the New Testament), and the consequent ending of infant Baptism. Disputations were held with the leaders of the Anabaptist group in January and March 1525, but these were abortive. The first rebaptisms took place in February, and widespread propaganda was initiated. Seeing its authority flouted, the council imprisoned the leaders and finally, after a further useless disputation in November 1525, brought them under a capital sentence. In theological refutation of the movement, Zwingli wrote a special work, *On Baptism* (1525), in which his main emphasis was on the significance of water Baptism as a covenant sign. During the following years he devoted many other tracts to the subject, culminating in his *Tricks of the Catabaptists* (1527).

Meanwhile, his thinking and practice in relation to the mass had led to a sharp disagreement with Martin Luther. The two agreed in rejecting the eucharistic sacrifice. They also agreed in rejecting the medieval notion of a change of substance in the sacrament. Luther, however, felt himself bound by the words "This is my body" to teach the real presence of Christ's body and blood not in place of, but in, with, and under the bread and wine. Zwingli, on the other hand, convinced that the word "is" has the force of "signifies," did not maintain a "real" presence but simply the divine presence of Christ or his presence to the believer by the power of the Holy Spirit, as signified by the elements. He stated his views in two Latin tracts (1525) and the more popular work, *On the Lord's Supper* (1526). Luther and his supporters responded with much acrimony, refusing to see in the Swiss movement a true work of evangelical reformation. Through the good offices of Philip the Magnanimous, landgrave of Hesse, the Colloquy of Marburg (1529) was arranged with a view to reconciliation; Luther, Zwingli, and Martin Bucer all participated. Cordial agreement was reached on most issues, but the critical gulf remained in relation to the sacramental presence, and Luther refused the hand of fellowship extended by Zwingli and Bucer.

Zwingli would undoubtedly have welcomed agreement with Luther for political as well as theological reasons, for he saw a growing danger in the isolation of

the Reforming cantons. The forest cantons had organized themselves against the alliance, and there was a
real threat of imperial intervention. In offensive
defense, the alliance attacked the forest cantons at
Kappel, 10 miles south of Zürich in 1529, and enforced
terms on the opposing districts. Attempts also were
made to link up with Strassburg and allied reforming
cities, but these were at first unsuccessful despite the
help of Hesse. The results of division were seen at the
Diet of Augsburg (1530), in which the evangelical groups
presented three different confessions, including
Zwingli's *Fidei Ratio*.

Lacking other friends, Zwingli turned to Venice and
France, partly in view of their political hostility to the
empire, partly in the hope of persuading the rulers to
accept evangelical views. His *Exposition of the Faith* (1531)
was addressed to Francis I of France to clear up misunderstandings and enlist his sympathy. The project faded,
however, and in 1531 Zwingli urged on the alliance a further reduction of the forest cantons. Instead, Bern
initiated a useless policy of economic sanctions that
simply provoked the foresters to attack Zürich in
October 1531. In the resultant Second War of Kappel,
Zwingli accompanied the Zürich forces as chaplain and
was killed in the battle, the spot where he fell being
now marked by an inscribed boulder.

The later preoccupation of Zwingli with ecclesiastical politics should not obscure his true contribution to
faith and order. He accepted the supreme authority of
the Scripture, although he applied it rigorously to all
doctrines and practices. He laid influential stress on the
divine sovereignty, though this was tempered by a
milder view of original sin and a wide hope of salvation.
His rejection of the sacraments as means of obtaining
grace and as forms of intervention between the soul and

God underlay the deepened conception of other Reformation leaders such as Bullinger, Pietro Martire Vermigli, and John Calvin. If he accepted lay authority in church government as exerted through the council, his personal influence averted both the subservient Erastianism (the supremacy of lay authority in ecclesiastical matters) of Lutheranism and exhausting conflict, as at Geneva. Obvious defects of disjointedness and intellectualism mark his writings. Behind them, however, lay an open, warm, and friendly disposition, and they embody a boldly striking attempt to rethink all Christian doctrine in consistently biblical terms.

SAINT IGNATIUS OF LOYOLA

(b. 1491, Loyola, Castile [Spain]—d. July 31, 1556, Rome [Italy]; canonized March 12, 1622; feast day July 31)

Saint Ignatius of Loyola, a Spanish theologian, was one of the most influential figures in the Catholic Reformation of the 16th century, and the founder of the Society of Jesus (Jesuits) in Paris in 1534.

Ignatius was born in the ancestral castle of the Loyolas in the Basque province of Guipúzcoa. The youngest son of a noble and wealthy family, Ignatius became, in 1506, a page in the service of a relative, Juan Velázquez de Cuéllar, treasurer of the kingdom of Castile. In 1517 Ignatius became a knight in the service of another relative, Antonio Manrique de Lara, Duke of Nájera and viceroy of Navarre, who employed him in military undertakings and on a diplomatic mission.

While defending the citadel of Pamplona against the French, Ignatius was hit by a cannonball on May 20, 1521, sustaining a bad fracture of his right leg and damage to his left. This event closed the first period of his life, during which he was, on his own admission, "a man given to the vanities of the world, whose chief delight consisted in martial exercises, with a great and vain desire to win renown" (*Autobiography*, 1). Although his morals were far from stainless, Ignatius was in his early years a proud rather than sensual man. He stood just under five feet two inches in height and had in his youth an abundance of hair of a reddish tint. He delighted in music, especially sacred hymns.

It is the second period of Ignatius's life, in which he turned toward a saintly life, that is the better known. After treatment at Pamplona, he was transported to Loyola in June 1521. There his condition became so serious that for a time it was thought he would die. When out of danger, he chose to undergo painful surgery to correct blunders made when the bone was first set. The result was a convalescence of many weeks, during which he read a life of Christ and a book on the lives of the saints, the only reading matter the castle afforded. He also passed time in recalling tales of martial valour and in thinking of a great lady whom he admired. In the early stages of this enforced reading, his attention was centred on the saints. The version of the lives of the saints he was reading contained prologues to the various lives by a Cistercian monk who conceived the service of God as a holy chivalry. This view of life profoundly moved and attracted Ignatius. After much reflection, he resolved to imitate the holy austerities of the saints in order to do penance for his sins.

In February 1522 Ignatius bade farewell to his family and went to Montserrat, a place of pilgrimage in northeastern Spain. He spent three days in confessing the sins of his whole life, hung his sword and dagger near the statue of the Virgin Mary as symbols of his abandoned ambitions, and, clothed in sackcloth, spent the night of March 24 in prayer. The next day he went to Manresa, a town 30 miles from Barcelona, to pass the decisive months of his career, from March 25, 1522, to mid-February 1523. He lived as a beggar, ate and drank sparingly, scourged himself, and for a time neither combed nor trimmed his hair and did not cut his nails. Daily he attended mass and spent seven hours in prayer, often in a cave outside Manresa.

The sojourn at Manresa was marked by spiritual trials as well as by joy and interior light. While sitting one day on the banks of Cardoner River, "the eyes of his understanding began to open and, without seeing any vision, he understood and knew many things, as well spiritual things as things of the faith" (Autobiography, 30). At Manresa, he sketched the fundamentals of his little book *The Spiritual Exercises*. Until the close of his studies at Paris (1535), he continued to make some additions to it. Thereafter there were only minor changes until Pope Paul III approved it in 1548. *The Spiritual Exercises* is a manual of spiritual arms containing a vital and dynamic system of spirituality. During his lifetime, Ignatius used it to give spiritual retreats to others, especially to his followers. The booklet is indeed an adaptation of the Gospels for such retreats.

The remainder of the decisive period was devoted to a pilgrimage to Jerusalem. Ignatius left Barcelona in March 1523 and, traveling by way of Rome, Venice, and Cyprus, reached Jerusalem on September 4. He would have liked to have settled there permanently, but the Franciscan custodians of the shrines of the Latin church would not listen to this plan. After visiting Bethany, the Mount of Olives, Bethlehem, the Jordan River, and Mount of Temptation, Ignatius left Palestine on October 3 and, passing through Cyprus and Venice, reached Barcelona in March 1524.

"After the pilgrim had learned that it was God's will that he should not stay in Jerusalem, he pondered in his heart what he should do and finally decided to study for a time in order to be able to help souls" (*Autobiography*, 50). So Ignatius, who in his *Autobiography* refers to himself as the "pilgrim," describes his decision to acquire as good an education as the circumstances permitted. He probably could have reached the priesthood in a few years. He chose to defer this goal for more than 12 years and to undergo the drudgery of the classroom at an age when most men have long since finished their training. Perhaps his military career had taught him the value of careful preparation. At any rate, he was convinced that a well-trained man would accomplish in a short time what one without training would never accomplish.

Ignatius studied at Barcelona for nearly two years. In 1526 he transferred to Alcalá. By this time he had acquired followers, and the little group had assumed a distinctive garb; but Ignatius soon fell under suspicion of heresy and was imprisoned and tried. Although found innocent, he left Alcalá for Salamanca. There not only was he imprisoned but his companions were also apprehended. Again he won acquittal but was forbidden to teach until he had finished his studies. This prohibition induced Ignatius to leave his disciples and Spain.

He arrived in Paris on Feb. 2, 1528, and remained there as a student until 1535. He lived on alms, and in 1528 and 1529 he went to Flanders to beg from Spanish merchants. In 1530 he went to England for the same purpose. In Paris Ignatius soon had another group of disciples whose manner of living caused such a stir that he had to explain himself to the religious authorities. This episode finally convinced him that he must abstain from public religious endeavour until he reached the priesthood.

During his long stay in the French capital, Ignatius won the coveted M.A. at the Collège de Sainte-Barbe. He also gathered the companions who were to be cofounders with him of the Society of Jesus, among them Francis Xavier, who became one of the order's greatest missionaries. On Aug. 15, 1534, he led the little band to nearby Montmartre, where they bound themselves by vows of poverty, chastity, and obedience, though as yet without the express purpose of founding a religious order.

Early in 1535, before the completion of his theological studies, Ignatius left Paris for reasons of health. He spent more than six months in Spain and then went to Bologna and Venice where he studied privately. On Jan. 8, 1537, his Parisian companions joined him in Venice. All were eager to make the pilgrimage to Jerusalem, but war between Venice and the Turkish Empire rendered this impossible. Ignatius and most of his companions were ordained on June 24, 1537. There followed 18 months during which they acquired experience in the ministry while also devoting much time to prayer. During these months, although he did not as yet say mass, Ignatius had one of the decisive experiences of his life. He related to his companions that on a certain day, while in prayer, he seemed to see Christ with the cross on his shoulder and beside him the Eternal Father, who said, "I wish you to take this man for your servant," and Jesus took him and said, "My will is that you should serve us." On Christmas Day 1538 Ignatius said his first mass at the Church of St. Mary Major in Rome. This ends the third period of his life, that of his studies, which were far from a formality. Diego Laínez, a cofounder of the Society of Jesus and an intelligent observer, judged that despite handicaps Ignatius had as great diligence as any of his fellow students. He certainly became in the difficult field of ascetic and mystical theology one of the surest of Catholic guides.

The final period of Loyola's life was spent in Rome or its vicinity. In 1539 the companions decided to form a permanent union, adding a vow of obedience to a superior elected by themselves to the vows of poverty, chastity, and obedience to the Roman pontiff that they had already taken. In 1540 Pope Paul III approved the plan of the new order. Loyola was the choice of his companions for the office of general.

The Society of Jesus developed rapidly under his hand. When he died there were about 1,000 Jesuits divided into 12 administrative units, called provinces. Three of these were in Italy, a like number in Spain, two in Germany, one in France, one in Portugal, and two overseas in India and Brazil. Loyola was, in his last years, much occupied with Germany and India, to which he sent his famous followers Peter Canisius and Francis Xavier. He also dispatched missionaries to the Congo region and to Ethiopia. In 1546 Loyola secretly received into the society Francis Borgia, Duke of Gandía and viceroy of Catalonia. When knowledge of this became public four years later it created a sensation. Borgia organized the Spanish provinces of the order and became third general.

Loyola left his mark on Rome. He founded the Roman College, embryo of the Gregorian University, and the Germanicum, a seminary for German candidates for the priesthood. He also established a home for fallen women and one for converted Jews.

Although at first Loyola had been somewhat opposed to placing his companions in colleges as educators of youth, he came in the course of time to recognize the value of the educational apostolate and in his last years was busily engaged in laying the foundations of the system of schools that was to stamp his order as largely a teaching order.

Probably the most important work of his later years was the composition of the Constitutions of the Society of Jesus. In them he decreed that his followers were to abandon some of the traditional forms of the religious life, such as chanting the divine office, physical punishments, and penitential garb, in favour of greater adaptability and mobility; they also renounced chapter government by the members of the order in favour of a more authoritative regime, and their vows were generally of such a nature that separation from the order was easier than had been usual in similar Catholic groups. The Society of Jesus was to be above all an order of apostles "ready to live in any part of the world where there was hope of God's greater glory and the good of souls." Loyola insisted on long and thorough training of his followers. Convinced that women are better ruled by women than by men, after some hesitation he resolutely excluded a female branch of the order. The special vow of obedience to the pope was called by Loyola "the cause and principal foundation" of his society.

While general of the order, Loyola was frequently sick. In January 1551 he became so ill that he begged his associates, though to no purpose, to accept his resignation as superior. Despite his condition he continued to direct the order until his death in July 1556. Since his days at Manresa, Loyola had practiced a form of prayer that was later published in *The Spiritual Exercises* and appears to have rivaled that of the greatest mystics.

Ignatius Loyola was beatified by Pope Paul V in 1609 and canonized by Pope Gregory XV in 1622. In 1922 he was declared patron of all spiritual retreats by Pope Pius XI. His achievements and those of his followers form a chapter in the history of the Roman Catholic Church that cannot be neglected by those who desire to understand that institution. English translations of Ignatius's two most important works are *The Spiritual Exercises of St. Ignatius*, translated by L. J. Puhl (1951); and *The Constitutions of the Society of Jesus*, translated and with an introduction and a commentary by G. E. Ganss (1970).

MENNO SIMONS

(b. 1496, Witmarsum, Friesland [Netherlands] — d. Jan. 31, 1561, near Lübeck, Holstein [Germany])

Menno Simons was a Dutch priest, an early leader of the peaceful wing of Dutch Anabaptism, whose followers formed the Mennonite Church.

Little is known about Menno's early life. He was born into a Dutch peasant family, and his father's name was Simon. At an early age he was enrolled in a monastic school, possibly at the Franciscan monastery in Bolsward, to prepare for the priesthood. In March 1524, at the age of 28, he was ordained at Utrecht and assigned to the parish at Pingjum, near the place of his birth. Seven years later he became the village priest in his home parish at Witmarsum.

Though Menno was to become a leading advocate of ethical Christianity, his initial concern was doctrinal. During his first year as a priest, he questioned the real presence of Christ in the bread and wine of the Eucharist. His concerns may have developed because of the antisacramental tendencies prevalent in the Netherlands at that time, tendencies that developed from the humanism of Erasmus and the ethical concerns of the Brethren of the Common Life. These doubts led Menno to read both the Bible and the writings of Martin Luther. At first he read the Bible with real fear, for he knew this step had driven Luther and the Swiss Reformer Huldrych Zwingli out of the Roman Catholic Church, but he soon agreed with them that biblical authority ought to be primary in the life of the believer and in the church. By 1528 he was known as an Evangelical preacher, though he continued as parish priest.

From doubts about the Eucharist, Menno moved gradually to questions about infant baptism and the meaning of church membership. His study of the New Testament led him to the firm conviction that only persons of mature faith, who acknowledged Jesus as Lord and had counted the cost of following him, could be eligible for membership in the church. Only such persons could be baptized as a seal (sign of guarantee) of the covenant and a witness to all the world. The grace of Christ was sufficient for children until they reached the age of accountability and made a conscious choice either for or against him. The experience of conversion came to be central to all of Menno's life and theology.

Meanwhile, the revolutionary wing of early Dutch Anabaptism continued its agitation. Members of that wing, under the leadership of the millenarian John of Leiden, had taken control of the town of Münster and were under siege from the bishop and local nobles. On April 7, 1535, the Olde Klooster near Bolsward, which had been occupied by the Anabaptists as a staging area for aid to Münster, fell before the onslaught of the state militia. Among those killed were members of Menno's congregation and Peter Simons, who may have been his brother. This prompted him to preach openly against the errors of the revolutionaries. In doing so, he articulated with increasing clarity what he believed to be the true nature of a believers' church: pure doctrine, scriptural use of sacraments, ethical obedience, love of neighbour, a clear and open witness to the faith, and a willingness to suffer. The fall of Münster on July 25, 1535, increased pressure within him to help those whom he considered to be misguided spirits. This bold and outspoken ministry soon jeopardized his safety, and in January 1536 he went into hiding after a spiritual struggle of 11 years.

In describing his decision, he wrote,

> Pondering these things my conscience tormented me so that I could no longer endure it....If I through bodily fear do not lay bare the foundation of the truth, nor use all my powers to direct the wandering flock who would gladly do their duty if they knew it, to the true pastures of Christ—oh, how shall their shed blood, shed in the midst of transgression, rise against me at the judgment of the

Almighty and pronounce sentence against my poor, miserable soul!

Menno spent a year in hiding, finding a sense of direction for his future work. During this time he wrote *Van de geestlijke verrijsenisse* ("The Spiritual Resurrection"), *De nieuwe creatuere* ("The New Birth"), and *Christelycke lering-hen op den 25. Psalm* ("Meditation on the Twenty-fifth Psalm"). Late in 1536 or early in 1537, he received believer's baptism, was called to leadership by the peaceful Anabaptist group founded in 1534 by Obbe Philips, and was ordained by Obbe. He also married. From this time on his life was in constant danger as a heretic. In 1542 the Holy Roman emperor Charles V himself issued an edict against him, promising 100 guilders reward for his arrest. One of the first Anabaptist believers to be executed for sheltering Menno was Tyaard Renicx of Leeuwarden, in 1539.

From 1543 to 1544 Menno worked in East Friesland, where in January 1544 he had a major interview or debate with the Polish Reformer Jan Laski, or Johannes à Lasco (b. 1499, Warsaw, Poland—d. 1560). The next two years, 1544–46, were spent in the Rhineland, after which Menno traveled from his new home base in Holstein, near Oldesloe, northeast of Hamburg, until his death in 1561. Here he found time for extensive writing and established a printing press to circulate Anabaptist works. His travels took him not only back to the Netherlands but also to Danzig (now Gdańsk, Poland).

Menno was not the founder of the Mennonite Church nor the most articulate spokesman of early Anabaptist theology. His greatness lay rather in the leadership he gave to northern Anabaptism during its formative first generation, a leadership maintained through his calm, biblically

oriented approach and through his writings, which consolidated the insights of the movement. Though these
writings often seem tedious and excessively polemical,
they delineated the Anabaptist faith he defended against
both Catholic and Protestant attacks on the one hand and
distortions by zealots from within the movement on the
other. During the last years of his life he was troubled particularly by some of his own brethren, who pressed for
great rigour in the application of the ban (expulsion from
the church) and other measures of discipline. More than
40 of his writings are extant.

JOHN CALVIN

(b. July 10, 1509, Noyon, Picardy, France—d. May 27, 1564, Geneva,
Switzerland)

John Calvin was a theologian and ecclesiastical statesman. He was the leading French Protestant Reformer
and the most important figure in the second generation of
the Protestant Reformation. His interpretation of
Christianity, advanced above all in his *Institutio Christianae
religionis* (1536 but elaborated in later editions; *Institutes of
the Christian Religion*), and the institutional and social pat-
terns he worked out for Geneva deeply influenced
Protestantism elsewhere in Europe and in North America.
The Calvinist form of Protestantism is widely thought to
have had a major impact on the formation of the modern
world.

Calvin was of middle-class parents. His father, a lay
administrator in the service of the local bishop, sent him
to the University of Paris in 1523 to be educated for the
priesthood but later decided that he should be a lawyer;
from 1528 to 1531, therefore, Calvin studied in the law
schools of Orléans and Bourges. He then returned to Paris.

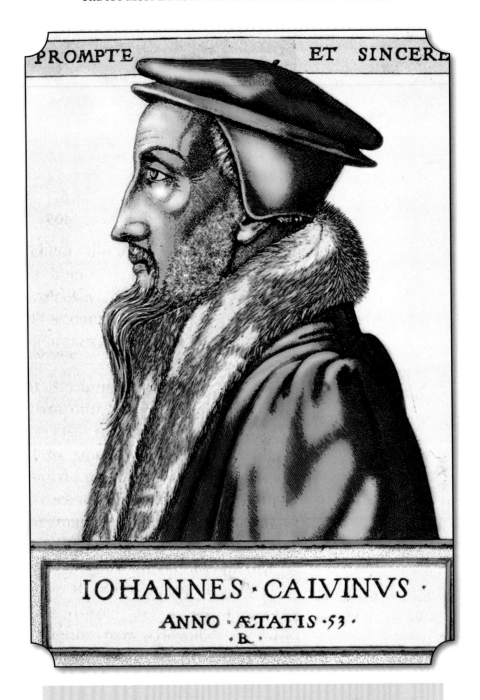

John Calvin, portrait by Konrad Meyer, 19th century.

During these years he was also exposed to Renaissance humanism, influenced by Erasmus and Jacques Lefèvre d'Étaples, which constituted the radical student movement of the time. This movement, which antedates the Reformation, aimed to reform church and society on the model of both classical and Christian antiquity, to be established by a return to the Bible studied in its original languages. It left an indelible mark on Calvin. Under its influence he studied Greek and Hebrew as well as Latin, the three languages of ancient Christian discourse, in preparation for serious study of the Scriptures. It also intensified his interest in the classics; his first publication (1532) was a commentary on Seneca's essay on clemency. But the movement, above all, emphasized salvation of individuals by grace rather than good works and ceremonies.

Calvin's Paris years came to an abrupt end late in 1533. Because the government became less tolerant of this reform movement, Calvin, who had collaborated in the preparation of a strong statement of theological principles for a public address delivered by Nicolas Cop, rector of the university, found it prudent to leave Paris. Eventually he made his way to Basel, then Protestant but tolerant of religious variety. Up to that point, however, there is little evidence of Calvin's conversion to Protestantism, an event difficult to date because it was probably gradual. His beliefs before his flight to Switzerland were probably not incompatible with Roman Catholic orthodoxy. But they underwent a change when he began to study theology intensively in Basel. Probably in part to clarify his own beliefs, he began to write. He began with a preface to a French translation of the Bible by his cousin Pierre Olivétan and then undertook what became the first edition of the *Institutes*, his masterwork, which, in its successive revisions, became the single most important statement of Protestant belief. Calvin published later editions in both Latin and French, containing elaborated and in a few cases revised teachings and replies to his critics. The final versions appeared in 1559 and 1560. The *Institutes* also reflected the findings of Calvin's massive biblical commentaries, which, presented extemporaneously in Latin as lectures to ministerial candidates from many countries, make up the largest proportion of his works. In addition he wrote many theological and polemical treatises.

The 1536 *Institutes* had given Calvin some reputation among Protestant leaders. Therefore, on discovering that Calvin was spending a night in Geneva late in 1536, the Reformer and preacher Guillaume Farel, then struggling to plant Protestantism in that town, persuaded him to remain to help in this work. The Reformation was in trouble in Geneva, a town of about 10,000 where Protestantism had only the shallowest of roots. Other towns in the region, initially ruled by their prince-bishops, had successfully won self-government much earlier, but Geneva had lagged behind in this process largely because its prince-bishop was supported by the neighbouring Duke of Savoy. There had been iconoclastic riots in Geneva in the mid-1520s, but these had negligible theological foundations. Protestantism had been imposed on religiously unawakened Geneva chiefly as the price of military aid from Protestant Bern. The limited enthusiasm of Geneva for Protestantism, reflected by a resistance to religious and moral reform, continued almost until Calvin's death. The resistance was all the more serious because the town council in Geneva, as in other Protestant towns, exercised ultimate control over the church and the ministers, all French refugees. The main issue was the right of excommunication, which the ministers regarded as essential to their authority but which the council refused to concede. The uncompromising attitudes of Calvin and Farel finally resulted in their expulsion from Geneva in May 1538.

Calvin found refuge for the next three years in the German Protestant city of Strasbourg, where he was pastor of a church for French-speaking refugees and also lectured on the Bible; there he published his commentary on the Letter of Paul to the Romans. There too, in 1540, he married Idelette de Bure, the widow of a man he had converted from Anabaptism. Although none of their children survived infancy, their marital relationship proved to be extremely warm. During his Strasbourg years Calvin also learned much about the administration of an urban church from Martin Bucer, its chief pastor. Meanwhile Calvin's attendance at various international religious conferences made him acquainted with other Protestant leaders and gave him experience in debating with Roman Catholic theologians. Henceforth he was a major figure in international Protestantism.

In September 1541 Calvin was invited back to Geneva, where the Protestant revolution, without strong leadership, had become increasingly insecure. Because he was now in a much stronger position, the town council in November enacted his Ecclesiastical Ordinances, which provided for the religious education of the townspeople, especially children, and instituted Calvin's conception of church order. It also established four groups of church officers: pastors and teachers to preach and explain the Scriptures, elders representing the congregation to administer the church, and deacons to attend to its charitable responsibilities. In addition it set up a consistory of pastors and elders to make all aspects of Genevan life conform to God's law. It undertook a wide range of disciplinary actions covering everything from the abolition of Roman Catholic "superstition" to the enforcement of sexual morality, the regulation of taverns, and measures against dancing, gambling, and swearing. These measures were resented by a significant element of the population, and the arrival of increasing numbers of French religious refugees in Geneva was a further cause of native discontent. These tensions, as well as the persecution of Calvin's followers in France, help to explain the trial and burning of Michael Servetus, a Spanish theologian preaching and publishing unorthodox beliefs. When Servetus unexpectedly arrived in Geneva in 1553, both sides felt the need to demonstrate their zeal for orthodoxy. Calvin was responsible for Servetus's arrest and conviction, though he had preferred a less brutal form of execution.

The struggle over control of Geneva lasted until May 1555, when Calvin finally prevailed and could devote himself more wholeheartedly to other matters. He had constantly to watch the international scene and to keep his Protestant allies in a common front. Toward this end he engaged in a massive correspondence with political and religious leaders throughout Protestant Europe. He also continued his commentaries on Scripture, working through the whole New Testament except the Revelation to John and most of the Old Testament. Many of these commentaries were promptly published, often with dedications to such European rulers as Queen Elizabeth, though Calvin had too little time to do much of the editorial work himself. Committees of amanuenses took down what he said, prepared a master copy, and then presented it to Calvin for approval. During this period Calvin also established the Genevan Academy to train students in humanist learning in preparation for the ministry and positions of secular leadership. He also performed a wide range of pastoral duties, preaching regularly and often, doing numerous weddings and baptisms, and giving spiritual advice. Worn out by so many responsibilities and suffering from a multitude of ailments, he died in 1564.

JOHN KNOX

(b. c. 1514, near Haddington, East Lothian, Scotland—d. Nov. 24, 1572, Edinburgh)

John Knox, the foremost leader of the Scottish Reformation, set the austere moral tone of the Church of Scotland and shaped the democratic form of government it adopted. He was influenced by George Wishart, who was burned for heresy in 1546, and the following year Knox became the spokesman for the Reformation in Scotland. After a period of intermittent imprisonment and exile in England and on the European continent, in 1559 he returned to Scotland, where he supervised the preparation of the constitution and liturgy of the Reformed Church. His most important literary work was his *History of the Reformation in Scotland.*

Almost nothing is known of Knox's life before 1540, the accounts given by his earlier biographers being mostly fanciful. Of his parentage it is known only that his mother's name was Sinclair (Knox used the name John Sinclair as an incognito in times of danger), that his father's name was William, and that he and both Knox's grandfathers had fought, and two of them had died—perhaps at the Battle of Flodden against Henry VIII's troops. The family may have been farmers.

It is supposed that Knox trained for the priesthood under the scholar John Major, most probably at the University of St. Andrews. Knox did not take a master's degree, however, but he ended his training with a mind imbued with that delight in abstract thought and dialectical disputation which, even in that age, was recognized throughout Europe as typical of Scottish scholarship. He was in priest's orders by 1540, and in 1543 he was known to be also practicing as an apostolic notary in the Haddington area, which would seem to indicate that he was in good standing with the ecclesiastical authorities.

Two years later, however, Knox was in more equivocal company as tutor to the sons of two gentlemen of East Lothian who were deeply involved in the intrigues of political Protestantism. Under their protection, George Wishart, a Scottish Reformation leader who was to become an early martyr for the cause, began a preaching tour in the Lothians in December 1545. Knox was much in his company, and Knox's complete conversion to the Reformed faith dates from his contact with Wishart, whose memory he cherished ever afterward. Wishart was burned for heresy in March 1546 by Cardinal David Beaton, archbishop of St. Andrews, who, rather than the weak governor, was the real ruler of Scotland. Wishart's execution began a chain of events that profoundly altered Knox's life. Three months later, Beaton was murdered by Protestant conspirators who fortified themselves in St. Andrews castle.

Meantime, Knox, accompanied by his pupils, was moving from place to place to escape persecution and arrest. His desire was to go to Germany to study there at the Protestant seats of learning, but his employers sent word to him to take their sons to St. Andrews and continue their education under the protection of the castle. Thus, in April 1547, less than a year after the cardinal's murder and against his own desire, Knox arrived with his pupils in St. Andrews—still an unknown man. The three months that he spent there transformed him, against his own predisposition, into the acknowledged spokesman and protagonist of the Reformation movement in Scotland. The Protestants in the castle had become involved in controversy with the university; several of them, becoming aware that a man of uncommon gifts had joined them, pressed upon Knox's conscience the duty of taking up "the public office and charge of preaching."

Knox's inclination was for the quiet of the study and the schoolroom, not for the responsibilities and perils of the life of a preacher of a proscribed and persecuted faith. He resisted the call with tears, and only after great hesitation was he persuaded to preach in the town of St. Andrews a sermon that convinced friend and foe alike that the great spokesman of Scottish Protestantism had been found. This was the turning point of Knox's life; from this time forward he regarded himself as called to preaching by God, and he was the more certain of the divine origin and compulsion of the call in that it ran counter to every inclination of his own.

At the end of June 1547, French assistance reached the governor of Scotland. The garrison of St. Andrews castle, bombarded from without and assailed by plague within, capitulated on terms that were not kept; Knox and others were carried off to slavery in the French galleys. English intervention secured his release 19 months later, though with permanently broken health.

In England the Protestant government of Edward VI was endeavouring to hurry clergy and people into the Reformation faster, if anything, than most of them were willing to go. For this program preachers and propagandists were urgently required; and because a return to a Scotland under Roman Catholic rule was impossible for Knox at this time, the English government promptly made him one of a select corps of licensed preachers and sent him north to propagate the Reformation in the turbulent garrison town of Berwick-upon-Tweed. He brought order to the town and established a congregation on Puritan lines, and there he met Marjorie Bowes, who was to become his wife. Early in 1551 he was given a new assignment in Newcastle and a little later was appointed to be one of the six royal chaplains whose duties included periodic residence at, and preaching before, the court as well as itinerant evangelism in areas where the regular clergy were lacking in Protestant zeal. He later refused to accept the bishopric of Rochester and the vicarage of Allhallows, London, but continued, under the patronage of the government, to exercise an itinerant ministry, mainly, but not exclusively, in Buckinghamshire, Kent, and London.

In three respects Knox left his mark on the Church of England: he took part in the shaping of its articles; he secured the insertion into The Book of Common Prayer of the so-called black rubric, which denies the corporal presence of Christ in the consecrated bread and wine used in Holy Communion and explains that kneeling at communion implies no adoration of the elements; and he was one of the chief foster fathers of English Puritanism, a reform movement started within the state church with a view to the more rigorous application of Reformation principles in doctrine and worship.

On the accession of Mary Tudor, a Roman Catholic, to the throne in 1553, Knox was one of the last of the Protestant leaders to flee the country. He escaped to the Continent disturbed by the realization that the fate of "true religion" in England had turned on the religious opinions of one woman. He could see no security for the Reformation anywhere if the personal whim of a sovereign was permitted to settle the religion of a nation. Might it not be legitimate for Protestant subjects, in such circumstances, to resist—if necessary by force—the subversion of their religion by a Roman Catholic ruler? Knox formulated his fateful conclusion, later to be applied in Scotland, that God-fearing magistrates and nobility have both the right and the duty to resist, if necessary by force, a ruler who threatens the safety of true religion. Also in 1554 Knox published his *Faithful Admonition* to the Protestants who remained in England. Its extremism and intemperate language served to increase the sufferings of those to whom it was addressed; and, coming as it did from one who was in comparative safety, it alienated many in England from him.

In the same year, on the insistence of John Calvin, Knox became minister of a congregation of English refugees, mainly Puritan, in Frankfurt am Main; but he remained there for only a few months. He then became minister of the growing congregation of English exiles in Geneva, a pastorate that lasted until his final return to Scotland in 1559, but was interrupted at the outset by a visit (1555–56) to Berwick and a nine-month sojourn in Scotland, in the course of which he married Marjorie Bowes. She died, having borne him two sons, in 1560.

In Edinburgh Knox was astounded by the progress made by the Reformed cause and by the eager reception given to him by all classes in the community. To the nobility, in visits to their country houses, he propounded his doctrine of "justifiable resistance" to Roman Catholic rulers who attacked the faith of Protestant subjects and urged them to withdraw from all the rites and ceremonies of the Roman Church and to band themselves together for the defense of Protestantism in case that should prove necessary. A peremptory summons from his congregation called him back to Geneva; but he left to the faithful in Scotland an important *Letter of Wholesome Counsel* (1556) enjoining not only private family worship but also weekly meetings of believers for corporate Bible study and discussion. From these weekly meetings, Reformed congregations grew apace, and from the leaders of these congregations came the elders of the Reformed Church.

Geneva was to Knox a beloved city in which he spent the happiest years of his life, highly esteemed, in peace, and among kindred souls. From this period (1556–58) dates his elaborate and rather tedious treatise on Predestination as well as his first blast of the trumpet against the monstruous regiment [rule] of women, in which he states with uncurbed vehemence the common belief of his day that the exercise of authority by women is contrary to both natural law and revealed religion. The pamphlet was aimed at the three women who were holding the reins of government in England, France, and Scotland and were oppressing Protestantism; but, unfortunately for Knox, publication coincided with the accession in England of the Protestant Elizabeth I, who indignantly and permanently debarred the rash author from her realm.

In Scotland, matters reached a crisis in the spring of 1559. Two years earlier the Protestant lords had signed a "band," or covenant, on Knox's advice, pledging themselves to foster and defend "the Congregation of the Lord" and its ministers (hence their name "Lords of the Congregation"). The queen regent, the French-born Mary of Guise, had deemed it politic to make concessions to them. But when hostilities between Spain and France ended early in 1559, opening the possibility of stronger French intervention in Scotland, the queen regent felt that the time had come to call a final halt to the expansion of Protestantism. To this end she summoned the Protestant preachers, as ringleaders of the growing Protestant insubordination, to appear before her on May 10 at Stirling. The Protestants replied by recalling Knox from Geneva, and the Protestant lords, lairds, and commoners mustered at Dundee. On May 4, Knox joined them and they advanced to Perth, where, after a vehement sermon by Knox, the friaries were sacked.

By the end of June, Edinburgh was temporarily in Protestant hands and Knox was preaching in St. Giles's; but the triumph was illusory and Knox knew it. The voluntary army of Protestants could not keep the field for more than a few weeks; the mercenary army of the queen regent could keep the field indefinitely and strike a crushing blow as Protestant strength declined. At this juncture Henry II of France died and power fell into the hands of the Guises, the brothers of the queen regent and uncles of the young queen of France—Mary, Queen of Scots and consort of Francis II, the new king of France. Strong French intervention in Scotland was now assured in furtherance of the Guise plan to displace Queen Elizabeth of England and to unite France, Scotland, and England under Francis II, of France, and Mary. Thus a political issue of critical international importance cut athwart the religious issue in Scotland. A French victory in Scotland would place Elizabeth and England in peril. It therefore behooved England to make common cause with the Scottish Protestants. Knox lost no opportunity to drive this fact home to Elizabeth. The autumn and winter of 1559 saw the Scottish Protestants in desperate plight. Only Knox's superhuman exertions and indomitable spirit kept the cause in being. In the blackest hour Knox put fresh heart into the despairing Protestant leaders and staved off defeat at the hands of the government's French mercenaries. On Knox's resolution alone in these months hung the fate not only of Scottish Protestantism but of Elizabeth's England as well.

In the spring of 1560, Elizabeth at last consented to English action. In April, 10,000 English troops joined the Scottish Protestants, the queen regent died in Edinburgh castle, and the disheartened French gave up. By treaty, French and English troops were then withdrawn, leaving the victorious Scottish Protestants to set their own house in order. Queen Mary was a Roman Catholic and an absentee in France, and all her sympathies were with the defeated side. The Scottish Parliament had never exercised much power, but now, meeting in August without royal authority, it proceeded to grapple with the religious issue. The Scots Confession (hurriedly prepared by Knox and three others) was adopted, and papal jurisdiction was abolished.

Knox, aided by a committee of distinguished churchmen, laid before the Scottish Parliament the *First Book of Discipline* containing proposals for the constitution and finance of the Reformed Church. Worship was to be regulated by the *Book of Common Order* (also called Knox's Liturgy), according to which congregations were to be governed by elders elected annually by the people and the elders were to aid the minister to maintain firm moral discipline among the people. Ministers were to be elected by the people but to be appointed only after rigorous examination of life and doctrine by their ministerial brethren. The ablest ministers were to be appointed superintendents of areas roughly corresponding to the old dioceses; they were to supervise the ministers and congregations in the area and were to be assisted by provincial synods of ministers and elders. In the high place given to the laity, Knox's system contains the most essential element of later Presbyterianism.

The *Book of Discipline* proceeds to outline a most elaborate educational scheme and plans for a much-needed scheme of systematic aid of the poor. Finally it urges that the endowments of the old church should be made available for the financing of these admittedly costly schemes of the new church. But the proposals thus outlined foundered on the rock of finance. The endowments of the old church were plunder in a poor land for the nobility, who had scant sympathy with Knox's "devout imaginings." Parliament shelved the financial problem by the temporary expedient of granting to the remaining Roman Catholic clergy the life-rent of their benefices, provided they contributed to the maintenance of the Reformed Church out of their revenues. Knox was deeply embittered by the enforced abandonment of his schemes for education and poor relief and by the scant provision for the Reformed Church.

Mary arrived in Scotland in 1561 already persuaded that Knox was to be her archenemy and that the country could not hold them both. Knox, who hoped at first that the young queen would prove pliable, soon reached a similar conviction. The first three of his audiences with Mary were polite skirmishes; in the fourth, battle was joined in grim earnest. Hearing that Mary was contemplating marriage with Don Carlos of Spain, a match that would have had fatal consequences for the Scottish Reformation and probably for England as well, Knox sounded the Protestant alarm. Mary, enraged at this intervention by a heretic preacher and commoner in affairs of state, berated Knox with hysterical fury and charged him with treason, but the Privy Council refused to convict him. Knox filled Mary's cup of bitterness in 1564 by marrying, without the royal assent, Margaret Stewart, a 17-year-old distant relative of the queen.

In 1564 Mary dismissed her Protestant advisers and undertook the mismanagement of her own affairs. For a time the Reformed Church was in real danger, but in 1567 came Mary's ruin and abdication, and Knox's old friend James Stewart, earl of Moray, became regent. In him the Reformed Church would have found a powerful patron, but he was murdered and the country plunged into a struggle between the supporters of the queen and those of the regency. Knox was involved in the turmoil, but he suffered a paralytic stroke. When Edinburgh became a battleground between the factions in 1571, the leaders on both sides insisted on his removal to safety in St. Andrews, from where he returned in 1572 to die. When the news of the St. Bartholomew's Day Massacre of French Protestants reached Scotland, Knox dragged himself to his pulpit in

St. Giles's and drove home the lesson of that tragedy. He stood one last time in the pulpit of St. Giles's, to introduce his successor.

SAINT TERESA OF ÁVILA

(b. March 28, 1515, Ávila, Spain — d. Oct.4, 1582, Alba de Tormes)

Saint Teresa of Ávila was a Spanish nun, one of the great mystics and religious women of the Roman Catholic Church, and an author of spiritual classics. She was the originator of the Carmelite Reform, which restored and emphasized the austerity and contemplative character of primitive Carmelite life. St. Teresa was elevated to doctor of the church in 1970 by Pope Paul VI, the first woman to be so honoured.

Her mother died in 1529, and, despite her father's opposition, Teresa entered, probably in 1535, the Carmelite Convent of the Incarnation at Ávila. Within two years her health collapsed, and she was an invalid for three years, during which time she developed a love for mental prayer. After her recovery, however, she stopped praying. She continued for 15 years in a state divided between a worldly and a divine spirit, until, in 1555, she underwent a religious awakening.

In 1558 Teresa began to consider the restoration of Carmelite life to its original observance of austerity, which had relaxed in the 14th and 15th centuries. Her reform required utter withdrawal so that the nuns could meditate on divine law and, through a prayerful life of penance, exercise what she termed "our vocation of reparation" for the sins of mankind. In 1562, with Pope Pius IV's authorization, she opened the first convent (St. Joseph's) of the Carmelite Reform. A storm of hostility came from municipal and religious personages, especially because the convent existed without endowment, but she staunchly insisted on poverty and subsistence only through public alms.

John Baptist Rossi, the Carmelite prior general from Rome, went to Ávila in 1567 and approved the reform, directing Teresa to found more convents and to establish monasteries. In the same year, while at Medina del Campo, Spain, she met a young Carmelite priest, Juan de Yepes (later St. John of the Cross, the poet and mystic), who she realized could initiate the Carmelite Reform for men. A year later Juan opened the first monastery of the Primitive Rule at Duruelo, Spain.

Despite frail health and great difficulties, Teresa spent the rest of her life establishing and nurturing 16 more convents throughout Spain. In 1575, while she was at the Sevilla (Seville) convent, a jurisdictional dispute erupted between the friars of the restored Primitive Rule, known as the Discalced (or "Unshod") Carmelites, and the observants of the Mitigated Rule, the Calced (or "Shod") Carmelites. Although she had foreseen the trouble and endeavoured to prevent it, her attempts failed. The Carmelite general, to whom she had been misrepresented, ordered her to retire to a convent in Castile and to cease founding additional convents; Juan was subsequently imprisoned at Toledo in 1577.

In 1579, largely through the efforts of King Philip II of Spain, who knew and admired Teresa, a solution was effected whereby the Carmelites of the Primitive Rule were given independent jurisdiction, confirmed in 1580 by a rescript of Pope Gregory XIII. Teresa, broken in health, was then directed to resume the reform. In journeys that covered hundreds of miles, she made exhausting missions and was fatally stricken en route to Ávila from Burgos.

Teresa's ascetic doctrine has been accepted as the classical exposition of the contemplative life, and her spiritual writings are among the most widely read. Her *Life of the Mother Teresa of Jesus* (1611) is autobiographical; the *Book of the Foundations* (1610) describes the establishment of her convents. Her writings on the progress of the Christian soul toward God are recognized masterpieces: *The Way of Perfection* (1583), *The Interior Castle* (1588), *Spiritual Relations*, *Exclamations of the Soul to God* (1588), and *Conceptions on the Love of God*. Of her poems, 31 are extant; of her letters, 458.

ISAAC BEN SOLOMON LURIA

born 1534, Jerusalem, Palestine, Ottoman Empire—d. Aug. 5, 1572, Safed, Syria [now Zefat, Israel])

Isaac ben Solomon Luria was the eponymous founder of the Lurianic school of Kabbala (Jewish esoteric mysticism).

Luria's youth was spent in Egypt, where he became versed in rabbinic studies, engaged in commerce, and eventually concentrated on study of the Zohar, the central work of Kabbala. In 1570 he went to Safed in Galilee, where he studied under Moses ben Jacob Cordovero, the greatest Kabbalist of the time, and developed his own Kabbalistic system. Although he wrote few works beyond three famous hymns, Luria's doctrines were recorded by his pupil Ḥayyim Vital, who presented them in a voluminous posthumous collection.

Luria's father was an Ashkenazi (an Eastern European Jew), while his mother was a Sephardi (of Iberian-North African Jewish stock). Legend has it that the prophet Elijah appeared to his father and foretold the birth of the son, whose name was to be Isaac. As a child, Luria was described as a young genius, "a Torah scholar who could silence all opponents by the power of his arguments," and also as possessed of divine inspiration.

The main source for his life story is an anonymous biography, *Toledot ha-Ari* ("Life of the Ari"), written or perhaps edited some 20 years after his death, in which factual and legendary elements are indiscriminately mingled. According to the *Toledot*, Luria's father died while Isaac was a child, and his mother took him to Egypt to live with her well-to-do family. While there, he became versed in rabbinic studies, including Halakha (Jewish law), and even wrote glosses on a famous compendium of legal discussions, the *Sefer ha-Halakhot* of Isaac ben Jacob Alfasi. He also engaged in commerce during this period.

While still a youth, Luria began the study of Jewish mystical learning and lived for nearly seven years in seclusion at his uncle's home on an island in the Nile River. His studies concentrated on the Zohar (late 13th–early 14th century), the central and revered work of the Kabbala, but he also studied the early Kabbalists (12th–13th century). The greatest Kabbalist of Luria's time was Moses ben Jacob Cordovero of Safed (modern Ẓefat), in Palestine, whose work Luria studied while still in Egypt. During this period he wrote a commentary on the Sifra di-tzeni'uta ("Book of Concealment"), a section of the Zohar. The commentary still shows the influence of classical Kabbala and contains nothing of what would later be called Lurianic Kabbala.

Early in 1570 Luria journeyed to Safed, the mountain town in Galilee that had become a centre of the Kabbalistic movement, and he studied there with Cordovero. At the same time, he began to teach Kabbala according to a new system and attracted many pupils. The greatest of these was Ḥayyim Vital, who later set Luria's teachings down in writing. Luria apparently expounded his teachings only in esoteric circles; not everyone was allowed to take part in these studies. While he devoted most of his time to the instruction of his pupils, he probably made his living in trade, which prospered at that time in Safed, situated as it was at the crossroads between Egypt and Damascus.

At the time of Luria's arrival in Safed, the group of Kabbalists gathered there around Cordovero had already developed a unique style of living and observed special rituals, going out, for instance, into the fields to welcome the sabbath, personified as the Sabbath Queen. With Luria's arrival, new elements were added to these excursions, such as communion with the souls of the *zaddikim* (men of outstanding piety) by means of special *kawwanot* (ritual meditations) and *yiḥudim* ("unifications") that were in essence a kind of lesser redemption whereby the souls were lifted up from the *kelipot* ("shells"; i.e., the impure, evil forms) into which they were banned until the coming of the Messiah.

The strong influence of Luria's personality helped to bring about in Safed an atmosphere of spiritual intensity, messianic tension, and the fever of creation that accompanies the sense of a great revelation. Deep devoutness, asceticism, and withdrawal from the world marked the Kabbalists' way of life. Luria apparently looked upon himself as the Messiah ben Joseph, the first of the two messiahs in Jewish tradition, who is fated to be killed in the wars (of Gog and Magog) that will precede the final redemption. In Safed there was an expectation (based on the Zohar) that the Messiah would appear in Galilee in the year 1575.

Even though he did not distinguish himself as a writer, as is evident from his own remarks about the difficulty of writing, Luria composed three hymns that became widely known and part of the cultural heritage of the Jewish people. These are hymns for the three sabbath meals, which became part of the Sephardic sabbath ritual and were printed in many prayer books. The three meals were linked by means of mystical "intention" or meditation (kawwana) to three partzufim (aspects of the Godhead). The hymns are known as "Azamer be-she-vaḥim" ("I Will Sing on the Praises"), "Asader seʿudata" ("I Will Order the Festive Meal"), and "Bene hekh-ala de-khesifin" ("Sons of the Temple of Silver"). They are mystical, erotic songs about "the adornment (or fitting) of the bride"—i.e., the sabbath, who was identified with the community of Israel—and on the other *partzufim: arikh anpin* (the long-suffering: the countenance of grace) and *ze ʿir anpin* (the impatient: the countenance of judgment).

During his brief sojourn in Safed—a scant two years before his death—Luria managed to construct a many-faceted and fertile Kabbalistic system from which many new elements in Jewish mysticism drew their nourishment. He set down almost none of his doctrine in writing, with the exception of a short text that seems to be only a fragment: his commentary on the first chapter of the Zohar—"*Be-resh hormanuta de-malka*"—as well as commentaries on isolated passages of the Zohar that were collected by Ḥayyim Vital, who attests to their being in his teacher's own hand. Luria died in an epidemic that struck Safed in August 1572.

What is called Lurianic Kabbala is a voluminous collection of Luria's Kabbalistic doctrines, recorded after his death by Ḥayyim Vital and appearing in two versions under different editorship. Because of this work, Lurianic Kabbala became the new thought that influenced all Jewish mysticism after Luria, competing with the Kabbala of Cordovero. Vital laboured much to give Lurianic Kabbala its form as well as to win legitimization for it.

Lurianic Kabbala propounds a theory of the creation and subsequent degeneration of the world and a practical method of restoring the original harmony. The theory is based on three concepts: *tzimtzum* ("contraction," or "withdrawal"), *shevirat ha-kelim* ("breaking of the vessels"), and *tiqqun* ("restoration"). God as the Infinite (En Sof) withdraws into himself in order to make room for the creation, which occurs by a beam of light from the Infinite into the newly provided space. Later the divine light is enclosed in finite "vessels," most of which break under the strain, and the catastrophe of the "breaking of the vessels" occurs, whereby disharmony and evil enter the world. Hence comes the struggle to rid the world of evil and accomplish the redemption of both the cosmos and history. This event occurs in the stage of tiqqun, in which the divine realm itself is reconstructed, the divine sparks returned to their source, and Adam Qadmon, the symbolic "primordial man," who is the highest configuration of the divine light, is rebuilt. Man plays an important role in this process through various kawwanot used during prayer and through mystical intentions involving secret combinations of words, all of which is directed toward the restoration of the primordial harmony and the reunification of the divine name.

The influence of Luria's Kabbala was far-reaching. It played an important role in the movement of the false messiah Shabbetai Tzevi in the 17th century and in the popular Ḥasidic (mystical-pietistic) movement a century later.

ARMAND-JEAN DU PLESSIS, CARDINAL ET DUC DE RICHELIEU

(b. Sept. 9, 1585, Richelieu, Poitou, France—d. Dec. 4, 1642, Paris)

Armand-Jean du Plessis, cardinal et duc de Richelieu was the chief minister to King Louis XIII of France from 1624 to 1642. His major goals were the establishment of royal absolutism in France and the end of Spanish-Habsburg hegemony in Europe.

The family du Plessis de Richelieu was of insignificant feudal origins but, by intermarriage with the legal and administrative classes, rose to some prominence and acquired the seigneury of Richelieu in Poitou. Armand-Jean's father, François du Plessis, seigneur de Richelieu, was grand provost (chief magistrate) to Henry III, and his mother, Suzanne de la Porte, was the daughter of a councillor of the Parlement of Paris (the supreme judicial assembly). In his intelligence, administrative competence, and instinct for hard work, he resembled his middle-class ancestors.

He was five years old when his father died, leaving estates that had been ruined by inflation and mismanagement during the Wars of Religion (1562–98), and he was conscious from his earliest years of the threat of penury. This inspired in him the ambition to restore the honour of his house and evoked in him the sense of grandeur he was to attribute vicariously to France. His provident mother, with three boys and two girls, set about reorganizing the family's precarious resources. The principal of these was the benefice of the bishopric of Luçon near La Rochelle, which had been granted by

A portrait of Cardinal de Richelieu was painted by Philippe de Champaigne. It is in the Louvre in Paris, France.

Henry III to the Richelieus under the Concordat of 1516. Unrest of the cathedral chapter threatened a revocation of the grant, and it became necessary for a member of the family to be consecrated bishop as soon as possible. Henri, the eldest son, was heir to the seigneury of Richelieu; and Alphonse, the second son, had become a Carthusian monk; so the obligation fell on Armand-Jean, who was a student.

The prospect of a career in the church was not displeasing to the thin, pale, and at times sickly boy, for he had an inclination toward learning, a facility for debate, and a relish for the prospect of governing the lives of others. Because he was below the canonical age for consecration upon the completion of his studies, he needed a papal dispensation. To gain it he went to Rome, where Paul V fell victim to the young man's skill as a charmer. On April 17, 1607, at the age of 22, he was ordained a priest and was consecrated to the see of Luçon. He found on his arrival a diocese ruined by the Wars of Religion, a hostile chapter, and a demoralized clergy, but his opponents quickly succumbed to the unaccustomed authority that radiated from the episcopal palace.

Richelieu was the first bishop in France to implement in his diocese the reforms decreed by the Council of Trent, and he was also the first theologian to write in French and to establish the conventions of vernacular theological exposition. He was a hard-working, conscience-stricken man, combatting forces dedicated to divisive political and social ends—a man obsessed with order as a superior moral end.

The France on which the bishop of Luçon pondered gave every indication of falling again into the disorder of the Wars of Religion. The assassination of Henry IV in 1610 released separative forces that were endemic in the administrative system. The government of the queen mother, Marie de Médicis, as regent for Louis XIII, was corrupt, and the magnates of the realm, motivated by personal self-interest, struggled to control it. Their disobedience was accompanied by predatory expeditions of armed men and complex negotiations with the court, and on one of these occasions the bishop of Luçon found himself an intermediary, which led to his being elected one of the representatives of the clergy of Poitou to the Estates-General of 1614. He put all his energy into persuading the assembly of his talents and the court of his support for royal authority. In a clash between the clergy and the Third Estate (the middle classes, artisans, and peasants) on the subject of the relationship between the crown and the papacy, he played a conciliatory role, and he was prominent in moves of the clergy to persuade the Third Estate that the decrees of the Council of Trent should be promulgated.

Some months later he was appointed chaplain to the new queen, Anne of Austria, which held the promise of eventual entry into the royal council, which, Richelieu had argued at the Estates-General, should accord first place to prelates of distinction. Clever negotiations with another disobedient faction led to his appointment as a secretary of state in 1616.

Up to this time Richelieu had had no insight into international relations, and the regard for Spain with which he was credited was probably genuine because he had had no occasion to question Spain's ambitions. His year of office, however, coincided with war between Spain (ruled by a Habsburg dynasty) and Venice, which invoked its alliance with France. The resultant involvement persuaded Richelieu of the vulnerability of France to Habsburg political and economic encirclement, the domestic ramifications of various European movements in the religious controversy between Catholics and Protestants, and the dependence of the small states in France's borderlands upon an equilibrium of power between France and Spain.

Richelieu's tenure of office was terminated in April 1617 when a palace revolution overthrew the regency of Marie de Médicis. Richelieu was banished to Luçon and then exiled to the papal city of Avignon, where he sought distraction from his melancholy in writing. A rebellion of the princes, gravitating this time to Marie de Médicis as the focus of opposition to the royal council, led in 1619 to the king recalling Richelieu to his mother's entourage on the assumption that he would exercise a moderating influence. The ascendency that he gained over her, however, did not lead to her submission. There followed four years of intricate negotiation and even overt hostilities during which the king's nomination of Richelieu for a cardinal's hat became one of the issues involved in a settlement. A revolt of the Huguenots and the death of the king's favourite brought about Marie de Médicis's recall to the council and Richelieu's promotion.

In 1624 another crisis, over the Valtellina in northern Italy, led to a ministerial reconstruction and to the cardinal's appointment as secretary of state for commerce and marine and chief of the royal council. Four years later the title of first minister was to be created for this office. The controversy occurred when the Protestant Swiss canton of Grisons invoked a treaty of protection with France against Spanish ambitions in the Valtellina valley. The struggle had ramifications throughout Europe as the Protestants made common cause with Grisons and the Catholics with the Habsburgs. Richelieu recognized that vacillation would threaten domestic stability, and so he struck, expelling the papal troops. It was an action that gained for Richelieu an instant reputation for decision and ruthlessness. It also disillusioned those who had seen in him a defender of Catholic interests and of a Franco-Spanish alliance.

From his first days in office Richelieu was the object of conspiracies to remove him, and the success of his security organization in ferreting out the disaffected and his manipulation of state trials made him misunderstood, feared, and detested. Yet according to the standards of the age, his administration of justice did not depart from the moral principles that he believed to underlie all government.

The goals that Richelieu set himself were to counter Habsburg hegemony in Europe, which threatened France's independence of action, and "to make the king absolute in his kingdom in order to establish therein order," but at no time was Richelieu powerful enough to achieve his domestic ends by overt measures. A respecter of law and history, he accepted the necessity of working with the traditional framework of administration. His sense of the feasible and his gift for seeing both sides of a question resulted in a pragmatism in practice that often contradicted his proclaimed theories, and he confused his critics by unexpected compromise and moderation.

Richelieu's great intellectual capacity enabled him to penetrate to the essence of events, and his tremendous willpower drove him to incessant work. In his theory of politics he shared the rationalism of contemporary philosophers, believing in "the light of natural reason." While he did not doubt the capacity of the mind to know what is naturally enjoined, he participated in the prevailing pessimism about man's will to act accordingly. A twofold view of moral causes, the natural and the divine, provided a philosophical axiom for state supervision of conduct in both the secular and the spiritual spheres. Sin and civil disobedience were, to Richelieu, but two aspects of disorder.

The gravest divisive factor in French society was religion. To Richelieu the Huguenots constituted a state within a state, with the civil government of major cities in their hands and considerable military force at their disposal. Yet Richelieu was prepared to tolerate this religious dissent so long as it did not amount to a political challenge. In this attempt to preserve social harmony at the expense of confessional difference he failed at first, for the Huguenot community was foolishly drawn into the intrigues of the Protestant magnates, who instigated England to war with France. Richelieu laid siege in 1628 to La Rochelle, the Huguenot centre, but it took a year to reduce the city, during which time Spain took advantage of the distraction to extend its hegemony in northern Italy at the expense of France's allies. While promising Richelieu help to combat the Protestants, Spain in fact subsidized their leaders, in order to keep the French government preoccupied, and seized the strategic fortress of Casale in northern Italy. Again Richelieu acted with surprising vigour. The moment La Rochelle fell, he led the army in winter over the Alps and checked the Spanish design. This reverse was countered by the Habsburgs with the introduction of imperial garrisons into parts of the duchy of Lorraine, which were claimed as fiefs of France. There followed intricate diplomatic maneuvers, culminating in Richelieu's dramatic refusal to ratify the peace Treaty of Regensburg in 1630, and the Habsburgs' appeal to Pope Urban VIII to excommunicate Louis XIII for this supposed breach of faith.

This was Richelieu's moment of greatest political insecurity. His relationship with the king was distant, and Catholic zealots provoked Marie de Médicis into a state of hysteria concerning the man who, she believed, had deprived her of influence. On Richelieu's return from

Italy in 1630, she tried to influence her son to dismiss his minister. The king, however, perceived that the issue was his own independence or his mother's domination and that there was no one but Richelieu who could relieve him of the responsibility of decisions at a moment of bewildering complications. After a day of suspense, he supported the cardinal and thereafter did not waver in his support. Marie de Médicis and the king's brother Gaston fled to the Spanish Netherlands, there to constitute a focus of sedition that Richelieu countered by a fatal involvement with the enemies of the Habsburgs. The central objective of his foreign policy was to restore the equilibrium in the empire that Habsburg victories had disturbed. Although Bavaria was disposed to seek French protection, the emperor's military successes and the Edict of Restitution occasioned a new mutual antagonism of Catholics and Protestants, which made neutrality of the Catholic League an impossibility.

Richelieu's German policy fell into ruins as a result of his grant of subsidies to Gustav II Adolf of Sweden, who was then engaged in the conquest of Pomerania. The subsidies liberated Gustav Adolf from constraint, and he fell on southern Germany, became embroiled with the armies of the Catholic League, and so consolidated the imperial and Catholic causes. The war spilled over the Rhine, and France's client states were by degrees drawn into the Habsburg orbit. The seizure by Spain in 1635 of the archbishop of Trier, who was under French protection, led to France's alignment with the Protestant powers in the Thirty Years' War.

This involvement on behalf of the Protestants was regarded by many Catholics in his own time and later as a betrayal of the church by one of its princes, and Richelieu has been criticized for intensifying a war whose horrors have rarely been equaled. That Richelieu was drawn unwillingly by events into the vortex is clear, just as it is clear that the cost paid in social suffering and economic decline, leading to more frequent agrarian revolts, was high. Almost as soon as war broke out with Spain in 1635, Richelieu initiated secret peace negotiations and renewed them repeatedly. His justification for war was the same as that for rigorous domestic discipline: only the statesman, furnished with all available information and equipped for judicious appraisal of events, is competent to judge policy.

In economic matters Richelieu was an amateur. He committed war expenditure with little regard for the difficulties of raising revenue, and he was given to economic improvisation that was often unsound, but he eschewed doctrinaire views and retained flexibility of mind. Whereas he was early influenced by the theories of the economist Antoine de Montchrestien, who argued for economic self-sufficiency so as to conserve specie, he was later persuaded that the drain of specie could be compensated for by trade. He promoted products and industries that could give France an export advantage and discouraged imports of luxury goods. Glassmaking, tapestry and silk, sugar, and the extractive industries attracted his interest. He planned canal systems and promoted overseas trading companies, in which he was a shareholder and which began the process of French colonization in Canada and the West Indies, and he gained economic footholds in Morocco and Persia.

His vast horizon reflected in part his concern with the French religious missions, which spread in Africa, the Middle East, and America and which extended French influence and created a vast intelligence network that fostered his political and economic designs. He laid the foundations for the French navy by buying ships from the

Dutch, and, though he failed to have much influence on seapower, he developed shipping connections with the Baltic. The legal reforms of his period were spasmodic and often frustrated by the Parlement, and how much of their content is due to him is questionable. The Code Michaud of 1629—which regulated industry and trade, companies, public offices, the church, and the army and standardized weights and measures—was promulgated under his authority, although he may not have been its architect.

In his last years Richelieu found himself involved in religious conflict, in opposition to the pope, and in a struggle with the French church over the allocation of revenues to the financing of the war. His relationship with Urban VIII became strained over diplomatic grievances, church administration, and his own ambitions to extend French political influence by acquiring benefices for himself in the Holy Roman Empire. In spite of these conflicts, Richelieu remained orthodox in his views on the relationship between church and state and resisted the Gallican challenge to the absolutism of papal authority.

The theocratic concept of the state that resulted from his notion of kingship caused Richelieu to regard heresy as political dissidence, and he harried the apparently unorthodox, such as the first Jansenists, on the ground that they disturbed the spiritual and secular orders, just as he harried the recalcitrant nobles and stamped out dueling. Although there were canonical irregularities in his life, notably in the matter of pluralism (the multiplication of ecclesiastical benefices), there is no evidence of a serious departure from the principles or practices of the church. His accumulation of wealth was excessive even by the standards of the age, but it was largely dedicated to public service and to patronage of the arts and of the University of Paris. Richelieu was a playwright and musician of some talent, and his establishment of the French Academy is one of his best-remembered achievements.

His last months were agitated by the most dangerous of all the conspiracies against his life, that of the youthful royal favourite Cinq-Mars, who was exposed by Richelieu's secret service and died on the block. The cardinal's health, bad for some years, had deteriorated, and it was virtually from his deathbed that he was compelled to dictate to the king five propositions respecting royal behaviour toward ministers that he considered essential for proper government. He died in 1642 and was buried in the chapel of the Sorbonne, which he had financed.

CORNELIUS OTTO JANSEN

(b. Oct. 28, 1585, Acquoi, near Leerdam, Holland—d. May 6, 1638, Ypres, Flanders, Spanish Netherlands [now in Belgium])

Cornelius Otto Jansen was a Flemish leader of the Roman Catholic reform movement known as Jansenism. He wrote biblical commentaries and pamphlets against the Protestants. His major work was *Augustinus*, published by his friends in 1640. Although condemned by Pope Urban VIII in 1642, it was of critical importance in the Jansenist movement.

Jansen entered the University of Leuven (Louvain), in the Spanish Netherlands in 1602 to study theology. According to the custom adopted by the humanists of the Renaissance, Jansen Latinized his name to Cornelius Jansenius. His teacher, Jacques Janson, taught the doctrine of the theologian Michael Baius (Michel de Bay), who had died at Leuven in 1589. According to the latter, man is affected from his birth by the sin of Adam, his ancestor. His instincts lead him necessarily to evil. He can be saved only by the grace of Christ, accorded to a small number of the elect who have been chosen in advance and destined to enter the Kingdom of Heaven. This doctrine, inspired by certain writings of St. Augustine, attracted Jansen and another student who had come to study at Leuven, a Frenchman named Jean Duvergier de Hauranne, who was to become a leader of the Jansenist movement. The two young men became friends in Paris, where Jansen went in 1604. They decided to revive theology, which they believed the theologians of the Sorbonne had reduced to subtle and vain discussions among Scholastics. Jansen and Duvergier thought that it was necessary to render to God the homage owed by men and that the pride of the Renaissance savants had alienated Christians from the Jesus who loved the simple and the humble.

In 1611 Jansen followed Duvergier to the home of the latter's parents, located in the outskirts of Bayonne. The bishop of the city entrusted to Jansen the direction of the episcopal college there from 1612 to 1614. For three years afterward the young Dutchman, with Duvergier, dedicated himself to the study of the writings of the early Church Fathers.

In 1617 Jansen returned to Leuven, where he directed the college of Sainte-Pulchérie, created for Dutch students. A violent dispute had arisen at Leuven between the disciples of Baius and the Jesuits, who considered as dangerous the doctrines of this theologian, who had been condemned by Pope Pius V in 1567. Jansen then undertook a thorough study of the works of Augustine by which Baius had been inspired. He read them, he declared, 10 times consecutively. But he devoted himself most particularly to the texts drafted by Augustine to combat the doctrine of Pelagius, who had held that, in spite of the fault committed by Adam, man continues to be entirely free to do good and to obtain salvation by means of his own merits. Jansen then began his great work, the *Augustinus*. For him, the divine grace that alone can save man is not due at all to his good actions. It is, he claimed, a gratuitous gift by means of which Christ leads the elect to eternal life, but the multitude, "the mass of perdition," is doomed to damnation. Thus, men are predestined to obtain grace or to suffer condemnation. In reality, Augustine had not envisaged the fate of human beings with such great rigour. He had even proclaimed the power of man's free will at the time when he was engaged in the struggle against the Manichaeans. But Augustine had then been constrained to enclose the liberty of man within strict limits, in order to refute the affirmations of Pelagius, who had radically reduced the value of the divine grace obtained by Jesus on the cross.

Jansen was so fascinated by Augustine's treatise against the Pelagians that he apparently lost sight of Augustine's works against the Manichaeans.

Jansen also wrote commentaries on the evangelists and on the Old Testament—notably on the Pentateuch—as well as a "Discourse on the Reformation of the Inner Man." He was likewise the author of pamphlets directed against the Protestants.

Having acquired the degree of doctor in theology at Leuven, Jansen became the rector of that university in 1635, and in 1636 he became bishop of Ypres. The Jesuit scholar René Rapin asserted in his book *Histoire du Jansénisme* (1861) that Jansen had obtained his mitre as a result of the personal intervention of the king of Spain, Philip IV. This sovereign had recognized him for having published a pamphlet entitled *Mars Gallicus*, in which he strongly criticized the policy of the French cardinal and prime minister, Richelieu, who had contracted an alliance with the Dutch Protestants against Spain. In 1638, a short time after his elevation to the episcopate, Jansen died of the plague. In 1640 his friends published at Leuven the work he had dedicated to St. Augustine, under the title *Augustinus Cornelii Jansenii, Episcopi, seu Doctrina Sancti Augustini de Humanae Naturae, Sanitate, Aegritudine, Medicina adversus Pelagianos et Massilienses* ("The Augustine of Cornelius Jansen, Bishop, or On the Doctrines of St. Augustine Concerning Human Nature, Health, Grief, and Cure Against the Pelagians and Massilians").

This book had cost its author 22 years of effort. In the epilogue Jansen declared: "I leave my work to the judgment of the Roman Church. . . . I retract all that she will decide that I ought to (must) retract."

GEORGE FOX

(b. July 1624, Drayton-in-the-Clay, Leicestershire, Eng.—died Jan. 13, 1691, London)

The founder of the Society of Friends, or Quakers, was an Englishman named George Fox. He was a man who lived by his principles. Despite severe persecution no one could halt his preaching or his disrespect for the Church of England, which he considered irreligious. Once he even refused to leave prison when given his freedom. Because he had been imprisoned unjustly, he demanded pardon as well as release.

George Fox was born in July 1624, at Drayton, in Leicestershire. His parents were Puritans. As a boy George was extremely religious. When he was 19, he became disgusted by the sinfulness of many Christians. He left his family and went off alone. After much thought and reading of the Bible, Fox came to the conclusion that God was to be found only within the soul of each individual.

Fox was 23 when he began his ministry by traveling from village to village. He preached his new belief of the Inner Light and soon won many converts. England was torn by civil war, however, and the authorities did not like this sect that claimed equality for all and refused to take up arms or swear allegiance. Hundreds were jailed. Fox wrote his *Journal* and pamphlets supporting his beliefs while in prison.

After Oliver Cromwell became ruler of England, Fox found a refuge at the home of Judge Fell, Cromwell's chancellor of the duchy of Lancaster. Fox died in London on Jan. 13, 1691.

SHABBETAI TZEVI

(b. July 23, 1626, Smyrna, Ottoman Turkey [now İzmir, Turkey]—d. 1676, Dulcigno, Albania)

Shabbetai Tzevi was a false messiah who developed a mass following and threatened rabbinical authority in Europe and the Middle East.

As a young man, Shabbetai steeped himself in the influential body of Jewish mystical writings known as the Kabbala. His extended periods of ecstasy and his strong personality combined to attract many disciples, and at the age of 22 he proclaimed himself the messiah.

Driven from Smyrna by the aroused rabbinate, he journeyed to Salonika (now Thessaloníki), an old Kabbalistic centre, and then to Constantinople (now Istanbul). There he encountered an esteemed and forceful Jewish preacher and Kabbalist, Abraham ha-Yakini, who possessed a false prophetic document affirming that Shabbetai was the messiah. Shabbetai then traveled to Palestine and after that to Cairo, where he won over to his cause Raphael Halebi, the wealthy and powerful treasurer of the Turkish governor.

With a retinue of believers and assured of financial backing, Shabbetai triumphantly returned to Jerusalem. There, a 20-year-old student known as Nathan of Gaza assumed the role of a modern Elijah, in his traditional role of forerunner of the messiah. Nathan ecstatically prophesied the imminent restoration of Israel and world salvation through the bloodless victory of Shabbetai, riding on a lion with a seven-headed dragon in his jaws. In accordance with millenarian belief, he cited 1666 as the apocalyptic year.

Threatened with excommunication by the rabbis of Jerusalem, Shabbetai returned to Smyrna in the autumn of 1665, where he was wildly acclaimed. His movement spread to Venice, Amsterdam, Hamburg, London, and several other European and North African cities.

At the beginning of 1666, Shabbetai went to Constantinople and was imprisoned on his arrival. After a few months, he was transferred to the castle at Abydos, which became known to his followers as Migdal Oz, the Tower of Strength. In September, however, he was brought before the sultan in Adrianople and, having been previously threatened with torture, became converted to Islam. The placated sultan renamed him Mehmed Efendi, appointed him his personal doorkeeper, and provided him with a generous allowance. All but his most faithful or self-seeking disciples were disillusioned by his apostasy. Eventually, Shabbetai fell out of favour and was banished, dying in Albania.

The movement that developed around Shabbetai Tzevi became known as Shabbetaianism. It attempted to reconcile Shabbetai's grandiose claims of spiritual authority with his subsequent seeming betrayal of the Jewish faith. Faithful Shabbetaians interpreted Shabbetai's apostasy as a step toward ultimate fulfillment of his messiahship and attempted to follow their leader's example. They argued that such outward acts were irrelevant as long as one remains inwardly a Jew. Those who embraced the theory of "sacred sin" believed that the Torah could be fulfilled only by amoral acts representing its seeming annulment. Others felt they could remain faithful Shabbetaians without having to apostatize.

After Shabbetai's death in 1676, the sect continued to flourish. The nihilistic tendencies of Shabbetaianism reached a peak in the 18th century with Jacob Frank, whose followers reputedly sought redemption through orgies at mystical festivals.

JOHN BUNYAN

(b. November 1628, Elstow, Bedfordshire, England—d. Aug. 31, 1688, London)

John Bunyan was a celebrated English minister and preacher, author of *The Pilgrim's Progress* (1678), the book that was the most characteristic expression of the Puritan religious outlook. His other works include doctrinal and controversial writings; a spiritual autobiography, *Grace Abounding* (1666); and the allegory *The Holy War* (1682).

Bunyan, the son of a brazier, or traveling tinker, was brought up "among a multitude of poor plowmen's children" in the heart of England's agricultural Midlands. He learned to read and write at a local grammar school, but he probably left school early to learn the family trade. Bunyan's mind and imagination were formed in these early days by influences other than those of formal education. He absorbed the popular tales of adventure that appeared in chapbooks and were sold at fairs like the great one held at Stourbridge near Cambridge (it provided the inspiration for Vanity Fair in *The Pilgrim's Progress*). Though his family belonged to the Anglican church, he also became acquainted with the varied popular literature of the English Puritans: plain-speaking sermons, homely moral dialogues, books of melodramatic judgments and acts of divine guidance, and John Foxe's *The Book of Martyrs*. Above all he steeped himself in the English Bible; the Authorized Version was but 30 years old when he was a boy of 12.

Bunyan speaks in his autobiography of being troubled by terrifying dreams. It may be that there was a pathological side to the nervous intensity of these fears; in the religious crisis of his early manhood his sense of guilt took the form of delusions. But it seems to have been abnormal sensitiveness combined with the tendency to exaggeration that caused him to look back on himself in youth as "the very ringleader of all . . . that kept me company into all manner of vice and ungodliness."

In 1644 a series of misfortunes separated the country boy from his family and drove him into the world. His mother died in June, his younger sister Margaret in July; in August his father married a third wife. The English Civil Wars had broken out, and in November he was mustered in a Parliamentary levy and sent to reinforce the garrison at Newport Pagnell. The governor was Sir Samuel Luke, immortalized as the Presbyterian knight of the title in Samuel Butler's Hudibras. Bunyan remained in Newport until July 1647 and probably saw little fighting.

His military service, even if uneventful, brought him in touch with the seething religious life of the left-wing sects within Oliver Cromwell's army, the preaching captains, and those Quakers, Seekers, and Ranters who were beginning to question all religious authority except that of the individual conscience. In this atmosphere Bunyan became acquainted with the leading ideas of the Puritan sectaries, who believed that the striving for religious truth meant an obstinate personal search, relying on free grace revealed to the individual, and condemning all forms of public organization.

Some time after his discharge from the army (in July 1647) and before 1649, Bunyan married. He says in his autobiography, *Grace Abounding*, that he and his first wife "came together as poor as poor might be, not having so much household-stuff as a dish or spoon betwixt us both." His wife brought him two evangelical books as her only dowry. Their first child, a blind daughter, Mary, was baptized in July 1650. Three more children, Elizabeth, John, and Thomas, were born to Bunyan's first wife before her death in 1658. Elizabeth, too, was baptized in the parish church there in 1654, though by that time her father had been baptized by immersion as a member of the Bedford Separatist church.

Bunyan's conversion to Puritanism was a gradual process in the years following his marriage (1650–55); it is dramatically described in his autobiography. After an initial period of Anglican conformity in which he went regularly to church, he gave up, slowly and grudgingly, his favourite recreations of dancing and bell ringing and sports on the village green and began to concentrate on his inner life. Then came agonizing temptations to spiritual despair lasting for several years. The "storms" of temptation, as he calls them, buffeted him with almost physical violence; voices urged him to blaspheme; the texts of Scriptures, which seemed to him to threaten damnation, took on personal shape and "did pinch him very sore." Finally one morning he believed that he had surrendered to these voices of Satan and had betrayed Christ: "Down I fell as a bird that is shot from the tree." In his psychopathic isolation he presents all the features of the divided mind of the maladjusted as they have been analyzed in the 20th century. Bunyan, however, had a contemporary psychological instrument for the diagnosis of his condition: the pastoral theology of 17th-century Calvinism, which interpreted the grim doctrine of election and predestination in terms of the real needs of souls, the evidence of spiritual progress in them, and the covenant of God's grace. Both techniques, that of the modern analyst and that of the Puritan preacher, have in common the aim of recovering the integrity of the self; and this was what Bunyan achieved as he emerged, from his period of spiritual darkness, gradually beginning to feel that his sin was "not unto death" and that there were texts to comfort as well as to terrify. He was aided in his recovery by his association with the Bedford Separatist church and its dynamic leader, John Gifford. He entered into full communion about 1655.

The Bedford community practiced adult baptism by immersion, but it was an open-communion church, admitting all who professed "faith in Christ and holiness of life." Bunyan soon proved his talents as a lay preacher. Fresh from his own spiritual troubles, he was fitted to warn and console others: "I went myself in Chains to preach to them in Chains, and carried that Fire in my own Conscience that I persuaded them to beware of." He was also active in visiting and exhorting church members, but his main activity in 1655–60 was in controversy with the early Quakers, both in public debate up and down the market towns of Bedfordshire and in his first printed works, *Some Gospel Truths Opened* (1656) and *A Vindication of Some Gospel Truths Opened* (1657). The Quakers and the open-communion Baptists were rivals for the religious allegiance of the "mechanics," or small tradesmen and artificers, in both town and country. Bunyan soon became recognized as a leader among the sectaries.

The Restoration of Charles II brought to an end the 20 years in which the separated churches had enjoyed freedom of worship and exercised some influence on government policy. On Nov. 12, 1660, at Lower Samsell in South Bedfordshire, Bunyan was brought before a local magistrate and, under an old Elizabethan act, charged with holding a service not in conformity with those of the Church of England. He refused to give an assurance that he would not repeat the offense, was condemned at the assizes in January 1661, and was imprisoned in the county jail. In spite of the courageous efforts of his second wife (he had married again in 1659) to have his case brought up at the assizes, he remained in prison for 12 years. A late 17th-century biography, added to the early editions of *Grace Abounding*, reveals that he relieved his family by making and selling "long Tagg'd laces"; prison conditions were lenient enough for him to be let out at times to visit friends and family and to address meetings.

During this imprisonment Bunyan wrote and published his spiritual autobiography (*Grace Abounding*, 1666). It reveals his incarceration to have been a spiritual opportunity as well as an ordeal, allowing "an inlet into the Word of God." Bunyan's release from prison came in March 1672 under Charles II's Declaration of Indulgence to the Nonconformists. The Bedford community had already chosen him as their pastor in January, and a new meetinghouse was obtained. In May he received a license to preach together with 25 other Nonconformist ministers in Bedfordshire and the surrounding counties. His nickname "Bishop Bunyan" suggests that he became the organizing genius in the area. When persecution was renewed he was again imprisoned for illegal preaching; the circumstances of this imprisonment have remained more obscure than those of the first, though it does not appear to have lasted longer than six months. A bond of surety for his release, dated June 1677, has survived, so it is likely that this second detention was in the first half of that year. Since *The*

Pilgrim's Progress was published soon after this, in February 1678, it is probable that he had begun to write it not in the second imprisonment but in the first, soon after the composition of *Grace Abounding*, and when the examination of his inner life contained in that book was still strong.

Bunyan's literary achievement, in his finest works, is by no means that of a naively simple talent, as has been the view of many of his critics. His handling of language, colloquial or biblical, is that of an accomplished artist. He brings to his treatment of human behaviour both shrewd awareness and moral subtlety, and he demonstrates a gift for endowing the conceptions of evangelical theology with concrete life and acting out the theological drama in terms of flesh and blood.

Bunyan thus presents a paradox since the impulse that originally drove him to write was purely to celebrate his faith and to convert others, and like other Puritans he was schooled to despise the adornments of style and to treat literature as a means to an end. Bunyan's effort to reach behind literary adornments so as to obtain an absolutely naked rendering of the truth about his own spiritual experience causes him in *Grace Abounding* to forge a highly original style. In this style, which is rich in powerful physical imagery, the inner life of the Christian is described; body and soul are so involved that it is impossible to separate bodily from mental suffering in the description of his temptations. He feels "a clogging and a heat at my breast-bone as if my bowels would have burst out"; a preacher's call to abandon the sin of idle pastimes "did benumb the sinews of my best delights"; and he can say of one of the texts of scripture that seemed to him to spell his damnation that it "stood like a mill-post at my back." The attempt to communicate the existential crisis of the human person without style had created a style of its own.

The use of a highly subjective prose style to express personal states of mind is Bunyan's first creative achievement, but he also had at his disposal the more traditional style he used in sermons, treatises, and scriptural exposition. In the allegories some of his greatest imaginative successes are due to his dreamlike, introspective style with its subtle personal music; but it is the workaday vigour and concreteness of the prose technique practiced in the sermons which provide a firm stylistic background to these imaginative flights.

Bunyan's great allegorical tale was published by Nathaniel Ponder in 1678. Because it recapitulates in symbolic form the story of Bunyan's own conversion, there is an intense, life-or-death quality about Christian's pilgrimage to the Heavenly City in the first part of the book. This sense of urgency is established in the first scene as Christian in the City of Destruction reads in his book (the Bible) and breaks out with his lamentable cry, "What shall I do?" It is maintained by the combats along the road with giants and monsters such as Apollyon and Giant Despair, who embody spiritual terrors. The voices and demons of the Valley of the Shadow of Death are a direct transcription of Bunyan's own obsessive and neurotic fears during his conversion. Episodes of stirring action like these alternate with more stationary passages, and there are various conversations between the pilgrims and those they encounter on the road, some pious and some providing light relief when hypocrites like Talkative and Ignorance are exposed. The halts at places of refreshment like the Delectable Mountains or the meadow by the River of Life evoke an unearthly spiritual beauty.

The narrative of *The Pilgrim's Progress* may seem episodic, but Calvinist theology provides a firm underlying ground plan. Only Christ, the Wicket Gate, admits Christian into the right road, and before he can reach it he has to be shown his error in being impressed by the pompous snob Worldly Wiseman, who stands for mere negative conformity to moral and social codes. Quite early in his journey Christian loses his burden of sin at the Cross, so he now knows that he has received the free pardon of Christ and is numbered among the elect. It might seem that all the crises of the pilgrimage were past, yet this initiation of grace is not the end of the drama but the beginning. Christian, and the companions who join him, Faithful and Hopeful, are fixed in the path of salvation, so that it is the horrors of the temptations they have to undergo that engage the reader's attention. The reader views Christian's agonized striving through his own eyes and shares Christian's uncertainty about the outcome.

Though conscientiously symbolic throughout, the narrative of *The Pilgrim's Progress* does not lose the feel of common life. In the character sketches and humorous passages scattered throughout the book, Bunyan's genius for realistic observation prevents the conversion allegory from becoming too inward and obsessed. Bunyan displays a sharp eye for behaviour and a sardonic sense of humour in his portrayals of such reprobates as Ignorance and Talkative; these moral types are endowed with the liveliness of individuals by a deft etching in of a few dominant features and gestures. And finally, Christian himself is a transcript from life; Bunyan, the physician of souls with a shrewd eye for backsliders, had faithfully observed his own spiritual growth.

The Pilgrim's Progress was instantly popular with all social classes upon its publication, though it was perhaps the last great expression of the folk tradition of the common people before the divisive effects of modern enlightened education began to be felt.

Bunyan continued to tend the needs of the Bedford church and the widening group of East Anglian churches associated with it. As his fame increased with his literary reputation, he also preached in Congregational churches in London. Bunyan followed up the success of *The Pilgrim's Progress* with other works. His *The Life and Death of Mr. Badman* (1680) is more like a realistic novel than an allegory in its portrait of the unrelievedly evil and unrepentant tradesman Mr. Badman. The book gives an insight into the problems of money and marriage when the Puritans were settling down after the age of persecution and beginning to find their social role as an urban middle class.

The Holy War (1682), Bunyan's second allegory, has a carefully wrought epic structure and is correspondingly lacking in the spontaneous inward note of *The Pilgrim's Progress*. The town of Mansoul is besieged by the hosts of the devil, is relieved by the army of Emanuel, and is later undermined by further diabolic attacks and plots against his rule. The metaphor works on several levels; it represents the conversion and backslidings of the individual soul, as well as the story of mankind from the Fall through to the Redemption and the Last Judgment; there is even a more precise historical level of allegory relating to the persecution of Nonconformists under Charles II. *The Pilgrim's Progress*, Second Part (1684), tells the story of the pilgrimage of Christian's wife, Christiana, and her children to the Celestial City. This book gives a more social and humorous picture of the Christian life than the First Part and shows Bunyan lapsing from high drama into comedy, but the great concluding passage on the summoning of the pilgrims to cross the River of Death is perhaps the finest single thing Bunyan ever wrote.

In spite of his ministerial responsibilities Bunyan found time to publish a large number of doctrinal and controversial works in the last 10 years of his life. He also composed rough but workmanlike verse of religious exhortation; one of his most interesting later volumes is the children's book *A Book for Boys and Girls* (1686), vigorous poems serving as comments on emblematic pictures.

Bunyan died in 1688, in London, after one of his preaching visits, and was buried in Bunhill Fields, the Nonconformists' traditional burying ground.

WILLIAM PENN

(b. Oct. 14, 1644, London, Eng.—d. July 30, 1718, Buckinghamshire)

William Penn, an English Quaker leader and advocate of religious freedom, oversaw the founding of the American Commonwealth of Pennsylvania as a refuge for Quakers and other religious minorities of Europe.

William was the son of Admiral Sir William Penn. He acquired the foundations of a classical education at the Chigwell grammar school in the Essex countryside, where he came under Puritan influences. After Admiral Penn's naval defeat in the West Indies in 1655, the family moved back to London and then to Ireland. In Ireland William heard Thomas Loe, a Quaker itinerant, preach to his family at the admiral's invitation, an experience that apparently intensified his religious feelings. In 1660 William entered the University of Oxford, where he rejected Anglicanism and was expelled in 1662 for his religious Nonconformity. Determined to thwart his son's religiosity, Admiral Penn sent his son on a grand tour of the European continent and to the Protestant college at Saumur, in France, to complete his studies. Summoned back to England after two years, William entered Lincoln's Inn and spent a year reading law. This was the extent of his formal education.

In 1666 Admiral Penn sent William to Ireland to manage the family estates. There he crossed paths again with Thomas Loe and, after hearing him preach, decided to join the Quakers (the Society of Friends), a sect of religious radicals who were reviled by respectable society and subject to official persecution.

After joining the sect, Penn would eventually be imprisoned four times for publicly stating his beliefs in word and print. He published 42 books and pamphlets in the seven years immediately following his conversion. In his first publication, the pamphlet *Truth Exalted* (1668), he upheld Quaker doctrines while attacking in turn those of the Roman Catholics, the Anglicans, and the Dissenting churches. It was followed by *The Sandy Foundation Shaken* (1668), in which he boldly questioned the Trinity and other Protestant doctrines. Though Penn subsequently qualified this anti-Trinitarianism in *Innocency with Her Open Face* (1669), he was imprisoned in the Tower of London, where he wrote his most famous book, *No Cross, No Crown* (1669). In this work he expounded the Quaker-Puritan morality with eloquence, learning, and flashes of humour, condemning the worldliness and luxury of Restoration England and extolling both Puritan conceptions of ascetic self-denial and Quaker ideals of social reform. *No Cross, No Crown* stands alongside the letters of St. Paul, Boethius's *Consolation of Philosophy*, and John Bunyan's *Pilgrim's Progress* as one of the world's finest examples of prison literature. Penn was released from the Tower in 1669.

It was as a protagonist of religious toleration that Penn would earn his prominent place in English history. In 1670 he wrote *The Great Case of Liberty of Conscience Once More Debated & Defended*, which was the most systematic and thorough exposition of the theory of toleration produced in Restoration England. Though Penn based his arguments on theological and scriptural grounds, he did not overlook rational and pragmatic considerations; he pointed out, for example, that the contemporary prosperity of Holland was based on "her Indulgence in matters of Faith and Worship."

That same year Penn also had an unexpected opportunity to strike another blow for freedom of conscience and for the traditional rights of all Englishmen. On Aug. 14, 1670, the Quaker meetinghouse in Gracechurch Street, London, having been padlocked by the authorities, he preached in the street to several hundred persons. After the meetings, he and William Mead were arrested and imprisoned on a trumped-up charge of inciting a riot. At his trial in the Old Bailey, Penn calmly and skillfully exposed the illegality of the proceedings against him. The jury, under the leadership of Edward Bushell, refused to bring in a verdict of guilty despite threats and abusive treatment. For their refusal the jurymen were fined and imprisoned, but they were vindicated when Sir John Vaughan, the lord chief justice, enunciated the principle that a judge "may try to open the eyes of the jurors, but not to lead them by the nose." The trial, which is also known as the Bushell's Case, stands as a landmark in English legal history, having established beyond question the independence of the jury. A firsthand account of the trial, which was a vivid courtroom drama, was published in *The People's Ancient and Just Liberties Asserted* (1670).

Admiral Penn died in 1670, having finally become reconciled to his son's Quakerism. Young Penn inherited his father's estates in England and Ireland and became, like his father, a frequenter of the court, where he enjoyed the friendship of King Charles II and his brother, the Duke of York (later James II). In 1672 Penn married Gulielma Springett, a Quaker by whom he had eight children, four of whom died in infancy. In the 1670s Penn was tirelessly active as a Quaker minister and polemicist, producing no fewer than 40 controversial tracts on religious doctrines and practice. In 1671 and 1677 he undertook preaching missions to Holland and northern Germany, where the contacts he established would later help him in peopling

Pennsylvania with thousands of Dutch and German emigrants. The later years of the decade were also occupied with political activities. In 1679 Penn supported the Parliamentary candidacy of the radical republican Algernon Sidney, going on the hustings twice—at Guildford and later at Bramber—for his friend. During these years he wrote a number of pamphlets on behalf of the radical Whigs, including *England's Great Interest in the Choice of this New Parliament* (1679), which is noteworthy as one of the first clear statements of party doctrine ever laid before the English electorate.

Penn had meanwhile become involved in American colonization as a trustee for Edward Byllynge, one of the two Quaker proprietors of West New Jersey. In 1681 Penn and 11 other Quakers bought the proprietary rights to East New Jersey from the widow of Sir John Carteret. In that same year, discouraged by the turn of political events in England, where Charles II was ruling without Parliament and prospects for religious freedom seemed dark, Penn sought and received a vast province on the west bank of the Delaware River, which was named Pennsylvania after his father (to whom Charles II had owed a large debt canceled by this grant). A few months later the Duke of York granted him the three "lower counties" (later Delaware). In Pennsylvania Penn hoped to provide a refuge for Quakers and other persecuted people and to build an ideal Christian commonwealth. "There may be room there, though not here" he wrote to a friend in America, "for such a holy experiment."

As proprietor, Penn seized the opportunity to create a government that would embody his Quaker-Whig ideas. In 1682 he drew up a Frame of Government for the colony that would, he said, leave himself and his successors "no power of doing mischief, that the will of one man may not hinder the good of a whole country." Freedom of worship in the colony was to be absolute, and all the traditional rights of Englishmen were carefully safeguarded. The actual machinery of government outlined in the Frame proved in some respects to be clumsy and unworkable, but Penn wisely included in the Frame an amending clause—the first in any written constitution—so that it could be altered as necessity required.

Penn himself sailed in the *Welcome* for Pennsylvania late in 1682, leaving his family behind, and found his experiment already well under way. The city of Philadelphia was already laid out on a grid pattern according to his instructions, and settlers were pouring in to take up the fertile lands lying around it. Presiding over the first Assembly, Penn saw the government of the "lower counties" united with that of Pennsylvania and the Frame of Government incorporated in the Great Law of the province. In a series of treaties based on mutual trust, he established good relations with the Lenni Lenape Indians. He also held an unsuccessful conference with Lord Baltimore, the proprietor of the neighbouring province of Maryland, to negotiate a boundary between it and Pennsylvania. When this effort proved unsuccessful, Penn was obliged in 1684 to return to England to defend his interests against Baltimore.

Before his return, he published *A Letter to the Free Society of Traders* (1683), which contained his fullest description of Pennsylvania and included a valuable account of the Lenni Lenape based on firsthand observation. With the accession of his friend the Duke of York as James II in 1685, Penn found himself in a position of great influence at court, whereby he was able to have hundreds of Quakers, as well as political prisoners such as John Locke, released from prison. Penn welcomed James's Declaration of Indulgence (1687) but received some criticism for doing so, since the declaration provided religious toleration at the royal pleasure rather than as a matter of fundamental right. But the Act of Toleration (1689), passed after James's abdication, finally established the principle for which Penn had laboured so long and faithfully.

Penn's close relations with James brought him under a cloud when William and Mary came to the throne, and for a time he was forced to live virtually in hiding to avoid arrest. He used this period of forced retirement to write more books. Among them were *An Essay Towards the Present and Future Peace of Europe* (1693), in which he proposed an international organization to prevent wars by arbitrating disputes, and *A Brief Account of the Rise and Progress of the People Called Quakers* (1694), which was the earliest serious effort to set down the history of the Quaker movement. Penn also drafted (1696) the first plan for a future union of the American colonies, a document that presaged the U.S. Constitution.

In 1696, his first wife having died in 1694, Penn married Hannah Callowhill, by whom he had seven children, five of whom lived to adulthood. Meanwhile, affairs had been going badly in Pennsylvania. For about two years (1692–94), while Penn was under suspicion, the government of the colony had been taken from him and given to that of New York. Afterwards, Pennsylvania's Assembly quarreled constantly with its Council and with Penn's deputy governors. The "lower counties" were unhappy at being unequally yoked with the larger province of Pennsylvania. Relations with the home government were strained by the Quakers' conscientious refusal to provide military defense. In 1699 Penn, his wife, and his secretary, James Logan, returned to the province. He settled many of the outstanding difficulties, though he was compelled to grant the Pennsylvania Assembly preeminence in 1701 in a revised constitution known as the Charter of Privileges. He also allowed the lower counties to form their own independent government.

After less than two years Penn's affairs in England demanded his presence, and he left the province in 1701, never to see it again. He confided his Pennsylvania interests to the capable hands of James Logan, who upheld them loyally for the next half century.

Penn's final years were unhappy. His eldest son, William, Jr., turned out a scapegrace. Penn's own poor judgment in choosing his subordinates (except for the faithful Logan) recoiled upon him: his deputy governors proved incompetent or untrustworthy, and his steward, Philip Ford, cheated him on such a staggering scale that Penn was forced to spend nine months in a debtors' prison. In 1712, discouraged at the outcome of his "holy experiment," Penn began negotiations to surrender Pennsylvania to the English crown. A paralytic stroke, which seriously impaired his memory and dulled his once-keen intellect, prevented the consummation of these negotiations. Penn lingered on, virtually helpless, until 1718, his wife undertaking to manage his proprietary affairs. Penn's collected works were published in 1726.

BA'AL SHEM ṬOV

(b. c. 1700, , probably Tluste, Podolia, Pol.—d. 1760, Medzhibozh)

Ba'al Shem Ṭov was the charismatic founder (c. 1750) of Ḥasidism, a Jewish spiritual movement characterized by mysticism and opposition to secular studies and Jewish rationalism. He aroused controversy by mixing with ordinary people, renouncing mortification of the flesh, and insisting on the holiness of ordinary bodily existence. He was also responsible for divesting Kabbala (esoteric Jewish mysticism) of the rigid asceticism imposed on it by Isaac ben Solomon Luria in the 16th century.

The Besht's life has been so adorned with fables and legends that a biography in the ordinary historical sense is not possible. He came from humble and obscure beginnings in a village known to contemporary Jews as Okop or Akuf, depending on the Hebrew vocalization. As a young orphan he held various semimenial posts connected with synagogues and Hebrew elementary religious schools. After marrying the daughter of the wealthy and learned Ephraim of Kuty, he retired to the Carpathian Mountains to engage in mystical speculation, meanwhile eking out his living as a lime digger. During this period his reputation as a healer, or ba'al shem, who worked wonders by means of herbs, talismans, and amulets inscribed with the divine name, began to spread. He later became an innkeeper and a ritual slaughterer and, about 1736, settled in the village of Medzhibozh, in Podolia. From this time until his death, he devoted himself almost entirely to spiritual pursuits.

Though the Besht gained no special renown as a scholar or preacher during his lifetime, he made a deep impression on his fellow Jews by going to the marketplace to converse with simple people and by dressing like them. Such conduct by a holy man was fiercely condemned in some quarters but enthusiastically applauded in others. The Besht defended his actions as a necessary "descent for the sake of ascent," a concept that eventually evolved into a sociotheological theory that placed great value on this type of spiritual ministration.

While still a young man, the Besht had become acquainted with such figures as Rabbi Naḥman of Gorodënka and Rabbi Naḥman of Kosov, already spoken of as creators of a new life, and with them he regularly celebrated the ritual of the three sabbath meals. In time it became customary for them to deliver pious homilies and discourses after the third meal, and the Besht took his turn along with the others. Many of these discourses were later recorded and have been preserved as the core of

Ba'al Shem Ṭov.

Hasidic literature. When the Besht's spiritual powers were put to a test by other members of the group—an indication that he probably was not yet recognized as the "first among equals"—he reportedly recognized a mezuzah (ritual object affixed to a doorpost) as ritually "unfit" by means of his clairvoyant powers.

The Besht gradually reached the point where he was prepared to renounce the strict asceticism of his companions. In words recorded by his grandson Rabbi Baruch of Medzhibozh, he announced:

> I came into this world to point a new way, to prevail upon men to live by the light of these three things: love of God, love of Israel, and love of Torah. And there is no need to perform mortifications of the flesh.

By renouncing mortification in favour of new rituals, the Besht in effect had taken the first step toward initiating a new religious movement within Judaism. The teaching of the Besht centred on three main points: communion with God, the highest of all values; service in ordinary bodily existence, proclaiming that every human deed done "for the sake of heaven" (even stitching shoes and eating) was equal in value to observing formal commandments; and rescue of the "sparks" of divinity that, according to the Kabbala, were trapped in the material world. He believed that such sparks are related to the soul of every individual. It was the Besht's sensitivity to the spiritual needs of the unsophisticated and his assurance that redemption could be attained without retreat from the world that found a ready response among his listeners, the common Jewish folk. He declared that they were, one and all, "limbs of the divine presence."

The Besht and his followers were fiercely attacked by

rabbinical leaders for "dancing, drinking, and making merry all their lives." They were called licentious, indifferent, and contemptuous of tradition—epithets and accusations that were wild exaggerations, to say the least.

An understanding of the Besht's view of the coming of the Messiah depends to a great extent on the interpretation of a letter attributed to, but not signed by, the Besht. It affirms that the author made "the ascent of the soul," met the Messiah in heaven, and asked him when he would come. The answer he received was: "when your well-springs shall overflow far and wide"—meaning that the Besht had first to disseminate the teaching of Ḥasidism. According to one view, the story indicates that the messianic advent was central in the Besht's belief; according to another, it effectively removes messianic redemption from central spiritual concern in the life that must be lived here and now.

During his lifetime, the Besht brought about a great social and religious upheaval and permanently altered many traditional values. In an atmosphere marked by joy, new rituals, and ecstasy, he created a new religious climate in small houses of prayer outside the synagogues. The changes that had occurred were further emphasized by the wearing of distinctive garb and the telling of stories. Though the Besht never did visit Israel and left no writings, by the time he died, he had given to Judaism a new religious dimension in Ḥasidism that continues to flourish to this day.

Among the Besht's most outstanding pupils was Rabbi Jacob Joseph of Polonnoye, whose books preserve many of the master's teachings. He speaks with holy awe of his religious teacher in tones that were echoed by other disciples, such as Dov Baer of Mezrechye, Rabbi Nahum of Chernobyl, Aryeh Leib of Polonnoye, and a second grandson, Rabbi Ephraim of Sydoluvka, who was but one of many to embellish the image of his grandfather with numerous legends.

JOHN WESLEY

(b. June 17, 1703, Epworth, Lincolnshire, Eng.—d. March 2, 1791, London)

John Wesley was an Anglican clergyman, evangelist, and founder, with his brother Charles, of the Methodist movement in the Church of England.

John Wesley was the second son of Samuel, a former Nonconformist (dissenter from the Church of England) and rector at Epworth, and Susanna Wesley. After six years of education at the Charterhouse, London, he entered Christ Church, Oxford University, in 1720. Graduating in 1724, he resolved to become ordained a priest; in 1725 he was made a deacon by the Bishop of Oxford and the following year was elected a fellow of Lincoln College. After assisting his father at Epworth and Wroot, he was ordained a priest on Sept. 22, 1728.

Recalled to Oxford in October 1729 to fulfill the residential requirements of his fellowship, John joined his brother Charles, Robert Kirkham, and William Morgan in a religious study group that was derisively called the Methodists because of their emphasis on methodical study and devotion. Taking over the leadership of the group from Charles, John helped the group to grow in numbers. The Methodists, also called the Holy Club, were known for their frequent communion services and for fasting two days a week. From 1730 on, the group added social services to their activities, visiting Oxford prisoners, teaching them to read, paying their debts, and attempting to find employment for them. The Methodists also extended their activities to workhouses and poor people, distributing food, clothes, medicine, and books and also running a school. When the Wesleys left the Holy Club in 1735, the group disintegrated.

Following his father's death in April 1735, John was persuaded by an Oxford friend, John Burton, and Col. James Oglethorpe, governor of the colony of Georgia in North America, to oversee the spiritual lives of the colonists and to missionize the Indians as an agent for the Society for the Propagation of the Gospel. Accompanied by Charles, who was ordained for this mission, John was introduced to some Moravian emigrants who appeared to him to possess the spiritual peace for which he had been searching. The mission to the Indians proved abortive, nor did Wesley succeed with most of his flock. He served them faithfully, but his stiff high churchmanship antagonized them. He had a naive attachment to Sophia Hopkey, niece of the chief magistrate of Savannah, who married another man, and Wesley unwisely courted criticism by repelling her from Holy Communion. In December 1737 he fled from Georgia; misunderstandings and persecution stemming from the Sophia Hopkey episode forced him to go back to England.

In London John met a Moravian, Peter Böhler, who convinced him that what he needed was simply faith, and he also discovered Martin Luther's commentary on the Letter of Paul to the Galatians, which emphasized the scriptural doctrine of justification by grace through faith alone. On May 24, 1738, in Aldersgate Street, London, during a meeting composed largely of Moravians under the auspices of the Church of England, Wesley's intellectual conviction was transformed into a personal experience while Luther's preface to the commentary to the Letter of Paul to the Romans was being read.

From this point onward, at the age of 35, Wesley viewed his mission in life as one of proclaiming the good news of salvation by faith, which he did whenever a pulpit was offered him. The congregations of the Church of England, however, soon closed their doors to him because of his enthusiasm. He then went to religious societies, trying to inject new spiritual vigour into them, particularly by introducing "bands" similar to those of the Moravians—i.e., small groups within each society that were confined to members of the same sex and marital status who were prepared to share intimate secrets with each other and to receive mutual rebukes. For such groups Wesley drew up Rules of the Band Societies in December 1738.

For a year he worked through existing church societies, but resistance to his methods increased. In 1739 George Whitefield, who later became a great preacher of the Evangelical revival in Great Britain and North America, persuaded Wesley to go to the unchurched masses. Wesley gathered converts into societies for continuing fellowship and spiritual growth, and he was asked by a London group to become their leader. Soon other such groups were formed in London, Bristol, and elsewhere. To avoid the scandal of unworthy members, Wesley published, in 1743, rules for the Methodist societies. To promote new societies he became a widely travelled itinerant preacher. Because most ordained clergymen did not favour his approach, Wesley was compelled to seek the services of dedicated laymen, who also became itinerant preachers and helped administer the Methodist societies.

Many of Wesley's preachers had gone to the American colonies, but after the American Revolution most returned to England. Because the Bishop of London would not ordain some of his preachers to serve in the United States, Wesley took it upon himself, in 1784, to do so. In the same year he pointed out that his societies operated independently of any control by the Church of England.

Toward the end of his life, Wesley became an honoured figure in the British Isles.

JONATHAN EDWARDS

(b. Oct. 5, 1703, East Windsor, Conn. [U.S.] — d. March 22, 1758, Princeton, N.J.)

Jonathan Edwards was the greatest theologian and philosopher of British American Puritanism, the stimulator of the religious revival known as the Great Awakening, and one of the forerunners of the age of Protestant missionary expansion in the 19th century.

Edwards's father, Timothy, was pastor of the church at East Windsor, Conn.; his mother, Esther, was a daughter of Solomon Stoddard, pastor of the church at Northampton, Mass. Jonathan was the fifth child and only son among 11 children; he grew up in an atmosphere of Puritan piety, affection, and learning. After a rigorous schooling at home, he entered Yale College in New Haven, Conn., at the age of 13. He was graduated in 1720 but remained at New Haven for two years, studying divinity. After a brief New York pastorate (1722–23), he received the M.A. degree in 1723; during most of 1724–26 he was a tutor at Yale. In 1727 he became his grandfather's colleague at Northampton. In the same year, he married Sarah Pierrepont, who combined a deep, often ecstatic, piety with personal winsomeness and practical good sense. To them were born 11 children.

The manuscripts that survive from his student days exhibit Edwards's remarkable powers of observation and analysis (especially displayed in "Of Insects"), the fascination that the English scientist Isaac Newton's optical theories held for him ("Of the Rainbow"), and his ambition to publish scientific and philosophical works in confutation of materialism and atheism ("Natural Philosophy"). Throughout his life he habitually studied with pen in hand, recording his thoughts in numerous hand-sewn notebooks; one of these, his "Catalogue" of books, demonstrates the wide variety of his interests.

Edwards did not accept his theological inheritance passively. In his "Personal Narrative" he confesses that, from his childhood on, his mind "had been full of objections" against the doctrine of predestination—i.e., that God sovereignly chooses some to salvation but rejects others to everlasting torment; "it used to appear like a horrible doctrine to me." Though he gradually worked through his intellectual objections, it was only with his conversion (early in 1721) that he came to a "delightful conviction" of divine sovereignty, to a "new sense" of God's glory revealed in Scripture and in nature. This became the centre of Edwards's piety: a direct, intuitive apprehension of God in all his glory, a sight and taste of Christ's majesty and beauty far beyond all "notional" understanding, immediately imparted to the soul (as a 1734 sermon title puts it) by "a divine and supernatural light." This alone confers worth on man, and in this consists his salvation. What such a God does must be right; hence, Edwards's cosmic optimism. The acceptance and affirmation of God as he is and does and the love of God simply because he is God became central motifs in all of Edwards's preaching.

Under the influence of Puritan and other Reformed divines, the Cambridge Platonists, and British philosopher-scientists such as Newton and Locke, Edwards began to sketch in his manuscripts the outlines of a "Rational Account" of the doctrines of Christianity in terms of contemporary philosophy. In the essay "Of Being," he argued from the inconceivability of absolute Nothing to the existence of God as the eternal omnipresent Being. It was also inconceivable to him that anything should exist (even universal Being) apart from consciousness; hence, material things exist only as ideas in perceiving minds; the universe depends for its being every moment on the knowledge and creative will of God; and "spirits only are properly substance." Further, if all knowledge is ultimately from sensation (Locke) and if a sense perception is merely God's method of communicating ideas to the mind, then all knowledge is directly dependent on the divine will to reveal; and a saving knowledge of God and spiritual things is possible only to those who have received the gift of the "new sense." This grace is independent of human effort and is "irresistible," for the perception of God's beauty and goodness that it confers is in its very nature a glad "consent." Nevertheless, God decrees conversion and a holy life as well as ultimate felicity; and he has so constituted things that "means of grace" (e.g., sermons, sacraments, even the fear of hell) are employed by the Spirit in conversion, though not as "proper causes." Thus, the predestinarian preacher could appeal to the emotions and wills of men.

At Stoddard's death in 1729, Edwards became sole occupant of the Northampton pulpit, the most important in Massachusetts outside of Boston. In his first published sermon, preached in 1731 to the Boston clergy and significantly entitled *God Glorified in the Work of Redemption, by the Greatness of Man's Dependence upon Him, in the Whole of It*, Edwards blamed New England's moral ills on its assumption of religious and moral self-sufficiency. Because God is the saints' whole good, faith, which abases man and exalts God, must be insisted on as the only means of salvation. The English colonists' enterprising spirit made them susceptible to a version of Arminianism (deriving from the Dutch theologian Jacobus Arminius), which was popular in the Anglican Church and spreading among dissenters; it minimized the disabling effects of original sin, stressed free will, and tended to make morality the essence of religion.

Against these ideas Edwards also delivered a series of sermons on "Justification by Faith Alone" in November

1734. The result was a great revival in Northampton and along the Connecticut River Valley in the winter and spring of 1734–35, during which period more than 300 of Edwards's people made professions of faith. His subsequent report, *A Faithful Narrative of the Surprising Work of God* (1737), made a profound impression in America and Europe, particularly through his description of the types and stages of conversion experience.

In 1740–42 came the Great Awakening throughout the colonies. George Whitefield, a highly successful evangelist in the English Methodist movement, and Gilbert Tennent, a Presbyterian minister from New Jersey, drew huge crowds; their "pathetical" (i.e., emotional) sermons resulted in violent emotional response and mass conversions. Edwards himself, though he held his own congregation relatively calm, employed the "preaching of terror" on several occasions, as in the Enfield sermon, "Sinners in the Hands of an Angry God" (1741).

The Awakening produced not only conversions and changed lives but also excesses, disorders, and ecclesiastical and civil disruptions. Though increasingly critical of attitudes and practices associated with the revival, to the extent of personally rebuking Whitefield, Edwards maintained that it was a genuine work of God, which needed to be furthered and purified. In defense and criticism of the Awakening he wrote *The Distinguishing Marks of a Work of the Spirit of God* (1741), *Some Thoughts Concerning the Present Revival of Religion in New England* (1742), and *A Treatise Concerning Religious Affections* (1746).

In the *Affections*, Edwards insisted, against the revival critics' ideal of sober, "reasonable" religion, that "the essence of all true religion lies in holy love," a love that proves its genuineness by its inner quality and practical results. In 1749 he edited, with "Reflections," the memoirs of David Brainerd, a young New Light revivalist who became a Presbyterian missionary to the Indians and died in 1747. The volume became a highly influential missionary biography. Edwards's *Humble Attempt to Promote Explicit Agreement and Visible Union of God's People in Extraordinary Prayer* (1747), written in support of a proposed international "concert of prayer" for "the Revival of Religion and the Advancement of Christ's Kingdom on Earth," helped to remove a major ideological barrier to missionary activity by arguing that the worst of the "great tribulations" (prophesied in the book of Revelation to John as preceding the millennium) were already past and that the church could thus look forward to an increasing success of the gospel among men.

Meanwhile, Edwards's relations with his own congregation had become strained; one reason for it was his changed views on the requirements for admission to the Lord's Supper. In the Halfway Covenant, baptized but unconverted children of believers might have their own children baptized by "owning the covenant"; Stoddard had instituted the subsequently widespread practice of admitting to the Eucharist all who were thus "in the covenant," even if they knew themselves to be unconverted. Edwards gradually came to believe that the profession required for admission to full communion should be understood to imply genuine faith, not merely doctrinal knowledge and good moral behaviour.

The public announcement of his position in 1749 precipitated a violent controversy that resulted in his dismissal. On July 1, 1750, Edwards preached his dignified and restrained "Farewell-Sermon." In the course of this controversy he wrote two books, *Qualifications for Communion* (1749) and *Misrepresentations Corrected, and Truth Vindicated, in a Reply to the Rev. Mr. Solomon Williams's Book* (1752), one to convince his congregation, the other to correct what he considered misrepresentations of his views by a kinsman, the pastor at Lebanon, Conn. Though Edwards himself was defeated, his position finally triumphed and provided New England Congregationalism with a doctrine of church membership more appropriate to its situation after disestablishment. In 1751 Edwards became pastor of the frontier church at Stockbridge, Mass., and missionary to the Indians there. Hampered by language difficulties, illness, Indian wars, and conflicts with powerful personal enemies, he nevertheless discharged his pastoral duties and found time to write his famous work on the *Freedom of Will* (1754). The will, said Edwards, is not a separate, self-determining faculty with power to act contrary to the strongest motives, as he understood the Arminians to teach. Rather, it is identical with feelings or preference, and a volition is simply the soul's "prevailing inclination" in action; the will "is as the greatest apparent good." Men are free to do as they please, and God therefore rightly holds them morally responsible for the quality of their volitions as expressions of their desires and intentions.

By 1757 Edwards had finished his *Great Christian Doctrine of Original Sin Defended* (1758), which was mainly a reply to the English divine John Taylor of Norwich, whose works attacking Calvinism (based on the thought of the 16th-century Protestant Reformer John Calvin) had "made a mighty noise in America." Edwards defended the doctrine not only by citing biblical statements about the corruption of man's heart but also by arguing that the empirical evidence of men's universal commission of sinful acts points to a sinful predisposition in every man. In answering Arminian objections to the notion that God "imputed" Adam's guilt to his posterity, Edwards proposed a novel theory of identity by divine "constitution" to account for men's unity with Adam and suggested that their innate corruption is not a judicial punishment for Adam's guilt but is really their own because of their participation (being one with him) in the sinful inclination that preceded Adam's sinful act. Edwards's was the first major contribution to the long debate about human nature in American theology and helped set the terms of that debate.

Edwards perceived the threat in Taylor's notion of man's innate goodness and autonomy; the whole Christian conception of supernatural redemption seemed to be at stake. He therefore planned further treatises, of which he completed two posthumously published dissertations: *Concerning the End for Which God Created the World* and *The Nature of True Virtue* (1765). God's glory, not human happiness, is his end in creation; but this is because God in his all-sufficient fullness must communicate himself by the exercise of his attributes. God can be said to aim at the creature's happiness, but it is a happiness that consists in contemplating and rejoicing in God's glory manifested in creation and redemption. Edwards defines true virtue as disinterested love (benevolence) toward God as Being in general and toward all lesser beings according to their degree of being. True virtue, therefore, does not spring from self-love or from any earthbound altruism (two prime 18th-century views); love to self, family, nation, or even mankind is good only if these lesser systems of being do not usurp the place of highest regard that belongs to God alone.

Edwards also projected books on other subjects, notably *A History of the Work of Redemption* (he had preached a series of sermons—posthumously published—on that subject in 1739), which was to be a complete theology combining biblical, historical, and systematic materials "in an entire new method." Late in 1757, however, he accepted the presidency of the College of New Jersey (later Princeton University) and arrived there in January. He had hardly assumed his duties when he contracted smallpox and died.

MOTOORI NORINAGA

(b. June 21, 1730, Matsuzaka, Japan—d. Nov. 5, 1801, Matsuzaka)

Motoori Norinaga was the most eminent scholar in Shintō and Japanese classics. His father, a textile merchant, died when Norinaga was 11 years old, but with his mother's encouragement he studied medicine in Kyōto and became a physician. In time he came under the influence of the National Learning (Kokugaku) movement, which emphasized the importance of Japan's own literature. Motoori applied careful philological methods to the study of the *Koji-ki*, *The Tale of Genji*, and other classical literature and stressed *mono no aware* ("sensitiveness to beauty") as the central concept of Japanese literature.

Motoori Norinaga.

Motoori's study of Japanese classics, especially the *Koji-ki*, provided the theoretical foundation of the modern Shintō revival.

Rejecting Buddhist and Confucian influence on the interpretation of Shintō, he instead traced the genuine spirit of Shintō to ancient Japanese myths and the sacred traditions transmitted from antiquity. Motoori also reaffirmed the ancient Japanese concept of *musubi* (the mysterious power of all creation and growth), which has become one of the main tenets of modern Shintō. While he accepted ethical dualism, he believed that evil existed for the sake of good, as an antithetic element of the dialectical higher good.

Motoori's 49-volume commentary on the *Koji-ki* (*Koji-ki-den*), completed in 1798 after 35 years of effort, is incorporated in the *Moto-ori Norinaga Zenshū*, 12 vol. (1926–27; "Complete Works of Motoori Norinaga").

ANN LEE

(b. Feb. 29, 1736, Manchester, Eng.—d. Sept. 8, 1784, Watervliet, N.Y., U.S.)

Ann Lee was a religious leader who brought the Shaker sect from England to the American colonies.

Lee was the unlettered daughter of a blacksmith who was probably named Lees. In her youth she went to work in a textile mill. At the age of 22 she joined a sect known as the Shaking Quakers, or Shakers, because of the shaking and dancing that characterized their worship. She married in 1762, a union that tradition holds was unhappy and may have influenced her later doctrinal insistence on celibacy.

In 1770, during a period of religious persecution by the English authorities, Lee was imprisoned and while in jail became convinced of the truth of certain religious ideas perceived in a vision. She came to believe that sexual lust impeded Christ's work and that only through celibacy could men and women further his kingdom on Earth. Four years later, commanded as the result of another vision, Lee persuaded her husband, brother, and six other followers to immigrate to America. There, her followers founded a settlement in the woods of Niskeyuna (now Watervliet), near Albany (in present-day New York State). Beginning with an influx of converts from nearby settlements, the Shaker movement grew and began to spread throughout New England to embrace thousands. Mother Ann, as she came to be known, was believed to have ushered in the millennium, for the Shakers asserted that as Christ had embodied the masculine half of God's dual nature, so she embodied the female half.

In 1780 Mother Ann was imprisoned for treason because of her pacifist doctrines and her refusal to sign an oath of allegiance. She was soon released and in 1781–83 toured New England. According to witnesses, she performed a number of miracles, including healing the sick by touch. After her death in 1784, her followers organized the United Society of Believers in Christ's Second Appearing, which was also known as the Millennial Church and, most commonly, as the Shakers, and which by 1826 had grown to encompass 18 Shaker villages in 8 states. The Shakers gradually disappeared as an active religious sect.

RICHARD ALLEN

(b. Feb. 14, 1760, Philadelphia, Pennsylvania [U.S.]—d. March 26, 1831, Philadelphia)

Richard Allen was the founder and first bishop of the African Methodist Episcopal Church, a major American denomination.

Soon after Allen was born, to slave parents, the family was sold to a Delaware farmer. At age 17 he became a Methodist convert and at 22 was permitted to preach. Two years later (1784), at the first general conference of the Methodist Episcopal Church at Baltimore, Allen was considered a talented candidate for the new denomination's ministry. In 1786 he bought his freedom and went to Philadelphia, where he joined St. George's Methodist Episcopal Church. Occasionally he was asked to preach to the congregation. He also con-

Richard Allen.

ducted prayer meetings for blacks. Restrictions were placed on the number permitted to attend these meetings, and Allen, dissatisfied, withdrew in 1787 to help organize an independent Methodist church. In 1787 he turned an old blacksmith shop into the first church for blacks in the United States. His followers were known as Allenites.

In 1799 Allen became the first African American to be officially ordained in the ministry of the Methodist Episcopal Church. The organization of the Bethel Society led in 1816 to the founding of the African Methodist Episcopal Church, which elected Allen its first bishop.

SAINT ELIZABETH ANN SETON

(b. Aug. 28, 1774, New York, N.Y. [U.S.]—d. Jan. 4, 1821, Emmitsburg, Md., U.S.; canonized 1975; feast day January 4)

Saint Elizabeth Ann Seton was the first native-born American to be canonized by the Roman Catholic Church. She was the founder of the Sisters of Charity, the first American religious society.

Elizabeth Bayley was the daughter of a distinguished physician. She devoted a good deal of time to working among the poor, and in 1797 she joined Isabella M. Graham and others in founding the first charitable institution in New York City, the Society for the Relief of Poor Widows with Small Children, serving as the organization's treasurer for seven years. She had married William M. Seton in 1794, and in 1803 they and the eldest of their five children traveled to Italy for his health. Nevertheless, in part perhaps as an aftereffect of his bankruptcy three years earlier, he died there in December. She returned to New York City and, as a result of her experiences and acquaintances in Italy, joined the Roman Catholic Church in 1805. She found it difficult to earn a living, partly because many friends and relatives shunned her after her conversion. For a time she operated a small school for boys. In 1808 Seton accepted an invitation from the Reverend William Dubourg, president of St. Mary's College in Baltimore, Maryland, to open a school for Catholic girls in that city. Several young women joined in her work, and in 1809 her long-held hope to found a religious community was realized when she and her companions took vows before Archbishop John Carroll and became the Sisters of St. Joseph, the first American-based Catholic sisterhood. A few months later Mother Seton and the sisters moved their home and school to Emmitsburg, Maryland, where they provided free education for the poor girls of the parish—an act later considered by many to be the beginning of Catholic parochial education in the United States. In 1812 the order became the Sisters of Charity of St. Joseph under a modification of the rule of the Sisters of Charity of St. Vincent de Paul. Houses of the order were opened in Philadelphia in 1814 and in New York City in 1817. Mother Seton continued to teach and work for the community until her death in 1821, by which time the order had 20 communities. In 1856 Seton Hall College (now University) was named for her. She was canonized in September 1975.

WILLIAM MILLER

(b. Feb. 15, 1782, Pittsfield, Mass., U.S.—d. Dec. 20, 1849, Low Hampton, N.Y.)

William Miller was an American religious enthusiast and leader of a movement called Millerism that sought to revive belief that the bodily arrival ("advent") of Christ was imminent.

Miller was a farmer, but he also held such offices as deputy sheriff and justice of the peace. In the War of 1812 he served as a captain of the 30th Infantry. After years of Bible study he began to preach in 1831 that the present world would end "about the year 1843." He based this belief primarily on a passage in the Book of Daniel (8:13–14). He published a pamphlet in 1833 and a book of lectures in 1836, the first of many publications. Principal organs of the Millerite movement were the *Signs of the Times* (Boston) and the *Midnight Cry* (New York). Miller estimated that between 50,000 and 100,000 believed in his views. When 1843 passed, some of his associates set Oct. 22, 1844, as the date of the Second Coming. This date brought the movement to a sharp climax. There is no historical foundation for stories that the Millerites engaged in such fanatical excesses as ascending hills, housetops, and trees in ascension robes. The last general conference met in Albany, N.Y., April 1845. Belief in the imminence of the advent was restated, but no date was set and no church organization created.

There are two principal Adventist bodies today—the Advent Christian Church, organized in 1861, and the much larger body of Seventh-day Adventists, organized in 1863—and several small Adventist bodies.

RALPH WALDO EMERSON

(b. May 25, 1803, Boston, Mass., U.S.—d. April 27, 1882, Concord, Mass.)

Ralph Waldo Emerson, an American lecturer, poet, and essayist, was the leading exponent of New England Transcendentalism.

Emerson was the son of the Reverend William Emerson, a Unitarian clergyman and friend of the arts. The son inherited the profession of divinity, which had attracted all his ancestors in direct line from Puritan days. The family of his mother, Ruth Haskins, was strongly Anglican, and among influences on Emerson were such Anglican writers and thinkers as Ralph Cudworth, Robert Leighton, Jeremy Taylor, and Samuel Taylor Coleridge.

On May 12, 1811, Emerson's father died, leaving the son largely to the intellectual care of Mary Moody Emerson, his aunt, who took her duties seriously. In 1812 Emerson entered the Boston Public Latin School, where his juvenile verses were encouraged and his literary gifts recognized. In 1817 he entered Harvard College, where he began his journals, which may be the most remarkable record of the "march of Mind" to appear in the United States. He graduated in 1821 and taught school while preparing for part-time study in the Harvard Divinity School.

Though Emerson was licensed to preach in the Unitarian community in 1826, illness slowed the progress of his career, and he was not ordained to the Unitarian ministry at the Second Church, Boston, until 1829. There he began to win fame as a preacher, and his position seemed secure. In 1829 he also married Ellen Louisa Tucker. When she died of tuberculosis in 1831, his grief drove him to question his beliefs and his profession. But in the previous few years Emerson had already begun to question Christian doctrines. His older brother William, who had gone to Germany, had acquainted him with the new biblical criticism and the doubts that had been cast on the historicity of miracles. From the first, Emerson's own sermons had been unusually free of traditional doctrine and were instead a personal exploration of the uses of spirit, showing an idealistic tendency and announcing his doctrine of self-reliance and self-sufficiency. Indeed, his sermons had divested Christianity of all external or historical supports and made its basis one's private intuition of the universal moral law and its test a life of virtuous accomplishment. Unitarianism had little appeal to him by now, and in 1832 he resigned from the ministry.

When Emerson left the church, he was in search of a more certain conviction of God than that granted by the historical evidences of miracles. He wanted his own revelation—i.e., a direct and immediate experience of God. When he left his pulpit he journeyed to Europe. In Paris he saw Antoine-Laurent de Jussieu's collection of natural specimens arranged in a developmental order that confirmed his belief in man's spiritual relation to nature. In England he paid memorable visits to Samuel Taylor Coleridge, William Wordsworth, and Thomas Carlyle. At home once more in 1833, he began to write *Nature* and established himself as a popular and influential lecturer. By 1834 he had found a permanent dwelling place in

Concord, Mass., and in the following year he married Lydia Jackson and settled into the kind of quiet domestic life that was essential to his work.

The 1830s saw Emerson become an independent literary man. During this decade his own personal doubts and difficulties were increasingly shared by other intellectuals. Before the decade was over his personal manifestos—*Nature*, "The American Scholar," and his "Divinity School Address"—had rallied together a group that came to be called the Transcendentalists, of which he was popularly acknowledged the spokesman. Emerson helped initiate Transcendentalism by publishing anonymously in Boston in 1836 a little book of 95 pages entitled *Nature*. Having found the answers to his spiritual doubts, he formulated his essential philosophy, and almost everything he ever wrote afterward was an extension, amplification, or amendment of the ideas he first affirmed in *Nature*.

Emerson's religious doubts had lain deeper than his objection to the Unitarians' retention of belief in the historicity of miracles. He was also deeply unsettled by Newtonian physics' mechanistic conception of the universe and by the Lockean psychology of sensation that he had learned at Harvard. Emerson felt that there was no place for free will in the chains of mechanical cause and effect that rationalist philosophers conceived the world as being made up of. This world could be known only through the senses rather than through thought and intuition; it determined men physically and psychologically; and yet it made them victims of circumstance, beings whose superfluous mental powers were incapable of truly ascertaining reality.

Emerson reclaimed an idealistic philosophy from this dead end of 18th-century rationalism by once again asserting the human ability to transcend the materialistic world of sense experience and facts and become conscious of the all-pervading spirit of the universe and the potentialities of human freedom. God could best be found by looking inward into one's own self, one's own soul, and from such an enlightened self-awareness would in turn come freedom of action and the ability to change one's world according to the dictates of one's ideals and conscience. Human spiritual renewal thus proceeds from the individual's intimate personal experience of his own portion of the divine "oversoul," which is present in and permeates the entire creation and all living things, and which is accessible if only a person takes the trouble to look for it. Emerson enunciates how "reason," which to him denotes the intuitive awareness of eternal truth, can be relied upon in ways quite different from one's reliance on "understanding"—i.e., the ordinary gathering of sense-data and the logical comprehension of the material world. Emerson's doctrine of self-sufficiency and self-reliance naturally springs from his view that the individual need only look into his own heart for the spiritual guidance that has hitherto been the province of the established churches. The individual must then have the courage to be himself and to trust the inner force within him as he lives his life according to his intuitively derived precepts.

Obviously these ideas are far from original, and it is clear that Emerson was influenced in his formulation of them by his previous readings of Neoplatonist philosophy, the works of Coleridge and other European Romantics, the writings of Emmanuel Swedenborg, Hindu philosophy, and other sources. What set Emerson apart from others who were expressing similar Transcendentalist notions were his abilities as a polished literary stylist able to express his thought with vividness and breadth of vision. His philosophical exposition has a peculiar power and an organic unity whose cumulative effect was highly suggestive and stimulating to his contemporary readers' imaginations.

In a lecture entitled "The American Scholar" (Aug. 31, 1837), Emerson described the resources and duties of the new liberated intellectual that he himself had become. This address was in effect a challenge to the Harvard intelligentsia, warning against pedantry, imitation of others, traditionalism, and scholarship unrelated to life. Emerson's "Address at Divinity College," Harvard University, in 1838 was another challenge, this time directed against a lifeless Christian tradition, especially Unitarianism as he had known it. He dismissed religious institutions and the divinity of Jesus as failures in man's attempt to encounter deity directly through the moral principle or through an intuited sentiment of virtue. This address alienated many, left him with few opportunities to preach, and resulted in his being ostracized by Harvard for many years. Young disciples, however, joined the informal Transcendental Club (founded in 1836) and encouraged him in his activities.

In 1840 he helped launch *The Dial*, first edited by Margaret Fuller and later by himself, thus providing an outlet for the new ideas Transcendentalists were trying to present to America. Though short-lived, the magazine provided a rallying point for the younger members of the school. From his continuing lecture series, he gathered his *Essays* into two volumes (1841, 1844), which made him internationally famous. In his first volume of *Essays* Emerson consolidated his thoughts on moral individualism and preached the ethics of self-reliance, the duty of self-cultivation, and the need for the expression of self. The second volume of *Essays* shows Emerson accommodating his earlier idealism to the limitations of real life; his later works show an increasing acquiescence to the state of things, less reliance on self, greater respect for society, and an awareness of the ambiguities and incompleteness of genius.

His *Representative Men* (1849) contained biographies of Plato, Swedenborg, Montaigne, Shakespeare, Napoleon, and Goethe. In *English Traits* he gave a character analysis of a people from which he himself stemmed. *The Conduct of Life* (1860), Emerson's most mature work, reveals a developed humanism together with a full awareness of man's limitations. It may be considered as partly confession. Emerson's collected *Poems* (1846) were supplemented by others in *May-Day* (1867), and the two volumes established his reputation as a major American poet.

By the 1860s Emerson's reputation in America was secure, for time was wearing down the novelty of his rebellion as he slowly accommodated himself to society. He continued to give frequent lectures, but the writing he did after 1860 shows a waning of his intellectual powers. A new generation knew only the old Emerson and had absorbed his teaching without recalling the acrimony it had occasioned. Upon his death in 1882 Emerson was transformed into the Sage of Concord, shorn of his power as a liberator and enrolled among the worthies of the very tradition he had set out to destroy.

Emerson's voice and rhetoric sustained the faith of thousands in the American lecture circuits between 1834 and the American Civil War. He served as a cultural middleman through whom the aesthetic and philosophical currents of Europe passed to America, and he led his countrymen during the burst of literary glory known as the American renaissance (1835–65). As a principal spokesman for Transcendentalism, the American tributary of European Romanticism, Emerson gave direction to a religious, philosophical, and ethical movement that above all stressed belief in the spiritual potential of every man.

BAHĀ' ALLĀH

(b. Nov. 12, 1817, Tehrān, Iran—d. May 29, 1892, Acre, Palestine [now 'Akko, Israel])

Bahā' Allāh was the founder of the Bahā'ī Faith upon his claim to be the manifestation of the unknowable God.

Mīrzā Ḥosayn was a member of the Shī'ite branch of Islam. He subsequently allied himself with Mīrzā 'Alī Moḥammad of Shīrāz, who was known as the Bāb (Arabic: "Gateway") and was the head of the Bābī, a Muslim sect professing a privileged access to final truth. After the Bāb's execution by the Iranian government for treason (1850), Mīrzā Ḥosayn joined Mīrzā Yaḥyā (also called Ṣobḥ-e Azal), his own half brother and the Bāb's spiritual heir, in directing the Bābī movement. Mīrzā Yaḥyā later was discredited, and Mīrzā Ḥosayn was exiled by orthodox Sunnī Muslims successively to Baghdad, Kurdistan, and Constantinople (Istanbul). There, in 1863, he publicly declared himself to be the divinely chosen *imām-mahdī* ("rightly guided leader"), whom the Bāb had foretold. The resulting factional violence caused the Ottoman government to banish Mīrzā Ḥosayn to Acre.

At Acre, Bahā' Allāh, as he was by then called, developed the formerly provincial Bahā'ī doctrine into a comprehensive teaching that advocated the unity of all religions and the universal brotherhood of man. Emphasizing social ethics, he eschewed ritual worship and devoted himself to the abolition of racial, class, and religious prejudices. His place of confinement in Acre became a centre of pilgrimage for Bahā'ī believers from Iran and the United States.

ISAAC MAYER WISE

(b. March 29, 1819, Steingrub, Bohemia, Austrian Empire [now in
Czech Republic] — d. March 26, 1900, Cincinnati, Ohio, U.S.)

Isaac Mayer Wise was a rabbi whose goal of uniting
American Jewry made him the greatest organizer of
Reform Jewish institutions in the United States.

After serving as a rabbi for two years in Radnice,
Bohemia, Wise immigrated in 1846 to Albany, N.Y., where
he was a rabbi for eight years. His congregation there was
the first in the United States to employ family pews; these
became a standard institution in Reform Judaism. In 1854
Wise accepted the pulpit of Bene Yeshurun in Cincinnati,
a post he retained for the rest of his life.

Although Wise failed in his efforts to unite American
Jews of all persuasions, he did bring about great unanimity
among Reform Jews. In addition, he succeeded in adapt-
ing Reform Judaism to American life. An astute politician,
he propagandized tirelessly for centralized Reform institutions in his English-language weekly, the *American
Israelite;* in his German-language paper, *Die Deborah*; and
in many rabbinical conferences.

The fruits of his efforts were the Union of American
Hebrew Congregations, a confederation of synagogues in
the Midwest and South that grew into an association of
American and Canadian Reform congregations; its educa-
tional arm, Hebrew Union College (now Hebrew Union
College–Jewish Institute of Religion), the first permanent
American rabbinical college, of which Wise was president
until his death; and the Central Conference of American
Rabbis, which became the legislative body of Reform
Judaism. Wise served as president of the Central
Conference until his death.

Because of the diversity of Reform prayer books, Wise
tried to compile a standard work and in 1857 published the

Minhag America ("American Usage"). It was superseded in 1894 by the Union Prayer Book, which came into being, in large part, because Wise had emphasized so often and so forcefully the need for a standard text. A believer in the universal mission of Judaism, he was a firm opponent of the establishment of a Jewish state in Palestine.

MARY BAKER EDDY

(b. July 16, 1821, Bow, near Concord, N.H., U.S.—d. Dec. 3, 1910, Chestnut Hill, Mass.)

Mary Baker Eddy was a Christian religious reformer and founder of the religious denomination known as Christian Science.

Mary Baker Eddy's family background and life until her "discovery" of Christian Science in 1866 greatly influenced her interest in religious reform. She was born to devout Congregationalists at a time when Puritan piety was a real, though residual, force in the religious life of New England. She struggled with serious illness from childhood, grieved over the death of a favourite brother when she was 20, became a widow at 22 after only a half year of marriage to George Glover, and in 1849 lost both her mother and her fiancé within three weeks of each other. Her marriage in 1853 to Daniel Patterson eventually broke down, ending in divorce 20 years later after he deserted her. In 1856 she was plunged into virtual invalidism after Patterson and her father conspired to separate her from her only child, a 12-year-old son from her first marriage. She would not see her son again for nearly 25 years, and they met only a few times thereafter.

Her understanding of her personal and physical misfortunes was greatly shaped by her Congregationalist upbringing. Her proclivity for religion was evident early on, and study of the Bible was the bedrock of her

Mary Baker Eddy.

religious life. She was especially influenced by ministers in the "New Light" tradition of Jonathan Edwards, which emphasized the heart's outflowing response to God's majesty and love.

Yet, as a teenager, she rebelled with others of her generation against the stark predestinarian Calvinism of what she called her father's "relentless theology." But whereas most Protestants who rejected Calvinism gravitated toward belief in a benign God, Eddy needed something more. Although she too believed in a benign God, she continued to ask how the reality of a God of love could possibly be reconciled with the existence of a world filled with so much misery and pain. She thus found herself confronting perhaps the most basic problem undermining Christian faith in her time.

Eddy's spiritual quest took an unusual direction during the 1850s with the new medical system of homeopathy. Losing faith in medical systems based on materialistic premises, she hit on what some today would call the placebo effect. Her conviction that the cause of disease was rooted in the human mind and that it was in no sense God's will was confirmed by her contact from 1862 to 1865 with Phineas P. Quimby of Maine, a pioneer in what would today be called suggestive therapeutics. The degree of Quimby's influence on her has been controversial, but, as his own son affirmed, her intensely religious preoccupations remained distinct from the essentially secular cast of Quimby's thought. Though personally loyal to Quimby, she soon recognized that his healing method was based in mesmerism, or mental suggestion, rather than in the biblical Christianity to which she was so firmly bound.

Injured in a severe fall shortly after Quimby's death in early 1866, she turned, as she later recalled, to a Gospel account of healing and experienced a moment of spiritual illumination and discovery that brought not only immediate recovery but a new direction to her life. "That short experience," she later wrote, "included a glimpse of the great fact that I have since tried to make plain to others, namely, Life in and of Spirit; this Life being the sole reality of existence. I learned that mortal thought evolves a subjective state which it names matter, thereby shutting out the true sense of Spirit."

While the precise extent of her injuries is unclear, the transforming effect of the experience is beyond dispute. From 1866 on, she gained increasing conviction that she had made a spiritual discovery of overwhelming authority and power. The next nine years of scriptural study, healing work, and teaching climaxed in 1875 with the publication of her major work, *Science and Health*, which she regarded as spiritually inspired. And it was in this major work that Eddy eventually included the basic tenets of the church:

1. As adherents of Truth, we take the inspired Word of the Bible as our sufficient guide to eternal Life. 2. We acknowledge and adore one supreme and infinite God. We acknowledge His Son, one Christ; the Holy Ghost or divine Comforter; and man in God's image and likeness. 3. We acknowledge God's forgiveness of sin in the destruction of sin and the spiritual understanding that casts out evil as unreal. But the belief in sin is punished so long as the belief lasts. 4. We acknowledge Jesus' atonement as the evidence of divine, efficacious Love, unfolding man's unity with God through Christ Jesus, the Way-shower; and we acknowledge that man is saved through Christ, through Truth, Life, and Love as demonstrated by the Galilean Prophet in healing the sick and overcoming sin and death. 5. We acknowledge that the crucifixion of Jesus and his resurrection served to uplift faith to

understand eternal Life, even the allness of Soul, Spirit, and the nothingness of matter. 6. And we solemnly promise to watch, and pray for that Mind to be in us which was also in Christ Jesus; to do unto others as we would have them do unto us; and to be merciful, just, and pure.

Although the first edition of *Science and Health* contained the essential structure of her teachings, Eddy continued to refine her statement of Christian Science in the years to come. For the rest of her life she continued to revise this "textbook" of Christian Science as the definitive statement of her teaching. In 1883 she added the words "with Key to the Scriptures" to the book's title to emphasize her contention that *Science and Health* did not stand alone but opened the way to the continuing power and truth of biblical revelation, especially the life and work of Jesus Christ.

To "reinstate primitive Christianity and its lost element of healing" was the stated purpose of the Church of Christ, Scientist, which she founded with 15 students in Lynn, Mass., in 1879. A promising move to Boston in 1882 began with a jolting setback: the death of her third husband, Asa Gilbert Eddy, on whose support she had relied since their marriage in 1877. Nonetheless, during her years in Boston from 1882 to 1889, Christian Science began to make an impact on American religious life.

Boston was an intellectual centre where new ideas, especially in religion, traveled fast. Eddy contributed to the ferment in the religious life of New England, especially since she maintained that her teaching, while thoroughly Christian, offered a distinct alternative to both liberal and orthodox forms of Christianity.

The demands on her were enormous during this period. Eddy taught hundreds of students in the

Massachusetts Metaphysical College, for which she obtained a charter in 1881. She continued to revise *Science and Health* and wrote a number of shorter works, including numerous articles for a monthly magazine she founded in 1883. And she also preached intermittently at Christian Science church services, which were attracting a growing number of disaffected mainstream Protestants.

Her successes in the 1880s, especially her conversions of mainstream Protestants, exposed her to growing criticism from concerned Boston ministers. The fledgling Christian Science movement was further threatened by internal schism and the rivalry of various "mind-cure" groups that appropriated her terminology but sought healing not through divine help but through the powers of the human mind, which she saw as engendering disease in the first place. In response to these challenges, Eddy's writings repeatedly underscore the biblical basis of her teachings and the Christian demands of practicing it. She also explicitly differentiated Christian Science from theosophy and spiritualism, both antecedents of 20th-century "New Age" movements.

Eddy moved to Concord, N.H., in 1889, and eventually settled into a house, called Pleasant View, with a small staff. During the next decade she gained both authority within the movement and public recognition outside it. In 1892 she reorganized the church she had founded in 1879, and over the next decade she established its present structure as The Mother Church—The First Church of Christ, Scientist—and its worldwide branches. In 1895 she published the *Manual of The Mother Church*, a slim book of bylaws that she continued to revise until her death and that she intended would govern the church in perpetuity.

Her growing public stature as a religious leader, together with the practical challenge her teachings posed to conventional religion and medicine, made her the subject of mounting controversy, as seen in a set of articles in 1902 and 1903 (published in book form in 1907 under the title *Christian Science*) by Mark Twain, who severely criticized Eddy while speaking at points warmly of her teaching. There was also a highly misleading series that ran in *McClure's Magazine* for two years and an unsuccessful lawsuit against her (the so-called "Next Friends Suit" of 1907) that Joseph Pulitzer's *New York World* newspaper orchestrated to question her mental competence.

Despite these personal attacks and occasional ill health (induced at least in part, she felt, by the hostility that fueled such attacks), Eddy accomplished much during the last decade of her long life. She put *Science and Health* through its last major revisions, completed the formal structuring of her church by entrusting greater responsibilities to its board of directors, and in 1908 founded the *Christian Science Monitor*, an international newspaper of recognized excellence.

Eddy's death in 1910 did not end the controversy over her character or her contribution to Christian thought and practice. Today's interest in women's studies, however, is prompting a fresh look at her life and influence, and feminists have often emphasized that her work had the effect of empowering women. Indeed, as she acknowledged, hers was a life of protest against conventional assumptions both in religion and in medicine. While she was not a feminist per se, she acted outside of conventional gender roles by founding and leading a significant American denomination, and she did support some feminist causes, such as woman suffrage and the right of women to hold property. In fact, she was praised by such figures as Clara Barton and Susan B. Anthony, who expressed some interest in her teaching as well.

Yet her aim was not to overturn traditional gender roles but to reinvigorate Christianity—to restore the role of spiritual healing in a living Christian faith. It is this tradition of spiritual healing that is perhaps the most controversial part of Eddy's legacy. Science is only beginning to grapple with some of the long-term questions raised by the church's practice of spiritual healing. These questions concern not only the medical evidence for spiritual healings, many of which have involved undiagnosed and psychosomatic disorders, but also the significance for religion of medically diagnosed conditions. While Eddy's character and the teachings of her church remain controversial, no single individual has focused more attention on this area of Christian experience.

DAYANANDA SARASVATI

(b. 1824, Tankāra, Gujarāt, India—d. Oct. 30, 1883, Ajmer, Rājputāna)

Dayananda Sarasvati was a Hindu ascetic and social reformer who was the founder (1875) of the Arya Samaj, a Hindu reform movement advocating a return to the temporal and spiritual authority of the Vedas, the earliest scriptures of India.

Dayananda received the early education appropriate for a young Brahman of a well-to-do family. At the age of 14 he accompanied his father on an all-night vigil at a Śiva temple. While his father and some others fell asleep, mice, attracted by the offerings placed before the image of the deity, ran over the image, polluting it. The experience set off a profound revulsion in the young boy against what he considered to be senseless idol worship. His religious doubts were further intensified five years later by the death of a beloved uncle. In a search for a way to overcome the limits of mortality, he was directed first toward Yoga (a system of mental and physical disciplines). Faced with the prospect of a marriage being arranged for him, he left home and joined the Sarasvatī order of ascetics.

For the next 15 years (1845–60) he traveled throughout India in search of a religious truth and finally became a disciple of Swami Birajananda. His guru, in lieu of the usual teacher's fees, extracted a promise from Dayananda (the name taken by him at the time of his initiation as an ascetic) to spend his life working toward a reinstatement of the Vedic Hinduism that had existed in pre-Buddhist India.

Dayananda first attracted wide public attention for his views when he engaged in a public debate with orthodox Hindu scholars in Benares (Vārānasi) presided over by the maharaja of Benares. The first meeting establishing the Arya Samaj (Society of Aryans [Nobles]) was held in Bombay on April 10, 1875. Although some of Dayananda's claims to the unassailable authority of the Vedas seem extravagant (for example, modern technological achievements such as the use of electricity he claimed to have found described in the Vedas), he furthered many important social reforms. He opposed child marriage, advocated the remarriage of widows, opened Vedic study to members of all castes, and founded many educational and charitable institutions. The Arya Samaj also contributed greatly to the reawakening of a spirit of Indian nationalism in pre-independence days.

Dayananda died after vigorous public criticism of a princely ruler, under circumstances suggesting that he might have been poisoned by one of the maharaja's supporters; but the accusation was never proved in court.

WILLIAM BOOTH

(b. April 10, 1829, Nottingham, Nottinghamshire, Eng.—d. Aug. 20, 1912, London)

William Booth was the founder and general (1878–1912) of the Salvation Army.

The son of a speculative builder, Booth was apprenticed as a boy to a pawnbroker. At 15 he underwent the experience of religious conversion and became a revivalist preacher. In 1849 he went to London, where he worked in a pawnbroker's shop at Walworth, hating the business but bound to it by the necessity of sending money home. At this period he met Catherine Mumford, his future wife and lifelong helpmate. In 1852 he had become a regular preacher of the Methodist New Connection, and in 1855 they were married. After nine years of ministry Booth broke loose from the New Connection and began his career as an independent revivalist.

Booth held the simple belief that eternal punishment was the fate of the unconverted. Coupled with this was a profound pity for the outcast and a hatred of dirt, squalor, and suffering. In 1864 Booth went to London and continued his services in tents and in the open air and founded at Whitechapel the Christian Mission, which became (in 1878) the Salvation Army. Booth modeled its "Orders and Regulations" on those of the British army. Its early "campaigns" excited violent opposition; a "Skeleton Army" was organized to break up the meetings, and for many years Booth's followers were subjected to fines and imprisonment as breakers of the peace. After 1889 these disorders were little heard of. The operations of the army were extended in 1880 to the United States, in 1881 to Australia, and later to the European continent, to India, to Ceylon (now Sri Lanka), and elsewhere—General Booth himself being an indefatigable traveler, organizer, and speaker.

In 1890 General Booth published *In Darkest England, and the Way Out*, in which he had the assistance of William Thomas Stead. He proposed to remedy pauperism and vice by means of: homes for the homeless; training centres to prepare emigrants for oversea colonies; rescue homes for fallen women; homes for released prisoners; legal aid for the poor; and practical help for the alcoholic. There was vast public support for the program; money was liberally subscribed, and a large part of the scheme was carried out. The opposition and ridicule with which Booth's work was for many years received gave way, toward the end of the 19th century, to very widespread sympathy as its results were more fully realized. The active encouragement of King Edward VII, at whose insistence in 1902 he was invited officially to be present at the coronation ceremony, marked the completeness of the change; and when, in 1905, General Booth went through England, he was received in state by the mayors and corporations of many towns. The fiery old man had become a great figure in English life.

HELENA BLAVATSKY

(b. Aug. 12 [July 31, Old Style], 1831, Yekaterinoslav, Ukraine, Russian Empire [now Dnipropetrovsk, Ukraine]—d. May 8, 1891, London, Eng.)

Helena Blavatsky was a Russian spiritualist, author, and cofounder of the Theosophical Society to promote theosophy, a pantheistic philosophical-religious system.

At the age of 17, Helena Hahn married Nikifor V. Blavatsky, a Russian military officer and provincial vice-governor, but they separated after a few months. She became interested in occultism and spiritualism and for many years traveled extensively throughout Asia, Europe, and the United States; she also claimed to have spent several years in India and Tibet studying under Hindu gurus. In 1873 she went to New York City, where she met and became a close companion of Henry Steel Olcott, and in

1875 they and several other prominent persons founded the Theosophical Society.

In 1877 her first major work, *Isis Unveiled*, was published. In this book she criticized the science and religion of her day and asserted that mystical experience and doctrine were the means to attain true spiritual insight and authority. Although *Isis Unveiled* attracted attention, the society dwindled. In 1879 Blavatsky and Olcott went to India; three years later they established the

Helena Blavatsky, detail of an oil painting by Hermann Schmiechen, 1884; in a private collection.

Theosophical Society headquarters at Adyar, near Madras, and began publication of the society's journal, *The Theosophist*, which Blavatsky edited from 1879 to 1888. The society soon developed a strong following in India.

Asserting that she possessed extraordinary psychic powers, Blavatsky, during journeys to Paris and London, was accused by the Indian press late in 1884 of concocting fictitious spiritualist phenomena. After protesting her innocence while on a tour of Germany, she returned to India in 1884 and met with an enthusiastic reception. The "Hodgson Report," the findings of an investigation in 1885 by the London Society for Psychical Research, declared her a fraud. Soon thereafter she left India in failing health. She lived quietly in Germany, Belgium, and finally in

London, working on her small, meditative classic *The Voice of Silence* (1889) and her most important work, *The Secret Doctrine* (1888), which was an overview of theosophical teachings. It was followed in 1889 by her *Key to Theosophy*. Her *Collected Writings* were published in 16 volumes (1950–91).

RAMAKRISHNA

(b. Feb. 18, 1836, Hooghly [now Hugli], Bengal state, India—d. Aug. 16, 1886, Calcutta [now Kolkata])

Ramakrishna was a Hindu religious leader who founded the school of religious thought that became the Ramakrishna Order.

Born into a poor Brahman (the highest-ranking social class) family, Ramakrishna had little formal schooling. He spoke Bengali and knew neither English nor Sanskrit. His father died in 1843, and his elder brother Ramkumar became head of the family. At age 23 Ramakrishna married Sarada Devi, a five-year-old girl, but, because of his advocacy of celibacy, the marriage was never consummated, even though they remained together until his death. (Sarada Devi was later deified and is still considered a saint by devotees who treat her as the Divine Mother.)

In 1852 poverty forced Ramkumar and Ramakrishna to leave their village to seek employment in Calcutta (now Kolkata). There they became priests in a temple dedicated to the goddess Kali. In 1856, however, Ramkumar died. Ramakrishna, now alone, prayed for a vision of Kali-Ma (Kali the Mother), whom he worshipped as the supreme manifestation of God. He wept for hours at a time and felt a burning sensation throughout his body while imploring the Divine Mother to reveal herself. When she did not, the young priest sank into despair. According to traditional accounts, Ramakrishna was on the verge of suicide when he was overwhelmed by an ocean of blissful light that he attributed to Kali. Visions of Kali or other deities brought ecstasy and peace; he once described Kali as "a limitless, infinite, effulgent ocean of spirit."

Soon after his first vision, Ramakrishna commenced on a series of *sadhanas* (austere practices) in the various mystical traditions, including Bengali Vaishnavism, Shakta Tantrism, Advaita Vedanta, and even Islamic Sufism and Roman Catholicism. (His interest in Roman Catholicism ended with a vision of "the great yogi" Jesus embracing him and then disappearing into his body.) After each of these sadhanas, Ramakrishna claimed to have had the same experience of *brahman*, the supreme power, or ultimate reality, of the universe. Later in life he became famous for his pithy parables about the ultimate unity of the different religious traditions in this formless Vedantic brahman. Indeed, seeing God in everything and everyone, he believed that all paths led to the same goal. "There are in a tank or pool," he said, various ghats (steps to the water). The Hindus draw out the liquid and call it *jal*. The Muslims draw out the liquid and call it *pani*. The Christians draw out the liquid and call it water, but it is all the same substance, no essential difference.

The message that all religions lead to the same end was certainly a politically and religiously powerful one, particularly because it answered in classical Indian terms the challenges of British missionaries and colonial authorities who had for almost a century criticized Hinduism on social, religious, and ethical grounds. That all religions could be seen as different paths to the same divine source or, even better, that this divine source revealed itself in traditional Hindu categories was welcome and truly liberating news for many Hindus.

A small band of disciples, most of them Western-educated, gathered around Ramakrishna in the early 1880s, drawn by the appeal of his message and by his charisma as a guru and ecstatic mystic. It was also about this time that Calcutta newspaper and journal articles first referred to him as "the Hindu saint" or as "the Paramahamsa" (a religious title of respect and honour).

After Ramakrishna's death, his message was disseminated through new texts and organizations. Notably, Ramakrishna's teachings are preserved in Mahendranath Gupta's five-volume Bengali classic *Sri Sri Ramakrishna Kathamrita* (1902–32; The Nectar-Speech of the Twice-Blessed Ramakrishna), best known to English readers as *The Gospel of Ramakrishna*, a remarkable text based on conversations with Ramakrishna from 1882 to 1886. Moreover, his disciple and successor Narendranath Datta (died 1902) became the world-traveling Swami Vivekananda and helped establish the Ramakrishna Order, whose teachings, texts, and rituals identified Ramakrishna as a new avatar ("incarnation") of God. The headquarters of the mission is in Belur Math, a monastery near Kolkata. The Ramakrishna Order also played an important role in the spread of Hindu ideas and practices in the West, particularly in the United States.

JOSEPH F. SMITH

(b. Nov. 13, 1838, Far West, Mo., U.S.—d. Nov. 19, 1918, Salt Lake City, Utah)

Joseph F. Smith was the sixth president (1901–18) of the Church of Jesus Christ of Latter-day Saints (the main Mormon denomination).

After his uncle Joseph Smith, the founder of Mormonism, and his father, Hyrum Smith, were murdered in Carthage, Ill., in 1844, he and his mother fled with the majority of the Mormons to Utah. Made an apostle of the church in 1866, Smith advanced within the hierarchy to the office of president in 1901. He also served on the city council of Salt Lake City and in the territorial legislature (1865–74, 1880, 1882). Smith had six wives, but he accepted the decision to give up polygamy reached by church leaders in 1890 and testified before a United States Senate committee that Mormons no longer accepted the practice.

Joseph Smith, detail from an oil painting by an unknown artist; in the Community of Christ Temple and Auditorium complex, Independence, Missouri.

CHARLES TAZE RUSSELL

(b. Feb. 16, 1852, Pittsburgh, Pa., U.S.—d. Oct. 31, 1916, Pampa, Texas)

Charles Taze Russell was the founder of the International Bible Students Association, the forerunner of the Jehovah's Witnesses.

By the time he was 20, Russell had left both Presbyterianism and Congregationalism because he could not reconcile the idea of an eternal hell with God's mercy. He had drifted into skepticism when a chance encounter with some followers of the Adventist movement begun by William Miller introduced him to the idea that the Bible could be used to predict God's plan of salvation, especially as the plan related to the end of the world.

With the help of tutors, Russell managed to master the use of Hebrew and Greek dictionaries to study the Bible, and he formed his first Bible classes in 1872. With N. H. Barbour of Rochester, N.Y., Russell published *Three Worlds and the Harvest of the World* in 1877. Basing his judgment on complex biblical calculations, he preached from 1877 that Christ's "invisible return" had occurred in 1874 and that the end of the Gentile times and the beginning of a golden age would come in 1914, followed by war between capitalism and communism or socialism, after which God's kingdom by Christ would rule the earth. Russell dedicated his life and his fortune to preaching Christ's

Charles Taze Russell, photograph by Eric Patterson, 1911.

millennial reign. In 1879 he started a Bible journal, later called *The Watch Tower*, and in 1884 he founded the Watch Tower Bible and Tract Society, which became an extensive publishing business. His own books and booklets (notably seven volumes of *Studies in the Scriptures*) reached a circulation of 16 million copies in 35 languages, and 2,000 newspapers published his weekly sermons. He was president of the society until his death.

Russell's movement survived the problem caused by the apparent failure of his eschatological prediction.

WOVOKA

(b. 1858?, Utah Territory—d. October 1932, Walker River Indian Reservation, Nev.)

Wovoka was an American Indian religious leader who spawned the second messianic Ghost Dance cult, which spread rapidly through reservation communities about 1890.

Wovoka's father, Tavibo, was a Paiute shaman and local leader; he had assisted Wodziwob, a shaman whose millenarian visions inspired the Round Dance movement of the 1870s. Wovoka (whose name means "the Cutter") worked during his early teens for a rancher, David Wilson, whose family name he adopted while among whites. The Wilsons employed a number of Paiutes (including Wovoka) on a seasonal basis. These employees resided together in a camp they built on the Wilson ranch, and they generally maintained traditional cultural practices throughout their employment.

By 1888 Wovoka himself had acquired a reputation as a spiritual leader; he began leading Round Dances about this time. In 1889 Wovoka told others that he had fallen into a trance state during which God informed him of momentous changes to come—that in two years the ancestors of his people would rise from the dead, buffalo would once again fill the plains, and the white colonizers would vanish. Wovoka also reported that God had provided instructions for ensuring these events: Indians were to accept American colonial hegemony, remain peaceful, and profess their faith in the resurrection of the dead (or ghosts) by taking part in a ritual dance, the so-called Ghost Dance. Wovoka's following increased quickly, and belief in his prophecies spread to other tribes. Wovoka was worshiped far and wide as a new messiah, but in some areas his pacifist message became distorted through repeated retellings. Notable among his new followers were the Sioux, many of whom were militant and saw the movement as a promise of ultimate revenge against American usurpers.

The religious frenzy engendered by Ghost Dancing frightened American and immigrant settlers, particularly in the Dakotas, the traditional home of most of the Sioux tribes; concurrently, the U.S. military was concerned that Sitting Bull would try to exploit the movement to engineer an uprising. Relations between Native Americans and settlers grew increasingly hostile, culminating in the massacre of about 200 Sioux men, women, and children by U.S. troops at Wounded Knee, S.D., on Dec. 29, 1890. After this tragic incident many of Wovoka's more militant followers despaired of Ghost Dance redemption, while others, particularly those from west of the Rocky Mountains, continued to practice Ghost Dance rituals as an integral part of indigenous culture. Though the popularity of the Ghost Dance religion waxed and waned over the 20th century and evolved toward a set of practices centred increasingly around individual rather than group worship, its tenets continued to be observed by some Native Americans in the early 21st century.

VIVEKANANDA

(b. Jan. 12, 1863, Calcutta [now Kolkata]—d. July 4, 1902, near Calcutta)

Vivekananda was a Hindu spiritual leader and reformer in India who attempted to combine Indian spirituality with Western material progress, maintaining that the two supplemented and complemented one another. His Absolute was a person's own higher self; to labour for the benefit of humanity was the noblest endeavour.

Born into an upper-middle-class Kayastha family in Bengal, he was educated at a Western-style university where he was exposed to Western philosophy, Christianity, and science. Social reform was given a prominent place in Vivekananda's thought, and he joined the Brahmo Samaj (Society of Brahma), dedicated to eliminating child marriage and illiteracy and determined to spread education among women and the lower castes. He later became the most notable disciple of Ramakrishna, who demonstrated the essential unity of all religions.

Always stressing the universal and humanistic side of the Vedas as well as belief in service rather than dogma, Vivekananda attempted to infuse vigour into Hindu thought, placing less emphasis on the prevailing pacifism and presenting Hindu spirituality to the West. He was an activating force behind the Vedanta (interpretation of the Upanishads) movement in the United States and England. In 1893 he appeared in Chicago as a spokesman for Hinduism at the World's Parliament of Religions and so captivated the assembly that a newspaper account described him as "an orator by divine right and undoubtedly the greatest figure at the Parliament." Thereafter he lectured throughout the United States and England, making converts to the Vedanta movement.

On his return to India with a small group of Western disciples in 1897, Vivekananda founded the Ramakrishna Mission at the monastery of Belur Math on the Ganges (Ganga) River near Calcutta (now Kolkata). Self-perfection and service were his ideals, and the order continued to stress them. He adapted and made relevant to the 20th century the very highest ideals of the Vedantic religion, and, although he lived only two years into that century, he left the mark of his personality on East and West alike.

MOHANDAS KARAMCHAND GANDHI

(b. Oct. 2, 1869, Porbandar, India—d. Jan. 30, 1948, Delhi)

Mohandas Karamchand Gandhi was an Indian law-yer, politician, social activist, and writer who became the leader of the nationalist movement against the British rule of India. As such, he came to be considered the father of his country. Gandhi is internationally esteemed for his doctrine of nonviolent protest (satyagraha) to achieve political and social progress.

In the eyes of millions of his fellow Indians, Gandhi was the Mahatma ("Great Soul"). The unthinking adoration of the huge crowds that gathered to see him all along the route of his tours made them a severe ordeal; he could hardly work during the day or rest at night. "The woes of the Mahatmas," he wrote, "are known only to the Mahatmas." His fame spread worldwide during his lifetime and only increased after his death. The name Mahatma Gandhi is now one of the most universally recognized on earth.

Gandhi was the youngest child of his father's fourth wife. His father—Karamchand Gandhi, who was the *dewan* (chief minister) of Porbandar, the capital of a small principality in western India (in what is now Gujarat State) under British suzerainty—did not have much in the way of a formal education. He was, however, an able administrator who knew how to steer his way between the capricious princes, their long-suffering subjects, and the headstrong British political officers in power.

Gandhi's mother, Putlibai, was completely absorbed in religion, did not care much for finery or jewelry, divided her time between her home and the temple, fasted frequently, and wore herself out in days and nights of nursing whenever there was sickness in the family. Mohandas grew up in a home steeped in Vaishnavism—worship of the Hindu god Vishnu—with a strong tinge of Jainism, a morally rigorous Indian religion whose chief tenets are nonviolence and the belief that everything in the universe is eternal. Thus, he took for granted vegetarianism, *ahimsa* (noninjury to all living beings), fasting for self-purification, and mutual tolerance between adherents of various creeds and sects.

The educational facilities at Porbandar were rudimentary; in the primary school that Mohandas attended, the children wrote the alphabet in the dust with their fingers. Luckily for him, his father became *dewan* of Rajkot, another princely state. Though Mohandas occasionally won prizes and scholarships at the local schools, his record was on the whole mediocre. One of the terminal reports rated him as "good at English, fair in Arithmetic and weak in Geography; conduct very good, bad handwriting." He was married at the age of 13 and thus lost a year at school. A diffident child, he shone neither in the classroom nor on the playing field. He loved to go out on long solitary walks when he was not nursing his by then ailing father (who died soon thereafter) or helping his mother with her household chores.

He had learned, in his words, "to carry out the orders of the elders, not to scan them." With such extreme passivity, it is not surprising that he should have gone through a phase of adolescent rebellion, marked by secret atheism, petty thefts, furtive smoking, and—most shocking of all for a boy born in a Vaishnava family—meat eating. His adolescence was probably no stormier than that of most children of his age and class. What was extraordinary was the way his youthful transgressions ended.

"Never again" was his promise to himself after each escapade. And he kept his promise. Beneath an unprepossessing exterior, he concealed a burning passion for self-improvement that led him to take even the heroes of Hindu mythology, such as Prahlada and Harishcandra—legendary embodiments of truthfulness and sacrifice—as living models.

In 1887 Mohandas scraped through the matriculation examination of the University of Bombay (now University of Mumbai) and joined Samaldas College in Bhavnagar (Bhaunagar). As he had to suddenly switch from his native language—Gujarati—to English, he found it rather difficult to follow the lectures.

Meanwhile, his family was debating his future. Left to himself, he would have liked to have been a doctor. But, besides the Vaishnava prejudice against vivisection, it was clear that, if he was to keep up the family tradition of holding high office in one of the states in Gujarat, he would have to qualify as a barrister. That meant a visit to England, and Mohandas, who was not too happy at Samaldas College, jumped at the proposal. His youthful imagination conceived England as "a land of philosophers and poets, the very centre of civilization." But there were several hurdles to be crossed before the visit to England could be realized. His father had left the family little property; moreover, his mother was reluctant to expose her youngest child to unknown temptations and dangers in a distant land. But Mohandas was determined to visit England. One of his brothers raised the necessary money, and his mother's doubts were allayed when he took a vow that, while away from home, he would not touch wine, women, or meat. Mohandas disregarded the last obstacle—the decree of the leaders of the Modh Bania subcaste (Vaishya caste), to which the Gandhis belonged, who forbade his trip to England as a violation of the Hindu religion—and sailed in September 1888. Ten days after his arrival, he joined the Inner Temple, one of the four London law colleges (The Temple).

Gandhi took his studies seriously and tried to brush up on his English and Latin by taking the University of London matriculation examination. But, during the three years he spent in England, his main preoccupation was with personal and moral issues rather than with academic ambitions. The transition from the half-rural atmosphere of Rajkot to the cosmopolitan life of London was not easy for him. As he struggled painfully to adapt himself to Western food, dress, and etiquette, he felt awkward. His vegetarianism became a continual source of embarrassment to him; his friends warned him that it would wreck his studies as well as his health. Fortunately for him he came across a vegetarian restaurant as well as a book providing a reasoned defense of vegetarianism, which henceforth became a matter of conviction for him, not merely a legacy of his Vaishnava background. The missionary zeal he developed for vegetarianism helped to draw the pitifully shy youth out of his shell and gave him a new poise. He became a member of the executive committee of the London Vegetarian Society, attending its conferences and contributing articles to its journal.

In the boardinghouses and vegetarian restaurants of England, Gandhi met not only food faddists but some earnest men and women to whom he owed his introduction to the Bible and, more important, the Bhagavadgita, which he read for the first time in its English translation by Sir Edwin Arnold. The *Bhagavadgita* (commonly known as the *Gita*) is part of the great epic the *Mahabharata* and, in the form of a philosophical poem, is the most popular expression of Hinduism. The English vegetarians were a motley crowd. They included socialists and humanitarians such as Edward Carpenter, "the British Thoreau"; Fabians such as George Bernard Shaw; and Theosophists such as Annie Besant. Most of them were idealists; quite a few were rebels who rejected the prevailing values of the late Victorian establishment, denounced the evils of the capitalist and industrial society, preached the cult of the simple life, and stressed the superiority of moral over material values and of cooperation over conflict. Those ideas were to contribute substantially to the shaping of Gandhi's personality and, eventually, to his politics.

Painful surprises were in store for Gandhi when he returned to India in July 1891. His mother had died in his absence, and he discovered to his dismay that the barrister's degree was not a guarantee of a lucrative career. The legal profession was already beginning to be overcrowded, and Gandhi was much too diffident to elbow his way into it. In the very first brief he argued in a court in Bombay (now Mumbai), he cut a sorry figure. Turned down even for the part-time job of a teacher in a Bombay high school, he returned to Rajkot to make a modest living by drafting petitions for litigants. Even that employment was closed to him when he incurred the displeasure of a local British officer. It was, therefore, with some relief that in 1893 he accepted the none-too-attractive offer of a year's contract from an Indian firm in Natal, South Africa.

Africa was to present to Gandhi challenges and opportunities that he could hardly have conceived. In the end he would spend more than two decades there, returning to India only briefly in 1896–97. The youngest two of his four children were born there.

Gandhi was quickly exposed to the racial discrimination practiced in South Africa. In a Durban court he was asked by the European magistrate to take off his turban; he refused and left the courtroom. A few days later, while traveling to Pretoria, he was unceremoniously thrown out of a first-class railway compartment and left shivering and brooding at the rail station in Pietermaritzburg. In the further course of that journey, he was beaten up by the white driver of a stagecoach because he would not travel on the footboard to make room for a European passenger, and finally he was barred from hotels reserved "for Europeans only." Those humiliations were the daily lot of Indian traders and labourers in Natal, who had learned to pocket them with the same resignation with which they pocketed their meagre earnings. What was new was not Gandhi's experience but his reaction. He had so far not been conspicuous for self-assertion or aggressiveness. But something happened to him as he smarted under the insults heaped upon him. In retrospect the journey from Durban to Pretoria struck him as one of the most creative experiences of his life; it was his moment of truth. Henceforth he would not accept injustice as part of the natural or unnatural order in South Africa; he would defend his dignity as an Indian and as a man.

While in Pretoria, Gandhi studied the conditions in which his fellow South Asians in South Africa lived and tried to educate them on their rights and duties, but he had no intention of staying on in South Africa. Indeed, in June 1894, as his year's contract drew to a close, he was back in Durban, ready to sail for India. At a farewell party given in his honour, he happened to glance through the *Natal Mercury* and learned that the Natal Legislative Assembly was considering a bill to deprive Indians of the right to vote. "This is the first nail in our coffin," Gandhi told his hosts. They professed their inability to oppose the bill, and indeed their ignorance of the politics of the colony, and begged him to take up the fight on their behalf.

Until the age of 18, Gandhi had hardly ever read a newspaper. Neither as a student in England nor as a budding barrister in India had he evinced much interest in politics. Indeed, he was overcome by a terrifying stage fright whenever he stood up to read a speech at a social gathering or to defend a client in court. Nevertheless, in July 1894, when he was barely 25, he blossomed almost overnight into a proficient political campaigner. He drafted petitions to the Natal legislature and the British government and had them signed by hundreds of his compatriots. He could not prevent the passage of the bill but succeeded in drawing the attention of the public and the press in Natal, India, and England to the Natal Indians' grievances. He was persuaded to settle down in Durban to practice law and to organize the Indian community. In 1894 he founded the Natal Indian Congress, of which he himself became the indefatigable secretary. Through that common political organization, he infused a spirit of solidarity in the heterogeneous Indian community. He flooded the government, the legislature, and the press with closely reasoned statements of Indian grievances. Finally, he exposed to the view of the outside world the skeleton in the imperial cupboard, the discrimination practiced against the Indian subjects of Queen Victoria in one of her own colonies in Africa. It was a measure of his success as a publicist that such important newspapers as *The Times* of London and *The Statesman* and *Englishman* of Calcutta (now Kolkata) editorially commented on the Natal Indians' grievances.

In 1896 Gandhi went to India to fetch his wife, Kasturba (or Kasturbai), and their two oldest children and to canvass support for the Indians overseas. He met prominent leaders and persuaded them to address public meetings in the country's principal cities. Unfortunately for him, garbled versions of his activities and utterances reached Natal and inflamed its European population. On landing at Durban in January 1897, he was assaulted and nearly lynched by a white mob. Joseph Chamberlain, the colonial secretary in the British Cabinet, cabled the government of Natal to bring the guilty men to book, but Gandhi refused to prosecute his assailants. It was, he said, a principle with him not to seek redress of a personal wrong in a court of law.

Gandhi was not the man to nurse a grudge. On the outbreak of the South African (Boer) War in 1899, he argued that the Indians, who claimed the full rights of citizenship in the British crown colony of Natal, were in duty bound to defend it. He raised an ambulance corps of 1,100 volunteers, out of whom 300 were free Indians and the rest indentured labourers. It was a motley crowd: barristers and accountants, artisans and labourers. It was Gandhi's task to instill in them a spirit of service to those whom they regarded as their oppressors. The editor of the *Pretoria News* offered an insightful portrait of Gandhi in the battle zone:

> After a night's work which had shattered men with much bigger frames, I came across Gandhi in the early morning sitting by the roadside eating a regulation army biscuit. Every man in [General] Buller's force was dull and depressed, and damnation was heartily invoked on everything. But Gandhi was stoical in his bearing, cheerful and confident in his conversation and had a kindly eye.

The British victory in the war brought little relief to the Indians in South Africa. The new regime in South Africa was to blossom into a partnership, but only between

Boers and Britons. Gandhi saw that, with the exception of a few Christian missionaries and youthful idealists, he had been unable to make a perceptible impression upon the South African Europeans. In 1906 the Transvaal government published a particularly humiliating ordinance for the registration of its Indian population. The Indians held a mass protest meeting at Johannesburg in September 1906 and, under Gandhi's leadership, took a pledge to defy the ordinance if it became law in the teeth of their opposition and to suffer all the penalties resulting from their defiance. Thus was born satyagraha ("devotion to truth"), a new technique for redressing wrongs through inviting, rather than inflicting, suffering, for resisting adversaries without rancour and fighting them without violence.

The struggle in South Africa lasted for more than seven years. It had its ups and downs, but under Gandhi's leadership, the small Indian minority kept up its resistance against heavy odds. Hundreds of Indians chose to sacrifice their livelihood and liberty rather than submit to laws repugnant to their conscience and self-respect. In the final phase of the movement in 1913, hundreds of Indians, including women, went to jail, and thousands of Indian workers who had struck work in the mines bravely faced imprisonment, flogging, and even shooting. It was a terrible ordeal for the Indians, but it was also the worst possible advertisement for the South African government, which, under pressure from the governments of Britain and India, accepted a compromise negotiated by Gandhi on the one hand and the South African statesman Gen. Jan Christian Smuts on the other.

"The saint has left our shores," Smuts wrote to a friend on Gandhi's departure from South Africa for India, in July 1914, "I hope for ever." A quarter century later, he wrote that it had been his "fate to be the antagonist of a man for whom even then I had the highest respect." Once, during his not-infrequent stays in jail, Gandhi had prepared a pair of sandals for Smuts, who recalled that there was no hatred and personal ill-feeling between them, and when the fight was over "there was the atmosphere in which a decent peace could be concluded."

As later events were to show, Gandhi's work did not provide an enduring solution for the Indian problem in South Africa. What he did to South Africa was indeed less important than what South Africa did to him. It had not treated him kindly, but, by drawing him into the vortex of its racial problem, it had provided him with the ideal setting in which his peculiar talents could unfold themselves.

Gandhi's religious quest dated back to his childhood, the influence of his mother and of his home life in Porbandar and Rajkot, but it received a great impetus after his arrival in South Africa. His Quaker friends in Pretoria failed to convert him to Christianity, but they quickened his appetite for religious studies. He was fascinated by the writings of Leo Tolstoy on Christianity, read the Qu'rān in translation, and delved into Hindu scriptures and philosophy. The study of comparative religion, talks with scholars, and his own reading of theological works brought him to the conclusion that all religions were true and yet every one of them was imperfect because they were "interpreted with poor intellects, sometimes with poor hearts, and more often misinterpreted."

Shrimad Rajchandra, a brilliant young Jain philosopher who became Gandhi's spiritual mentor, convinced him of "the subtlety and profundity" of Hinduism, the religion of his birth. And it was the *Bhagavadgita*, which Gandhi had first read in London, that became his "spiritual dictionary" and exercised probably the greatest single influence on his life. Two Sanskrit words in the *Gita* particularly fascinated him. One was *aparigraha* ("nonpossession"), which implies that people have to jettison the material goods that cramp the life of the spirit and to shake off the bonds of money and property. The other was *samabhava* ("equability"), which enjoins people to remain unruffled by pain or pleasure, victory or defeat, and to work without hope of success or fear of failure.

Those were not merely counsels of perfection. In the civil case that had taken him to South Africa in 1893, he had persuaded the antagonists to settle their differences out of court. The true function of a lawyer seemed to him "to unite parties riven asunder." He soon regarded his clients not as purchasers of his services but as friends; they consulted him not only on legal issues but on such matters as the best way of weaning a baby or balancing the family budget. When an associate protested that clients came even on Sundays, Gandhi replied: "A man in distress cannot have Sunday rest."

Gandhi's legal earnings reached a peak figure of £5,000 a year, but he had little interest in moneymaking, and his savings were often sunk in his public activities. In Durban and later in Johannesburg, he kept an open table; his house was a virtual hostel for younger colleagues and political coworkers. This was something of an ordeal for his wife, without whose extraordinary patience, endurance, and self-effacement Gandhi could hardly have devoted himself to public causes. As he broke through the conventional bonds of family and property, their life tended to shade into a community life.

Gandhi felt an irresistible attraction to a life of simplicity, manual labour, and austerity. In 1904—after reading John Ruskin's *Unto This Last*, a critique of capitalism—he set up a farm at Phoenix near Durban where he and his friends could live by the sweat of their brow. Six years later another colony grew up under Gandhi's fostering care near Johannesburg; it was named Tolstoy Farm for the Russian writer and moralist, whom Gandhi admired and corresponded with. Those two settlements were the precursors of the more-famous ashrams (religious retreats) in India, at Sabarmati near Ahmedabad (Ahmadabad) and at Sevagram near Wardha.

South Africa had not only prompted Gandhi to evolve a novel technique for political action but also transformed him into a leader of men by freeing him from bonds that make cowards of most men. "Persons in power," the British Classical scholar Gilbert Murray prophetically wrote about Gandhi in the *Hibbert Journal* in 1918,

> should be very careful how they deal with a man who cares nothing for sensual pleasure, nothing for riches, nothing for comfort or praise, or promotion, but is simply determined to do what he believes to be right. He is a dangerous and uncomfortable enemy, because his body which you can always conquer gives you so little purchase upon his soul.

Gandhi decided to leave South Africa in the summer of 1914, just before the outbreak of World War I. He and his family first went to London, where they remained for several months. Finally, they departed England in December, arriving in Bombay in early January 1915.

For the next three years, Gandhi seemed to hover uncertainly on the periphery of Indian politics, declining to join any political agitation, supporting the British war effort, and even recruiting soldiers for the British Indian Army. At the same time, he did not flinch from criticizing the British officials for any acts of high-handedness or from taking up the grievances of the long-suffering peasantry in Bihar and Gujarat. By February 1919, however, the British had insisted on pushing through—in the teeth of fierce Indian opposition—the Rowlatt Acts, which empowered the authorities to imprison without trial those suspected of sedition. A provoked Gandhi finally revealed a sense of estrangement from the British Raj and announced a satyagraha struggle. The result was a virtual political earthquake that shook the subcontinent in the spring of 1919. The violent outbreaks that followed—notably the Massacre of Amritsar, which was the killing by British-led soldiers of nearly 400 Indians who were gathered in an open space in Amritsar in the Punjab region (now in Punjab state), and the enactment of martial law—prompted him to stay his hand. However, within a year he was again in a militant mood, having in the meantime been irrevocably alienated by British insensitiveness to Indian feeling on the Punjab tragedy and Muslim resentment on the peace terms offered to Turkey following World War I.

By the autumn of 1920, Gandhi was the dominant figure on the political stage, commanding an influence never before attained by any political leader in India or perhaps in any other country. He refashioned the 35-year-old Indian National Congress (Congress Party) into an effective political instrument of Indian nationalism: from a three-day Christmas-week picnic of the upper middle class in one of the principal cities of India, it became a mass organization with its roots in small towns and villages. Gandhi's message was simple: it was not British guns but imperfections of Indians themselves that kept their country in bondage. His program, the nonviolent noncooperation movement against the British government, included boycotts not only of British manufactures but of institutions operated or aided by the British in India: legislatures, courts, offices, schools. The campaign electrified the country, broke the spell of fear of foreign rule, and led to the arrests of thousands of *satyagrahis*, who defied laws and cheerfully lined up for prison. In February 1922 the movement seemed to be on the crest of a rising wave, but, alarmed by a violent outbreak in Chauri Chaura, a remote village in eastern India, Gandhi decided to call off mass civil disobedience. That was a blow to many of his followers, who feared that his self-imposed restraints and scruples would reduce the nationalist struggle to pious futility. Gandhi himself was arrested on March 10, 1922, tried for sedition, and sentenced to six years' imprisonment. He was released in February 1924, after undergoing surgery for appendicitis. The political landscape had changed in his absence. The Congress Party had split into two factions, one under Chitta Ranjan Das and Motilal Nehru (the father of Jawaharlal Nehru, India's first prime minister) favouring the entry of the party into legislatures and the other under Chakravarti Rajagopalachari and Vallabhbhai Jhaverbhai Patel opposing it. Worst of all, the unity between Hindus and Muslims of the heyday of the noncooperation movement of 1920–22 had dissolved. Gandhi tried to draw the warring communities out of their suspicion and fanaticism by reasoning and persuasion. Finally, after a serious outbreak of communal unrest, he undertook a three-week fast in the autumn of 1924 to arouse the people into following the path of nonviolence. In December 1924 he was named president of the Congress Party, and he served for a year.

During the mid-1920s Gandhi took little interest in active politics and was considered a spent force. In 1927, however, the British government appointed a constitutional reform commission under Sir John Simon, a prominent English lawyer and politician, that did not contain a single Indian. When the Congress and other parties boycotted the commission, the political tempo rose. At the Congress session (meeting) at Calcutta in December 1928, Gandhi put forth the crucial resolution demanding dominion status from the British government within a year under threat of a nationwide nonviolent campaign for complete independence. Henceforth, Gandhi was back as the leading voice of the Congress Party. In March 1930 he launched the Salt March, a satyagraha against the

British-imposed tax on salt, which affected the poorest section of the community. One of the most spectacular and successful campaigns in Gandhi's nonviolent war against the British Raj, it resulted in the imprisonment of more than 60,000 people. A year later, after talks with the viceroy, Lord Irwin (later Lord Halifax), Gandhi accepted a truce (the Gandhi-Irwin Pact), called off civil disobedience, and agreed to attend the Round Table Conference in London as the sole representative of the Indian National Congress.

The conference, which concentrated on the problem of the Indian minorities rather than on the transfer of power from the British, was a great disappointment to the Indian nationalists. Moreover, when Gandhi returned to India in December 1931, he found his party facing an all-out offensive from Lord Irwin's successor as viceroy, Lord Willingdon, who unleashed the sternest repression in the history of the nationalist movement. Gandhi was once more imprisoned, and the government tried to insulate him from the outside world and to destroy his influence. That was not an easy task. Gandhi soon regained the initiative. In September 1932, while still a prisoner, he embarked on a fast to protest against the British government's decision to segregate the so-called untouchables (the lowest level of the Indian caste system) by allotting them separate electorates in the new constitution. The fast produced an emotional upheaval in the country, and an alternative electoral arrangement was jointly and speedily devised by the leaders of the Hindu community and the untouchables and endorsed by the British government. The fast became the starting point of a vigorous campaign for the removal of the disabilities of the untouchables, whom Gandhi referred to as Harijans, or "children of God." (That term has fallen out of favour, replaced by Dalit; Scheduled Castes is the official designation.)

In 1934 Gandhi resigned not only as the leader but also as a member of the Congress Party. He had come to believe that its leading members had adopted nonviolence as a political expedient and not as the fundamental creed it was for him. In place of political activity he then concentrated on his "constructive programme" of building the nation "from the bottom up"—educating rural India, which accounted for 85 percent of the population; continuing his fight against untouchability; promoting hand spinning, weaving, and other cottage industries to supplement the earnings of the underemployed peasantry; and evolving a system of education best suited to the needs of the people. Gandhi himself went to live at Sevagram, a village in central India, which became the centre of his program of social and economic uplift.

With the outbreak of World War II, the nationalist struggle in India entered its last crucial phase. Gandhi hated fascism and all it stood for, but he also hated war. The Indian National Congress, on the other hand, was not committed to pacifism and was prepared to support the British war effort if Indian self-government was assured. Once more Gandhi became politically active. The failure of the mission of Sir Stafford Cripps, a British cabinet minister who went to India in March 1942 with an offer that Gandhi found unacceptable, the British equivocation on the transfer of power to Indian hands, and the encouragement given by high British officials to conservative and communal forces promoting discord between Muslims and Hindus impelled Gandhi to demand in the summer of 1942 an immediate British withdrawal from India—what became known as the Quit India Movement.

In mid-1942 the war against the Axis Powers, particularly Japan, was in a critical phase, and the British reacted sharply to the campaign. They imprisoned the entire Congress leadership and set out to crush the party once and for all. There were violent outbreaks that were sternly suppressed, and the gulf between Britain and India became wider than ever before. Gandhi, his wife, and several other top party leaders (including Nehru) were confined in the Aga Khan Palace (now the Gandhi National Memorial) in Poona (now Pune). Kasturba died there in early 1944, shortly before Gandhi and the others were released.

A new chapter in Indo-British relations opened with the victory of the Labour Party in Britain 1945. During the next two years, there were prolonged triangular negotiations between leaders of the Congress, the Muslim League under Mohammad Ali Jinnah, and the British government, culminating in the Mountbatten Plan of June 3, 1947, and the formation of the two new dominions of India and Pakistan in mid-August 1947.

It was one of the greatest disappointments of Gandhi's life that Indian freedom was realized without Indian unity. Muslim separatism had received a great boost while Gandhi and his colleagues were in jail, and in 1946–47, as the final constitutional arrangements were being negotiated, the outbreak of communal riots between Hindus and Muslims unhappily created a climate in which Gandhi's appeals to reason and justice, tolerance and trust had little chance. When partition of the subcontinent was accepted—against his advice—he threw himself heart and soul into the task of healing the scars of the communal conflict, toured the riot-torn areas in Bengal and Bihar, admonished the bigots, consoled the victims, and tried to rehabilitate the refugees. In the atmosphere of that period, surcharged with suspicion and hatred, that was a difficult and heartbreaking task. Gandhi was blamed by partisans of both the communities. When persuasion failed, he went on a fast. He won at least two spectacular triumphs: in September 1947 his fasting stopped the rioting in Calcutta, and in January 1948 he shamed the city of Delhi into a communal truce. A few days later, on January 30, while he was on his way to his evening prayer meeting in Delhi, he was shot down by Nathuram Godse, a young Hindu fanatic.

SAINT JOHN XXIII

(b. Nov. 25, 1881, Sotto il Monte, Italy—d. June 3, 1963, Rome)

Saint John XXIII was one of the most popular popes of all time (reigned 1958–63), who inaugurated a new era in the history of the Roman Catholic Church by his openness to change (*aggiornamento*), shown especially in his convoking of the Second Vatican Council. He wrote several socially important encyclicals, most notably *Pacem in Terris.*

Angelo Giuseppe Roncalli was one of 13 children born to Giovanni Roncalli, a tenant farmer of Sotto il Monte, a tiny village 7 miles (11 km) from the Lombard city of Bergamo. The Roncallis were poor but not nearly as destitute as some later legends would have it. "We had the necessities of life," the pope used to say testily, "and we were strong and healthy." Though Angelo, the third child and oldest son of the family, went off to prepare for the priesthood as a child of 11, he continued to spend vacations with his family and remained close to them throughout his life.

No matter how powerful he became, however, he never helped any of the other Roncallis to advance in the world. "The world is only interested in making money...," he wrote to his brother Xaverio after becoming pope. "A great honour has come to our family," he acknowledged, but he urged Xaverio and the others to remain humble, seek no honours or preferments, and take no material advantage of their relationship to the pope. "At my own death," he concluded, "I shall not be denied the praise which did so much honour to the holiness of Pius X: born poor, he died poor." In his last will he bequeathed each of the living members of the family a legacy of less than $20—his total personal fortune.

Angelo the churchman, however, was destined to spend most of his life among the powerful and cultivated. Inevitably, that set him apart from the other Roncallis almost from the beginning. While still a seminarian, he was already beginning to feel out of place in Sotto il Monte, where he was charged with priggishness and "putting on airs." "Only three days of the holidays have passed and already I am weary of them," he recorded in the diary that he allowed to be published after his death. He was eager, he wrote, to return to Bergamo, with its orderly life of study, prayer, and genteel fellowship, and to escape from the petty gossip, suspicion, and jealousies of the village.

Roncalli was not an especially brilliant student. He did well enough, however, to be sent to Rome for theological studies in 1900. After only one year at the Seminario Romano, his education was interrupted when he was drafted into military service and assigned to an infantry company conveniently stationed at Bergamo. Later, as a priest, he returned to the army during World War I. Again he served in Bergamo, first as a hospital orderly and later as a military chaplain with the rank of lieutenant.

Even with the time out for military service, he was not yet 23 when he was ordained a priest in Rome on August 10, 1904. The next day he said his first mass at St. Peter's Basilica. After a visit to his family in Sotto il Monte, he returned to the Seminario Romano for further study. Eventually he received a doctorate in canon law.

As a graduate student in Rome, Roncalli took the first step that was to lead to the papacy a half century later. Simply because he was a priest of Bergamo, he was asked by the reigning pope, Pius X, to assist in the ceremony of consecration for a new bishop, Giacomo Radini-Tedeschi, who had been appointed to take over the diocese of Bergamo. The new bishop, a member of the Italian nobility, was much taken by the young priest and asked him to serve as his secretary.

Back in Bergamo, Don Angelo, in addition to his secretarial duties, was assigned to the faculty of the diocesan seminary. For the next nine years he served as a professor of theology and spiritual director of the young men preparing for ordination. As the bishop's right-hand man, he gained a wide range of pastoral experience.

Roncalli had great esteem for his superior, who was known as the most progressive prelate in Italy. After the bishop's death in 1914, he wrote an appreciative biography of the prelate and sent a copy to the pope, Benedict XV, who had been one of Radini-Tedeschi's personal friends.

With the war behind him, Roncalli was summoned to wider service in the church. In 1920 Pope Benedict, recalling Radini-Tedeschi's biographer, named him a director of the Italian organization for the support of foreign missions. The position was not notably significant in a church top-heavy with dignitaries, but it brought him into personal contact with a number of important clerical figures throughout Europe, and his name became recognizable in ecclesiastical Rome. He also gained some attention because of his work as a part-time historian who specialized in some of the minor activities of Saint Charles Borromeo, a cardinal of Milan who played an important role in the 16th-century Counter-Reformation. It was Roncalli's researches for this project that first brought him into contact with Monsignor Achille Ratti, the Milanese librarian who would become Pius XI.

Pius XI later remembered the Bergamo priest's gift for personal dealings and brought him into the Vatican's diplomatic service. Roncalli was appointed apostolic visitor to Bulgaria in March 1925. In keeping with custom, he was made an archbishop before he left Rome. He spent the next 10 years in that obscure but delicate post, where he was expected to protect the interests of a small Roman Catholic community in a country overwhelmingly Eastern Orthodox. His diary reveals that he was often lonely and discouraged in Bulgaria, but he carried out the assignment with tact, patience, and notable good humour. Still, he was not deemed to be among the best-qualified clerics in the papal diplomatic corps.

Roncalli's next assignment was equally unpromising. He was appointed apostolic delegate to Greece, which was combined with naming him head of the Vatican diplomatic mission to Turkey. Again he was called upon to represent powerless Catholic minorities in an Eastern Orthodox nation, Greece, and a Muslim nation, Turkey. He made his home in Istanbul, where he was generally ignored by both the Turkish government and the Vatican but was warmly appreciated in the diplomatic colony as an amiable host and affable dinner companion.

None of these posts loomed large in the Western-oriented Vatican, and the archbishop had good reason to believe that his career had reached a dead end. Later he confessed that he was stunned by the announcement, at the end of 1944, that he had been named papal nuncio to Charles de Gaulle's newly liberated France; his first thought was that an assignment error must have been made in Rome.

The French post was particularly delicate at the time. Roncalli's predecessor, Monsignor Valerio Valeri, had been close to the collaborationist General Philippe Pétain during the German occupation, and de Gaulle made it clear to the Vatican that, since Valeri had become persona non grata to the French people, he would have to be replaced immediately. France was still seething with a spirit of vengeance against former collaborators. It would be the new nuncio's obligation to deal with the ill will created by his predecessor and by the bishops who had cooperated with the hated Vichy government. Someone in the Vatican remembered the genial archbishop languishing in the Middle East, and it was decided that, though he was not noted for his political astuteness, perhaps he had precisely the qualifications needed under the circumstances. Roncalli was told that he would be expected to cool the atmosphere, reestablish the independence of the church, and gain the release of a number of German seminarians who were being held as prisoners of war. In addition, he had to deal with an outburst of radicalism among the younger French clergy, which the conservative forces in the Vatican Curia found highly disturbing.

His success in carrying out the assignment was acknowledged by the papacy when Archbishop Roncalli was named a cardinal by Pius XII. In January 1953 the red hat, the symbol of a cardinal, was conferred on him by the socialist president of France, Vincent Auriol.

As a cardinal, Roncalli immediately became eligible for one of the major Italian archbishoprics. Appointed patriarch of Venice at age 71, he had cause once more to believe that he had reached the end of the line. Thus, perhaps no one was more surprised than he when, after the death of Pius XII on October 9, 1958, he was elected pope on the 12th ballot—clearly a compromise candidate acceptable to all parties only because of his advanced years.

Perhaps a younger pontiff would have been less daring and innovative than John XXIII turned out to be. Soon after his coronation, he announced almost casually that he was summoning an ecumenical council—a general meeting of the bishops of the church—the first in almost a century. He said the idea came to him in a sudden inspiration. His purpose was to "bring the church up to date" (*aggiornamento*) and to work for its spiritual regeneration. He was the first pope since the Reformation who acknowledged frankly that Catholicism stood in need of reinvigoration and reform.

It was long a truism among church historians that councils are followed by upheaval and disorder in the church. The pope's decision, consequently, was received coolly by his conservative Curia, who were convinced that the church had prospered under Pius XII's leadership and who saw no good reason for the changes John envisioned. Some of the Vatican cardinals in fact did everything in their power to delay the council until the old man had passed from the scene and the project could be quietly dropped. But the pope pushed on with his plan and lived long enough to preside over the first session of the Second Vatican Council in the fall of 1962.

In keeping with his wishes, the council fathers pledged that they would be consistently positive. No condemnations or anathemas were to be made; political hostilities were to be ignored; and the church above all was to recognize that it was not the master but the servant of humanity. The pope made it clear that the Second Vatican Council was convened as a pastoral council. No new dogmas were to be pronounced, though old doctrines and disciplines were to be reexamined. What John sought, he said, was a "New Pentecost," a new outpouring of the Holy Spirit.

The council, according to John's design, would make a new start toward achieving Christian unity by putting aside the hostilities of the past and acknowledging the Catholics' share of responsibility for the scandal of a divided Christianity. With his long experiences among the Eastern Orthodox, John's interest in Christian ecumenism seemed natural enough, but no one in Rome was quite prepared for the extent of his openness. He received Eastern Orthodox, Anglican, and Protestant religious leaders with extreme cordiality and made sure they were invited to send observers to the Vatican Council. He removed certain words offensive to Jews from the official liturgy of the church. On one notable occasion, he introduced himself to a group of Jewish visitors with the biblical words, "I am Joseph your brother," referring to the Old Testament story of the meeting of the sons of the patriarch Jacob at the court of Egypt.

John traveled around Rome freely, breaking with the tradition that the pope, deprived of his former temporal power, was a "prisoner of the Vatican." In an attempt to depoliticize the church, he played down his position as ruler of the Vatican and emphasized his role as "servant of the servants of God," a traditional title of the pope. In that spirit he called on the president of Italy and cordially received the son-in-law of the Soviet premier, Nikita Khrushchev, in private audience. Among his other visitors were the archbishop of Canterbury—the first such meeting since the 14th century—the moderator of the Scottish Kirk, and a Shintō (the indigenous religion of Japan) high priest—the first such official in history to be received at the Vatican.

During the Cuban missile crisis of 1962, the pope publicly urged both the United States and the Soviet Union to exercise caution and restraint and won the appreciation of both President John F. Kennedy and Premier Khrushchev. His major encyclical, *Pacem in Terris* ("Peace on Earth"), addressed to all humankind, was received warmly throughout the world and praised by politicians as well as churchmen. Straightforward and frankly optimistic, it avoided the language of diplomacy and set forth the requirements for world peace in pro-foundly human terms. Distinguishing between the philosophy of Marxism and actual governments to which it gave birth, John suggested that peaceful coexistence between the West and the communist East was not only desirable but actually necessary if humankind was to sur-vive. He thereby diluted the religious energy that had been poured into the Cold War as a result of the militant policies shaped by his predecessor.

John saw himself as a reconciler. In statement after statement he emphasized the church's significance as a suprapolitical spiritual force in the world. His great-est claim on the world's affection, however, rested on the warmth of his personality rather than on any of his formal statements. He remained simple and unaf-fected, in spite of the baroque setting in which he found himself, and instinctively appealed directly to human values that everyone could understand. "Since you could not come to me, I came to you," he told the inmates of a Roman prison. When Jacqueline Kennedy, the wife of the president of the United States, came to call, he rehearsed "Mrs. Kennedy, Madame Kennedy" in his poor English. Then, when she appeared, he spon-taneously spread open his arms and cried out, "Jacqueline!" He once told a communist diplomat, "I know you are an atheist, but won't you accept an old man's blessing?" When a shabby peasant woman reached up to touch him as he was being carried through St. Peter's, he stopped to clasp her hand. "There is no reason why you shouldn't get as close as the king of Jordan did," he said. The roly-poly pon-tiff—he was short of stature and never overcame a tendency toward corpulence—gradually became a kind of father figure for the world. When he died in 1963, it was generally recognized that he had become one of the best-loved men in the world.

SIMON KIMBANGU

(b. c. Sept. 12, 1887, Nkamba, near Thysville, Congo Free State [now Mbanza-Ngungu, Democratic Republic of the Congo]—d. Oct. 10, 1951, Élisabethville, Belgian Congo [now Lubumbashi, Democratic Republic of the Congo])

Simon Kimbangu was a Congolese religious leader who founded a separatist church known as the Kimbanguist church.

Brought up in a British Baptist Missionary Society mission, Kimbangu suddenly became famous among the Bakongo people of Lower Congo in April 1921. He was reputed to heal the sick and raise the dead, and thousands came to hear his preaching. He was called Ngunza, the Kikongo word for "prophet" in the Baptist translation of the Bible.

Although Kimbangu's preaching had no overtly political content, Belgian authorities, alarmed by the disturbances that he provoked, arrested him and his immediate followers in September 1921. He was condemned to death, but his sentence was commuted; he spent the rest of his life in prison in Élisabethville. Meanwhile, his followers and imitators spread "Ngunzism," or, as it came to be called, Kimbanguism, in the Belgian Congo and the neighbouring French Congo and Angola. During the African nationalist ferment of the 1950s, Kimbanguists from Nkamba, led by the youngest of the prophet's three sons, Joseph Diangienda (Diangienda ku Ntima), founded the Kimbanguist church, which received official recognition in September 1959.

REINHOLD NIEBUHR

(b. June 21, 1892, Wright City, Missouri, U.S.—d. June 1, 1971,
Stockbridge, Massachusetts)

Reinhold Niebuhr was an American Protestant theologian who had extensive influence on political thought and whose criticism of the prevailing theological liberalism of the 1920s significantly affected the intellectual climate within American Protestantism. His exposure, as a pastor in Detroit, to the problems of American industrialism led him to join the Socialist Party for a time. A former pacifist, he actively persuaded Christians to support the war against Hitler and after World War II had considerable influence in the U.S. State Department. His most prominent theological work was *The Nature and Destiny of Man*, which was planned as a synthesis of the theology of the Reformation with the insights of the Renaissance.

Niebuhr was the son of Gustav and Lydia Niebuhr, who had emigrated to the United States at an early age from Germany. Gustav Niebuhr was a minister of the Evangelical Synod of North America, a denomination with a Lutheran and Reformed German background that merged into the Evangelical and Reformed Church in 1934. At an early age Reinhold Niebuhr decided to emulate his father and become a minister. He graduated from his denomination's Elmhurst College, Illinois (1910), and Eden Theological Seminary, St. Louis, Missouri (1913), and completed his theological education at Yale University, receiving a bachelor of divinity degree (1914) and a master of arts (1915). He was ordained to the ministry of the Evangelical Synod in 1915.

Niebuhr served as pastor of Bethel Evangelical Church in Detroit from 1915 to 1928. His earliest writings exhibit the religious liberalism and social idealism that pervaded the theological atmosphere of the time. But his experience in Detroit—and especially his exposure to the American automobile industry before labour was protected by unions and by social legislation—caused him to become a radical critic of capitalism and an advocate of socialism. His *Leaves from the Notebook of a Tamed Cynic* (1929) is an account of his years in Detroit. Niebuhr left the pastoral ministry in 1928 to teach at Union Theological Seminary in New York City, where he served as professor of applied Christianity (from 1930) and was a great intellectual and personal force until his retirement in 1960.

As a theologian Niebuhr is best known for his "Christian Realism," which emphasized the persistent roots of evil in human life. In his *Moral Man and Immoral Society* (1932) he stressed the egoism and the pride and hypocrisy of nations and classes. Later he saw these as ultimately the fruit of the insecurity and anxious defensiveness of humans in their finiteness; here he located "original sin." He emphasized the tendency for sin—in the form of destructive pride—to appear on every level of human achievement, especially where claims to perfection were made, either in religious or political terms. His powerful polemics against liberal beliefs in assured progress and radical utopian hopes have caused a neglect of his more-hopeful teaching concerning the image of God in all men that is never completely destroyed by sin and concerning "common grace" that is not dependent on recognized Christian redemption in personal or collective life. Also, he was himself a hopeful political activist and emphasized the good that could be achieved if pretentions were overcome. His outlook is well expressed in his statement that "the saints are tempted to continue to see that grace may abound, while sinners toil and sweat to make human relations a little more tolerable and slightly more just." He always had faith in what he called "indeterminate possibilities" for humanity in history as long as men did not deceive themselves into thinking that absolute solutions of historical problems were in their control. Though he did much to encourage the revival of the theology of the Reformation, with its emphasis on sin and grace—so-called Neo-orthodoxy—his salient theological work, *The Nature and Destiny of Man,* 2 vol. (1941–43), was planned by him as a synthesis both of the insights of the Reformation and of the Renaissance, with its hopefulness about cultural achievements.

His distance from the strongly Christocentric forms of Protestant Neo-orthodoxy can be seen in his unusual attitude toward the Jewish community. He was perhaps the first Christian theologian with ecumenical influence who developed a view of the relations between Christianity and Judaism that made it inappropriate for Christians to seek to convert Jews to their faith.

His early political activities were influenced by his socialist convictions (he was a founder of the Fellowship of Socialist Christians), and he ran for office several times on the Socialist ticket. In the 1930s he broke with the Socialist Party over its pacifist or noninterventionist attitude in foreign policy, and in the 1940s he became a left-wing, anti-Communist Democrat. He was a founder and for a time chairman of the Americans for Democratic Action and he was vice chairman of the Liberal Party in the state of New York. In the 1930s he was much influenced by Marxist theory, but he rejected Marxist absolutism and both the tactics of Communists in the United States and Stalinism in the Soviet Union.

He did much to persuade Christians influenced by pacifism to support the war against Hitler. He himself had been a pacifist as a result of his revulsion against World War I, but during the 1930s he became the strongest theological opponent of any form of pacifism that claimed to have universally applicable nonviolent solutions of political problems. Identifying himself with the resistance to Hitler within Germany, he opposed a vindictive peace after World War II, and he had considerable influence with the policy planners in the U.S. State Department. He was a strong supporter of the United States' resistance to Soviet political expansion in Europe during the postwar years. His political activity ended during the early stage of the Cold War, but his later thought showed his capacity to transcend the outlook of that period. His book *The Irony of American History* (1952), while justifying American anti-Communist policies, gave much attention to criticism of American messianism and the American tendency to engage in self-righteous crusades. He always attacked American claims to special virtue. Early he favoured the recognition by the United States of Communist China, and he was an early opponent of American participation in the Vietnam War. He regarded as an error attempts to impose U.S. solutions on the new countries that emerged out of the colonial empires after World War II.

In addition to the works mentioned above, Niebuhr's writings include *Faith and History: A Comparison of Christian and Modern Views of History* (1949), a theological orientation; *The Self and the Dramas of History* (1955), probably his profoundest philosophical work; and *The Structure of Nations and Empires* (1959), his chief systematic discussion of international relations. Four volumes of essays, some of which are essential for understanding Niebuhr's thought and his influence on events, are *Christianity and Power Politics* (1940); *Christian Realism and Political Problems* (1953); *Pious and Secular America* (1958); and *Faith and Politics: A*

Commentary on Religious, Social, and Political Thought in a Technological Age, ed. by Ronald H. Stone (1968). *Love and Justice*, ed. by D.B. Robertson (1957), is a collection of shorter writings showing Niebuhr's response to events; *Children of Light and Children of Darkness: A Vindication of Democracy and a Critique of Its Traditional Defence* (1944) is a brief but comprehensive discussion of social ethics.

Niebuhr was an editor of *The World Tomorrow*, a religious pacifist and socialist journal; *Christianity and Crisis*, a biweekly with wide-ranging social and religious concerns; and a quarterly, now discontinued, first named *Radical Religion* and later *Christianity and Society*. He married Ursula M. Keppel-Compton in 1931. His wife was herself a teacher of religion at Barnard College in New York City, and they worked closely together. After 1952 Niebuhr's public activities were seriously limited as the result of a stroke, but he was able to continue much of his teaching and writing.

BLESSED PAUL VI

(b. Sept. 26, 1897, Concesio, near Brescia, Italy—d. Aug. 6, 1978, Castel Gandolfo)

B lessed Paul VI was an Italian pope of the Roman Catholic Church (reigned 1963–78) during a period including most of the Second Vatican Council (1962–65) and the immediate postconciliar era, in which he issued directives and guidance to a changing Roman Catholic Church. His pontificate was confronted with the problems and uncertainties of a church facing a new role in the contemporary world.

The son of a middle-class lawyer—who was also a journalist and local political figure—and of a mother belonging to the same social background, Giovanni Battista Montini was in his early years educated mainly at home because of frail health. Later he studied in Brescia. Ordained priest on May 29, 1920, he was sent by his bishop to Rome for higher studies and was eventually recruited for the Vatican diplomatic service. His first assignment, in May 1923, was to the staff of the apostolic nunciature (papal ambassador's post) in Warsaw, but persistent ill health brought him back to Rome before the end of that same year. He then pursued special studies at the Ecclesiastical Academy, the training school for future Vatican diplomats, and at the same time resumed work at the Vatican Secretariat of State, where he remained in posts of increasing importance for more than 30 years.

In 1939 Montini was appointed papal undersecretary of state and later, in 1944, acting secretary for ordinary (or nondiplomatic) affairs. He declined an invitation to be elevated to the Sacred College of Cardinals in 1953. In the beginning of November 1954, Pope Pius XII appointed him archbishop of Milan, and Pope John XXIII named him cardinal in 1958. He was elected pope on June 21, 1963, choosing to be known as Paul VI.

The Montini pontificate began in the period following the difficult first session of the Second Vatican Council, in which the new pope had played an important, though not spectacular, part. His lengthy association with university students in the stormy atmosphere of the early days of the Fascist regime in Italy, in combination with the generally philosophical bent of his mind—developed by a long-standing habit of extensive and reflective reading—enabled him to bring to the perplexing problems of the times an academic understanding, coupled with the knowledge derived from long years of practical diplomatic experience. Paul VI guided the three remaining sessions of the Second Vatican Council, often developing points he had first espoused as cardinal archbishop of Milan. His chief concern was that the Roman Catholic Church in the 20th century should be a faithful witness to the tradition of the past, except when tradition was obviously anachronistic.

Upon the completion of the council (December 8, 1965), Paul VI was confronted with the formidable task of implementing its decisions, which affected practically every facet of church life. He approached this task with a sense of the difficulty involved in making changes in centuries-old structures and practices—changes rendered necessary by many rapid transformations in the social, psychological, and political milieu of the 20th century. Paul VI's approach was consistently one of careful assessment of each concrete situation, with a sharp awareness of the many varied complications that he believed could not be ignored.

This prevalently philosophical attitude was often construed by his critics as timidity, indecision, and uncertainty. Nonetheless, many of Paul VI's decisions in these crucial years called for courage. In July 1968, he published his encyclical *Humanae vitae* ("Of Human Life"), which reaffirmed the stand of several of his predecessors on the long-smoldering controversy over artificial means of birth prevention, which he opposed. In many sectors this encyclical provoked adverse reactions that may be described as the most violent attacks on the authority of papal teaching in modern times. Similarly, his firm stand on the retention of priestly celibacy (*Sacerdotalis caelibatus*, June 1967) evoked much harsh criticism. Paul VI later likened the large numbers of priests leaving the ministry to a "crown of thorns." He also was disturbed by the growing numbers of religious men and women asking for release from vows or who were abandoning out of hand their religious vows.

From the very outset of his years as pope, Paul VI gave clear evidence of the importance he attached to the study and the solution of social problems and to their impact on world peace. Social questions had already been prominent in his far-reaching pastoral program in Milan (1954–63). During those years he had traveled extensively in the Americas and in Africa, centring his attention mainly on concern for workers and for the poor. Such problems dominated his first encyclical letter, *Ecclesiam suam* ("His Church"), August 6, 1964, and later became the insistent theme of his celebrated *Populorum progressio* ("Progress of the Peoples"), March 26, 1967. This encyclical was such a pointed plea for social justice that in some conservative circles the pope was accused of Marxism.

In an address to the council fathers at the end of the first session of the Second Vatican Council, the then Cardinal Montini formulated a question that may be called the theme of his pastoral service as pontiff: "Church of Christ, what say you of yourself?" In an effort to answer this fundamental question, Paul VI undertook a series of apostolic journeys that were unparalleled occasions for a pope to set foot on every continent. His first journey was a pilgrimage to the Holy Land (January 1964), highlighted by his historic meeting with the Greek Orthodox patriarch of Constantinople, Athenagoras, in Jerusalem. At the end of that same year, he went to India, the first pope to visit Asia. The following year (October 4, 1965) he traveled to the headquarters of the United Nations in New York City, where he delivered a moving plea for peace to the General Assembly in special session. In 1967 he undertook short visits to Fátima (Portugal) and to Istanbul and Ephesus (Turkey), a journey that had special ecumenical significance: a second meeting with Athenagoras in the patriarch's own episcopal city (Constantinople). In August 1968 the pope went to Bogotá, and he appeared before the International Labour Organisation and the World Council of Churches in Geneva, in June 1969. The following month he was in Uganda, East Africa. In the autumn of 1970, he undertook the longest papal journey in modern history: 10 days spent in visits to Tehrān, East Pakistan, the Philippines, Western Samoa (now Samoa), Australia, Indonesia, Hong Kong, and Ceylon, each stop bringing Paul VI into personal contact with different peoples of the world. His arrival in Manila almost ended in tragedy when an attempt was made on his life within minutes of his descent from the plane, but with no serious injury.

The themes treated by Paul VI on these trips were basically the same: world peace, social justice, world hunger, illiteracy, brotherhood under God, and international cooperation.

On January 6, 1971, in the Clementine Hall in the Vatican, Paul VI conferred the Pope John XXIII Peace Prize on the Albanian-born Mother Mary Teresa Bojaxhiu, who had spent most of her life in India, where she had founded a special religious congregation of women dedicated to the alleviation of the countless ills of the poorest classes in the country. Paul VI declared on this occasion that the award was intended to centre attention on how even a humble individual without means can further world peace without fanfare, simply by proving in day-to-day action that "every man is my brother." Here, as in other instances, Paul's aim was to confront the world at large with the inescapable problems of justice and peace while at the same time proving conclusively that even these apparently insoluble problems can and must be settled with realistic courage and individual perseverance.

Paul VI's human concern found further expression in his efforts to lessen the long-standing tensions between the church of Rome and other churches and even with those professing no religion at all. He sought out closer understanding with numerous religious leaders throughout the world, both Christian and non-Christian, placing more emphasis on those aspects that unite the churches than on those that divide. To show that mutual acquaintance is at the very foundation of any plans or hopes for unity, Pope Paul met with prominent religious leaders from various communities in Great Britain, the United States, and the Soviet Union, as well as other countries. Paul VI also set up a special secretariat for nonbelievers, stressing the need of understanding and endeavouring to solve the problems posed by atheism.

Under his guidance the Roman Catholic Church drastically revised its legislation governing marriages between its own members and those who profess other faiths, expressing a firm desire to diminish the threat of human tragedy following possible clashes of individual consciences. For this reason Paul VI's *motu proprio* (a type of papal document) was welcomed and praised for its understanding of human problems and its desire to find a satisfactory solution to the problem of mixed marriages without demanding of either side any renunciation of basic principles of conscience.

In the rise of modern ecumenism, Paul VI saw excellent opportunities to encourage world brotherhood, which, he hoped, might further efforts for human well-being in the pursuit of happiness in unity of faith in God. On May 15, 1971, commemorating the 80th anniversary of Pope Leo XIII's encyclical *Rerum novarum* on the reform of the social order, Pope Paul issued a forceful apostolic letter, *Octogesima adveniens*, with particular insistence on the necessity of involvement of all human beings in the solution of the problems of justice and peace. In 2012 Pope Benedict XVI declared that Paul had lived "a life of heroic virtue." Two years later he was beatified by Benedict's successor, Francis I.

ELIJAH MUHAMMAD

(b. Oct. 7, 1897, Sandersville, Ga., U.S.—died Feb. 25, 1975, Chicago)

The son of a former slave, Elijah Muhammad established the Nation of Islam, sometimes called the Black Muslims, as an influential religious, political, and economic force among urban African Americans. He led the organization from 1934 until his death in 1975. Muhammad and his teachings became widely known in the 1950s as a result of the speaking tours of one of the growing organization's new young leaders, Malcolm X.

Elijah Robert Poole was born on Oct. 7, 1897, in Sandersville, Ga. He worked as a manual laborer in his youth. In 1923 he moved with his wife and two children to Detroit, Mich. The couple would eventually have six more children. In about 1930 Poole met Wallace D. Fard, also known as Fard Muhammad, the founder of the Lost-Found Nation of Islam. Poole claimed that he received the "word of Allah" from Fard, and he became Fard's assistant minister at Temple Number One in Detroit. Like Fard's other followers, Poole also adopted an Arabic name. In 1932 Muhammad established Temple Number Two in Chicago, Ill. He returned to Detroit in 1934 and took control of the Nation of Islam following Fard's disappearance. Muhammad developed a coherent theology for the organization and began attracting followers with his message that African Americans were the chosen people of Allah and that they would assert themselves over whites during the 20th century. These ideas, combined with many of the basic tenets of Islam, formed the basis of the disciplined, self-sufficient way of life of Nation of Islam members.

During World War II, Muhammad supported Japan because it was a nonwhite country, and he encouraged his followers to avoid the draft. He was imprisoned from 1942 to 1946 after being convicted of violating the Selective Service Act. In the years after the war Muhammad made a concentrated effort to increase the Nation of Islam's membership. Many African American prison inmates joined, including Malcolm Little, who converted in 1946 while serving time in a Boston, Mass., jail for burglary. Little changed his surname to "X" and quickly became a valuable asset to the organization, establishing many new mosques and founding its official publication, Muhammad Speaks, in 1961. Malcolm X eloquently expressed Muhammad's confrontational racial views, but by the mid-1960s he had fallen into disfavor with Muhammad, who suspended his well-known disciple from the Nation of Islam.

In his later years Muhammad expressed more moderate views of relations between African Americans and whites, whom he often had referred to as "blue-eyed devils." He continued to stress, however, the idea of a self-sufficient African American community. After suffering a fatal heart attack in Chicago on Feb. 25, 1975, Muhammad was succeeded by his son Wallace D. Muhammad, who eventually changed his name to Warith Deen Mohammed. Mohammed reformed the Nation of Islam, rejecting many of his father's teachings, including the claim that Elijah Muhammad was a prophet. He brought the organization into closer alignment with orthodox Sunni Islam and changed its name. In 1978 Louis Farrakhan and others dissatisfied with the reforms broke away to reestablish the Nation of Islam as originally envisioned by Muhammad.

DOROTHY DAY

(b. Nov. 8, 1897, New York, N.Y., U.S. — d. Nov. 29, 1980, New York, N.Y.)

Dorothy Day was an American journalist and reformer, cofounder of the *Catholic Worker* newspaper, and an important lay leader in its associated activist movement.

While a student at the University of Illinois on a scholarship (1914–16), Day read widely among socialist authors and soon joined the Socialist Party. In 1916 she returned to New York City and joined the staff of the *Call*, a socialist newspaper; she also became a member of the Industrial Workers of the World (IWW). In 1917 she moved to the staff of the Masses, where she remained until the magazine was suppressed by the government a few months later. After a brief period on the successor journal, the Liberator, Day worked as a nurse in Brooklyn (1918–19). For several years thereafter she continued in journalism in Chicago and in New Orleans, Louisiana. In 1927, following years of doubt and indecision, she joined the Roman Catholic Church, an act that for some time estranged her from her earlier radical associates.

In 1932 Day met Peter Maurin, a French-born Catholic who had developed a program of social reconstruction, which he initially called "the green revolution," based on communal farming and the establishment of houses of hospitality for the urban poor. The program, now called the Catholic Worker movement, aimed to unite workers and intellectuals in joint activities ranging from farming to educational discussions. In 1933 Day and Maurin founded the *Catholic Worker*, a monthly newspaper, to carry the idea to a wider audience. Within three years the paper's circulation had grown to 150,000, and the original St. Joseph's House of Hospitality in New York City had served as the pattern for similar houses in a number of other cities.

The Catholic Worker movement that Day inspired took radical positions on many issues as it grew, and Day, a professed anarchist, became widely regarded as one of the great Catholic lay leaders of the 20th century. During World War II the *Catholic Worker* was an organ for

Dorothy Day fighting the closing of House of Hospitality.

pacifism and supported Catholic conscientious objectors. Day protested the Vietnam War and was arrested in 1973 while demonstrating in California in support of Cesar Chavez and the United Farm Workers. Day died at the House of Hospitality on the Lower East Side of New York City.

Her autobiography, *The Long Loneliness*, was published in 1952. In the late 1990s steps were taken with the Vatican to begin the canonization process for Day; the Vatican granted the Archdiocese of New York permission to open her cause in March 2000.

RUHOLLAH KHOMEINI

(b. Sept. 24, 1902, Khomeyn, Iran—d. June 3, 1989, Tehrān)

Ruhollah Khomeini was an Iranian Shīʿite cleric who led the revolution that overthrew Mohammad Reza Shah Pahlavi in 1979 and who was Iran's ultimate political and religious authority for the next 10 years.

Khomeini was the grandson and son of mullahs (Shīʿite religious leaders). When he was about five months old, his father was killed on the orders of a local landlord. The young Khomeini was raised by his mother and aunt and then, after their deaths, by his older brother, Mortaza (later known as Ayatollah Pasandideh). He was educated in various Islamic schools, and he settled in the city of Qom about 1922. About 1930 he adopted the name of his home town, Khomayn (also spelled Khomeyn or Khomen), as his surname. As a Shīʿite scholar and teacher, Khomeini produced numerous writings on Islamic philosophy, law, and ethics, but it was his outspoken opposition to Iran's ruler, Mohammad Reza Shah Pahlavi, his denunciations of Western influences, and his uncompromising advocacy of Islamic purity that won him his initial following in Iran. In the 1950s he was acclaimed as an ayatollah, or major

Ruhollah Khomeini.

religious leader, and by the early 1960s he had received the title of grand ayatollah, thereby making him one of the supreme religious leaders of the Shīʿite community in Iran.

In 1962–63 Khomeini spoke out against the shah's reduction of religious estates in a land-reform program and against the emancipation of women. His ensuing arrest sparked antigovernment riots, and, after a year's imprisonment, Khomeini was forcibly exiled from Iran on Nov. 4, 1964. He eventually settled in the Shīʿite holy city of Al-Najaf, Iraq, from where he continued to call for the shah's overthrow and the establishment of an Islamic republic in Iran.

From the mid-1970s Khomeini's influence inside Iran grew dramatically owing to mounting public dissatisfaction with the shah's regime. Iraq's ruler, Ṣaddām Ḥussein, forced Khomeini to leave Iraq on Oct. 6, 1978. Khomeini then settled in Neauphle-le-Château, a suburb of Paris. From there his supporters relayed his tape-recorded messages to an increasingly aroused Iranian populace, and massive demonstrations, strikes, and civil unrest in late 1978 forced the departure of the shah from Iran on Jan. 16, 1979. Khomeini arrived in Tehrān in triumph on Feb. 1, 1979, and was acclaimed as the religious leader of Iran's revolution. He appointed a government four days later and on March 1 again took up residence in Qom. In December a referendum on a new constitution created an Islamic republic in Iran, with Khomeini named Iran's political and religious leader for life.

Khomeini himself proved unwavering in his determination to transform Iran into a theocratically ruled Islamic state. Iran's Shīʿite clerics largely took over the formulation of governmental policy, while Khomeini arbitrated between the various revolutionary factions and made final decisions on important matters requiring his personal authority. First his regime took political vengeance, with hundreds of people who had worked for the shah's regime reportedly executed. The remaining domestic opposition was then suppressed, its members being systematically imprisoned or killed. Iranian women were required to wear the veil, Western music and alcohol were banned, and the punishments prescribed by Islamic law were reinstated.

The main thrust of Khomeini's foreign policy was the complete abandonment of the shah's pro-Western orientation and the adoption of an attitude of unrelenting hostility toward both superpowers. In addition, Iran tried to export its brand of Islamic revivalism to neighbouring Muslim countries. Khomeini sanctioned Iranian militants' seizure of the U.S. embassy in Tehrān (Nov. 4, 1979) and their holding of American diplomatic personnel as hostages for more than a year. He also refused to countenance a peaceful solution to the Iran-Iraq War, which had begun in 1980 and which he insisted on prolonging in the hope of overthrowing Ṣaddām. Khomeini finally approved a cease-fire in 1988 that effectively ended the war.

Iran's course of economic development foundered under Khomeini's rule, and his pursuit of victory in the Iran-Iraq War ultimately proved futile. Khomeini, however, was able to retain his charismatic hold over Iran's Shīʿite masses, and he remained the supreme political and religious arbiter in the country until his death. His gold-domed tomb in Tehrān's Behesht-e Zahrāʾ cemetery has since become a shrine for his supporters. Ideologically, he is best remembered for having developed the concept of *velāyat-e faqīh* ("guardianship of the jurist") in a series of lectures and tracts first promulgated during exile in Iraq in the late 1960s and '70s. Khomeini argued therein for the establishment of a theocratic government administered by Islamic jurists in place of corrupt secular regimes. The Iranian constitution of 1979 embodies articles upholding this concept of juristic authority.

HASAN AL-BANNĀ'

(b. 1906, Egypt—d. February 1949, Cairo)

Ḥasan al-Bannā' was an Egyptian political and religious leader who established a new religious society, the Muslim Brotherhood, and played a central role in Egyptian political and social affairs.

At age 12 Ḥasan al-Bannā' joined the Society for Moral Behaviour, thus demonstrating at an early age the deep concern for religious affairs that characterized his entire life. In 1923 he enrolled at the Dār al-'Ulūm, a teacher-training school in Cairo, which maintained a traditional religious and social outlook. In 1927 he was assigned to teach Arabic in a primary school in the city of Ismailia (al-Ismā'īlīyah), near the Suez Canal, which was a focal point for the foreign economic and military occupation of Egypt. There he witnessed scenes that acutely distressed him and many other Muslims. In March 1928, with six workers from a British camp labour force, he created the Society of the Muslim Brothers (Arabic: al-Ikhwān al-Muslimūn), which aimed at a rejuvenation of Islam.

In the 1930s, at his own request, Ḥasan al-Bannā' was transferred to a teaching post in Cairo. By the advent of World War II the Muslim Brotherhood had grown enormously and had become a potent element on the Egyptian scene, attracting significant numbers of students, civil servants, urban labourers, and others, and representing almost every group in Egyptian society.

Many of the members came to view the Egyptian government as betraying the interests of Egyptian nationalism. For a while Ḥasan al-Bannā' tried to maintain a tactical alliance with the government, but he and his followers had become a threat to the central authorities. In the turmoil of the postwar years many elements of the society passed beyond his authority, and members were implicated in a number of assassinations, notably that of Prime Minister an-Nuqrāshī in December 1948. With the connivance of the government, Ḥasan al-Bannā' himself was assassinated the following year.

BLESSED MOTHER TERESA

(baptized Aug. 27, 1910, Skopje, Macedonia, Ottoman Empire [now in Republic of Macedonia]—d. Sept. 5, 1997, Calcutta [now Kolkata], India)

Blessed Mother Teresa was the founder of the Order of the Missionaries of Charity, a Roman Catholic congregation of women dedicated to the poor, particularly to the destitute of India. She was the recipient of numerous honours, including the 1979 Nobel Prize for Peace.

The daughter of an ethnic Albanian grocer, she went to Ireland in 1928 to join the Sisters of Loretto at the Institute of the Blessed Virgin Mary and sailed only six weeks later to India as a teacher. She taught for 17 years at the order's school in Calcutta (Kolkata).

In 1946 Sister Teresa experienced her "call within a call," which she considered divine inspiration to devote herself to caring for the sick and poor. She then moved into the slums she had observed while teaching. Municipal authorities, upon her petition, gave her a pilgrim hostel, near the sacred temple of Kali, where she founded her order in 1948. Sympathetic companions soon flocked to her aid. Dispensaries and outdoor schools were organized. Mother Teresa adopted Indian citizenship, and her Indian nuns all donned the sari as their habit. In 1950 her order received canonical sanction from Pope Pius XII, and in 1965 it became a pontifical congregation (subject only to the pope). In 1952 she established Nirmal Hriday ("Place for the Pure of Heart"), a hospice where the terminally ill could die with dignity. Her order also opened numerous centres serving the blind, the aged, and the disabled. Under Mother Teresa's guidance, the Missionaries of Charity built a leper colony, called Shanti Nagar ("Town of Peace"), near Asansol, India.

In 1962 the Indian government awarded Mother Teresa the Padma Shri, one of its highest civilian honours, for her services to the people of India. Pope Paul VI on his trip to India in 1964 gave her his ceremonial limousine, which she immediately raffled to help finance her leper colony. She was summoned to Rome in 1968 to found a home there, staffed primarily with Indian nuns. In recognition of her apostolate, she was honoured on Jan. 6, 1971, by Pope Paul, who awarded her the first Pope John XXIII Peace Prize. In 1979 she received the Nobel Peace Prize for her humanitarian work, and the following year the Indian government conferred on her the Bharat Ratna, the country's highest civilian honour.

In her later years Mother Teresa spoke out against divorce, contraception, and abortion. She also suffered ill health and had a heart attack in 1989. In 1990 she resigned as head of the order but was returned to office by a nearly unanimous vote—the lone dissenting voice was her own. A worsening heart condition forced her retirement, and the order chose the Indian-born Sister Nirmala as her successor in 1997. At the time of Mother Teresa's death, her order included hundreds of centres in more than 90 countries with some 4,000 nuns and hundreds of thousands of lay workers. Within two years of her death, the process to declare her a saint was begun, and Pope John Paul II issued a special dispensation to expedite the process of canonization. She was beatified on Oct. 19, 2003, reaching the ranks of the blessed in what was then the shortest time in the history of the church.

Although Mother Teresa displayed cheerfulness and a deep commitment to God in her daily work, her letters (which were collected and published in 2007) indicate that she did not feel God's presence in her soul during the last 50 years of her life. The letters reveal the suffering she endured and her feeling that Jesus had abandoned her at the start of her mission. Continuing to experience a spiritual darkness, she came to believe that she was sharing in Christ's Passion, particularly the moment in which Christ asks, "My God, my God, why have you forsaken me?" Despite this hardship, Mother Teresa integrated the feeling of absence into her daily religious life and remained committed to her faith and her work for Christ.

L. RON HUBBARD

(b. March 13, 1911, Tilden, Nebraska, U.S.—d. Jan. 24, 1986, San Luis Obispo, California)

L. Ron Hubbard was an American novelist and founder of the Church of Scientology. Hubbard grew up in Helena, Montana, and studied at George Washington University in Washington, D.C. In the 1930s and '40s he published short stories and novels in a variety of genres, including horror and science fiction. After serving in the navy in World War II, he published *Dianetics* (1950), which detailed his theories of the human mind. He eventually moved away from *Dianetics'* focus on the mind to a more religious approach to the human condition, which he called Scientology. After founding the Church of Scientology in 1954, Hubbard struggled to gain recognition of it as a legitimate religion and was often at odds with tax authorities and former members who accused the church of fraud and harassment. He lived many years on a yacht and remained in seclusion for his last six years.

BILLY GRAHAM

(b. Nov. 7, 1918, Charlotte, N.C., U.S.)

Billy Graham was an American evangelist whose large-scale preaching missions, known as crusades, and friendship with numerous U.S. presidents brought him to international prominence.

The son of a prosperous dairy farmer, Billy Graham grew up in rural North Carolina. In 1934, while attending a revival meeting led by the evangelist Mordecai Ham, he underwent a religious experience and professed his "decision for Christ." In 1936 he left his father's dairy farm to attend Bob Jones College (now Bob Jones University), then located in Cleveland, Tenn., but stayed for only a semester because of the extreme fundamentalism of the institution. He transferred to Florida Bible Institute (now Trinity College), near Tampa, graduated in 1940, and was ordained a minister by the Southern Baptist Convention. Convinced that his education was deficient, however, Graham enrolled at Wheaton College in Illinois. While at Wheaton, he met and married (1943) Ruth Bell, daughter of L. Nelson Bell, a missionary to China.

By the time Graham graduated from Wheaton in 1943, he had developed the preaching style for which he would become famous—a simple, direct message of sin and salvation that he delivered energetically and without condescension. "Sincerity," he observed many years later, "is the biggest part of selling anything, including the Christian plan of salvation." After a brief and undistinguished stint as pastor of Western Springs Baptist Church in the western suburbs of Chicago, Graham decided to become an itinerant evangelist. He joined the staff of a new organization called Youth for Christ in 1945 and in 1947 served as president of Northwestern Bible College in Minneapolis, Minn.

Graham's emergence as an evangelist came at a propitious moment for 20th-century Protestants. Protestantism in the United States was deeply divided as a result of controversies in the 1920s between fundamentalism and modernism (a movement that applied scholarly methods of textual and historical criticism to the study of the Bible). The public image of fundamentalists was damaged by the Scopes Trial of 1925, which concerned the teaching of Charles Darwin's theory of evolution in public schools in Tennessee; in his writings about the trial, the journalist and social critic H.L. Mencken successfully portrayed all fundamentalists as uneducated country bumpkins. In response to these controversies, most fundamentalists withdrew from the established Protestant denominations, which they regarded as hopelessly liberal, and retreated from the larger society, which they viewed as both corrupt and corrupting. Although Graham remained theologically conservative, he refused to be sectarian like other fundamentalists. Seeking to dissociate himself from the image of the stodgy fundamentalist preacher, he seized on the opportunity presented by new media technologies, especially radio and television, to spread the message of the gospel.

In the late 1940s Graham's fellow evangelist in Youth for Christ, Charles Templeton, challenged Graham to attend seminary with him so that both preachers could shore up their theological knowledge.

Graham considered the possibility at length, but in 1949, while on a spiritual retreat in the San Bernardino Mountains of southern California, he decided to set aside his intellectual doubts about Christianity and simply "preach the gospel." After his retreat, Graham began preaching in Los Angeles, where his crusade brought him national attention. He acquired this new fame in no small measure because newspaper magnate William Randolph Hearst, impressed with the young evangelist's preaching and anticommunist rhetoric, instructed his papers to "puff Graham." The huge circus tent in which Graham preached, as well as his own self-promotion, lured thousands of curious visitors—including Hollywood movie stars and gangsters—to what the press dubbed the "canvas cathedral" at the corner of Washington and Hill streets. From Los Angeles, Graham undertook evangelistic crusades around the country and the world, eventually earning international renown.

Despite his successes, Graham faced criticism from both liberals and conservatives. In New York City in 1954 he was received warmly by students at Union Theological Seminary, a bastion of liberal Protestantism; nevertheless, the theologian Reinhold Niebuhr, a professor at Union and one of the leading Protestant thinkers of the 20th century, had little patience for Graham's simplistic preaching. On the other end of the theological spectrum, fundamentalists such as Bob Jones, Jr., Carl McIntire, and Jack Wyrtzen never forgave Graham for cooperating with the Ministerial Alliance, which included mainline Protestant clergy, in the planning and execution of Graham's storied 16-week crusade at Madison Square Garden in New York in 1957. Such cooperation, however, was part of Graham's deliberate strategy to distance himself from the starchy conservatism and separatism of American fundamentalists. His entire career, in fact, was marked by an irenic spirit.

Graham, by his own account, enjoyed close relationships with several American presidents, from Dwight Eisenhower to George W. Bush. (Although Graham met with Harry Truman in the Oval Office, the president was not impressed with him.) Despite claiming to be apolitical, Graham became politically close to Richard Nixon, whom he had befriended when Nixon was Eisenhower's vice president. During the 1960 presidential campaign, in which Nixon was the Republican nominee, Graham met in Montreaux, Switz., with Norman Vincent Peale and other Protestant leaders to devise a strategy to derail the campaign of John F. Kennedy, the Democratic nominee, in order to secure Nixon's election and prevent a Roman Catholic from becoming president. Although Graham later mended relations with Kennedy, Nixon remained his favourite politician; indeed, Graham all but endorsed Nixon's reelection effort in 1972 against George McGovern. As Nixon's presidency unraveled amid charges of criminal misconduct in the Watergate Scandal, Graham reviewed transcripts of Oval Office tape recordings subpoenaed by Watergate investigators and professed to be physically sickened by his friend's use of foul language.

SUN MYUNG MOON

(b. Jan. 6, 1920, Kwangju Sangsa Ri, North P'yŏngan province, Korea [now in North Korea]—d. Sept. 3, 2012, Kap'yŏng, Kyŏnggi province, South Korea)

Sun Myung Moon was a South Korean religious leader who in 1954 founded the Holy Spirit Association for the Unification of World Christianity, better known as the Unification Church.

In his book *The Divine Principle* (1952), which is the basic scripture of the church, Moon wrote that at the age of 16 he had a vision of Jesus Christ in which he was told to carry out Christ's unfinished task. Moon believed that God chose him to save mankind from Satanism, and he regarded communists as Satan's representatives in the world.

Moon began to preach his doctrines in Korea in 1946. Two years later he was excommunicated by the Korean Presbyterian Church, and shortly thereafter he was imprisoned by the North Korean authorities for reasons that are not entirely clear. In 1950 he escaped—or was released—and fled to South Korea, where he founded what was to become the Unification Church. He built his Korean and Japanese enterprises, which included factories that produced armaments, paint, machinery, and ginseng tea, into a multimillion-dollar empire, and in the early 1970s he began full-scale missionary operations in the United States. As young people were drawn into the movement, Moon incurred widespread hostility from the parents of followers, who believed that their children had been unfairly indoctrinated. Other controversies also mounted over the movement's fund-raising techniques, as well as over immigration issues and tax manipulation.

Moon and his wife were respectively addressed as "Father" and "Mother" by disciples, for whom the two epitomized God's ideal family. In 1973 the Moons moved their headquarters to Tarrytown, New York, operating from there an international network of businesses. In 1982 Moon founded a newspaper, *The Washington Times*. That year he was also convicted of tax evasion, sentenced to 18 months in prison, and fined $25,000; he went to prison in 1984.

SAINT JOHN PAUL II

(b. May 18, 1920, Wadowice, Poland—died April 2, 2005, Vatican City)

The first Polish pope was John Paul II, who was the 264th bishop of Rome. His 26-year reign as head of the Roman Catholic Church—from 1978 until his death in 2005—was one of the longest in church history. John Paul II made extraordinary efforts to reach out to people around the world, to both Roman Catholics and those of other faiths. Traveling a far greater distance than did all the popes before him combined, he took 104 trips abroad. The crowds that came to hear him speak were sometimes among the largest ever assembled, and he reached still more people through televised broadcasts. He maintained an impressive touring schedule even after becoming visibly ill with Parkinson disease and severe arthritis in the 1990s.

John Paul II was also an ardent advocate for universal human rights and world peace. His experiences as a young man during World War II had profoundly demonstrated to him the importance of combatting violence, religious intolerance, and political oppression. He strove to improve the church's relationship with Judaism and Islam, becoming the first pope to enter a synagogue and the first to enter a mosque. A powerful opponent of Communism, his nonviolent activism was credited with helping lead to the peaceful dismantling of the Soviet Union. At the same time, he was a sharp critic of unbridled capitalism and Western-style materialism.

On theological issues, John Paul II was very conservative, more so than his three immediate predecessors. He did not, for instance, change the requirement that the clergy must remain celibate or bans on the ordination of women, homosexual activity, divorce, and artificial

Pope John Paul II waving to a crowd during a visit to Kraków, Poland, 1987.

contraception. He also vigorously opposed abortion and euthanasia, which he characterized as a "culture of death." Bishops and teachers of theology who disagreed with church doctrine were disciplined, and some were relieved of their posts. Among the problems the church encountered during John Paul II's reign were a drop in the number of priests and nuns and a decline in church attendance.

He was born Karol Józef Wojtyła on May 18, 1920, to working-class parents in Wadowice, Poland. His mother died when he was eight, and his older brother died a few years later. His father, a pious and disciplined man who was a lieutenant in the Polish army, became the dominant influence in his life. Wojtyła was an outgoing but serious boy, an excellent student, and an avid athlete who enjoyed playing soccer (association football) and skiing.

After graduating from high school as class valedictorian, Wojtyła entered Jagiellonian University in Kraków in 1938 to study literature and philology. After Germany invaded Poland in 1939, however, the Nazis closed the university. Wojtyła continued to study in secret. To avoid being deported to a concentration camp, he worked in a quarry and then in a chemical factory considered to be critical to the war effort; he later was the first pope in modern times to have worked as a laborer. He also was active in an underground theater group that produced plays in Polish, which was forbidden under Nazi rule.

During the war Wojtyła witnessed immeasurable cruelty and suffering, including the deportation and slaughter of the Jews of Kraków as well as of Polish priests and many of his professors. Amid these horrors, he was deeply influenced by the work of Jan Tyranowski, a tailor who ran a youth ministry for a local church. He introduced Wojtyła to the writings of the Carmelite Spanish mystics, and his example working with young people inspired hope that the church could change the troubled world. Wojtyła's father, his sole remaining close relative, died in 1941. He soon decided to become a priest and began studying in an illegal seminary. In August 1944, Nazi troops swept through Kraków, seizing all able-bodied men. For the rest of the war Wojtyła hid in the archbishop's palace, disguised as a cleric. After World War II ended, he studied at a seminary in Kraków.

Wojtyła was ordained in 1946. After receiving a Ph.D. degree in philosophy from Pontifical Angelicum University in Rome in 1948, he returned to Poland to become a parish priest and a student chaplain. He continued the study of ethics, earned a second doctorate, and taught ethics and theology at the Catholic University of Lublin. In 1958 he became the youngest Polish bishop when he was appointed auxiliary bishop of Kraków.

In the early 1960s Wojtyła participated in the Second Vatican Council. He so impressed the church leadership that he was named archbishop at the end of 1963. He became a cardinal in 1967. As a spokesman for the large Roman Catholic population of Poland, he defended the church and the right to freedom of worship within a Communist system that suppressed religious activity. Unable to use the government-controlled media, he began traveling throughout the country to talk to the people, and he became skilled at addressing large crowds.

Upon his election as pope on Oct. 16, 1978, he was only 58 years old. He was the first non-Italian pope in 455 years. John Paul II adopted both the name and the less formal style of his predecessor, John Paul I. To avoid a conflict with a soccer (association football) match, for example, he scheduled his coronation for noon. In matters of theology and most official policy, however, John Paul II supported traditional church doctrines. An exception was the customary Vatican policy of neutrality, which he abandoned as he campaigned for religious freedom and national independence, supporting, for example, Poland's Solidarity movement. His visits to Brazil, the Philippines, Haiti, Paraguay, Chile, and even non-Catholic South Korea were credited with weakening authoritarian rule in those countries.

In January 1979 John Paul II attended a conference of Latin American bishops in Mexico. He became the first pope to visit a Communist country when he traveled to his native Poland in June of that year. He was also the first pope to visit a United States president in the White House. In October he addressed the United Nations General Assembly while on his six-city tour of the United States. Dubbed the "pilgrim pope," he visited 44 nations in the first 10 years of his reign. Fluent in eight languages, he was often able to address crowds in their native tongue.

The pope was shot and seriously wounded during an assassination attempt by Mehmet Ali Agca, a Turkish gunman, in St. Peter's Square on May 13, 1981. On May 12, 1982, when the pope went to Portugal's Shrine of Our Lady of Fátima to give thanks for his recovery from the gun wounds, another attack on his life was attempted. A rebel Spanish priest, carrying a bayonet, was subdued by security guards. John Paul II forgave Agca in person in 1983. In 2000 the church announced that the 1981 attempt on the pope's life had been foretold in the third prophecy revealed to three children at Fátima in the early 20th century.

In December 1989 Mikhail Gorbachev became the first Soviet leader to visit the pope. During the visit Gorbachev pledged that all Soviet citizens (including Muslims and Jews) would be guaranteed greater religious freedom and invited the pope to visit the Soviet Union. The Roman Catholic Church and the Soviet Union reestablished diplomatic relations in 1990 after a break of 67 years.

At the invitation of Cuban President Fidel Castro, the pope visited Cuba in 1998. He preached against both the Communist government's long suppression of religion and the U.S. embargo against Cuba, which he described as "unjust and ethically unacceptable." The Cuban government released about 300 prisoners after his visit.

John Paul II was a champion for world peace throughout his pontificate. He firmly opposed, for example, violence in Northern Ireland, the Persian Gulf War, the NATO bombing of Yugoslavia in 1999, and the U.S.-led invasion of Iraq in 2003.

Throughout his reign, John Paul II also emphasized the need for the Roman Catholic Church to reconcile with other religions and to apologize for past wrongdoings, including brutalities committed against indigenous peoples, women, ethnic and racial minorities, people of other faiths, and suspected heretics. In a statement of 1998, he officially apologized for the church's failure to speak out against the Nazi persecution of the Jews. In 2000 he made a historic visit to Jerusalem, meeting with Israeli Prime Minister Ehud Barak at the Yad Vashem Holocaust memorial and with Muslim leaders at the Al-Aqsa Mosque. John Paul II also worked to heal the long breach between the Vatican and Italy, and in 2002 he became the first pope to address the Italian parliament.

An admirer of the scientific search for truth, the pope issued statements supporting the theory that the human body developed through the gradual process of evolution. He also acknowledged that the church had been wrong to denounce Galileo in the 17th century for teaching that the Earth revolves around the sun.

John Paul II canonized more than 480 people, more than doubling the number of Roman Catholic saints. Among them were the church's first Amerindian, Roma (Gypsy), and Chinese saints. He also broadened the membership of the Sacred College of Cardinals, appointing many new cardinals from developing countries. By the time of his death, John Paul II had installed nearly all the cardinals who were eligible to choose his successor.

During his reign, John Paul II revised several major church texts. On January 25, 1983, he approved the first revision of the Roman Catholic Church's canon law since it had been codified in 1917. The new code, however, did not change any of the more controversial prohibitions of the church. Although the rule on the celibacy of the clergy was not changed, some married priests were accepted into the church, mainly as transfers from other denominations. John Paul II also introduced the Reform of the Roman Curia and the new Code of Canons for the Eastern Catholic Churches. In 1992 he introduced the first revision to the Roman Catholic catechism in more than four centuries. On Oct. 16, 2002, the 24th anniversary of his election as pope, he added an additional set of meditations, or "mysteries," to the rosary, a method of reciting prayers that had not been changed in hundreds of years.

In 2002 the Roman Catholic Church faced widespread allegations, predominantly in the United States, that priests had sexually abused minors and that church leaders had long attempted to cover up the scandal. In April of that year, John Paul II summoned the U.S. cardinals to the Vatican to address the issue, and they later negotiated a new national policy for handling accusations of sexual misconduct.

In addition to issuing encyclicals and other official writings, John Paul II published volumes of poetry and books about faith and ethics, including *Love and Responsibility* (1960), a work on sexual morality. In *The Acting Person* (1969), he discussed his philosophy that a person's actions, and not his thoughts or statements, define what that person stands for. His other books include *Crossing the Threshold of Hope* (1994), *Gift and Mystery: On the 50th Anniversary of My Priestly Ordination* (1997), and *Memory and Identity* (2005).

Despite worsening health in his later years, John Paul II continued to travel and to maintain, as much as possible, the dynamic style of his pontificate, until he became seriously ill in early 2005. He died in Vatican City on April 2, 2005. In January 2011 the Vatican recognized the recovery of a French nun from Parkinson disease as a miracle performed by John Paul II; he was beatified on May 1, 2011, and canonized with Pope John XXIII on April 27, 2014.

MALCOLM X

(b. May 19, 1925, Omaha, Nebraska, U.S.—d. Feb. 21, 1965, New York, New York)

Malcolm X was an African American leader and prominent figure in the Nation of Islam, who articulated concepts of race pride and black nationalism in the early 1960s. After his assassination, the widespread distribution of his life story—*The Autobiography of Malcolm X* (1965)—made him an ideological hero, especially among black youth.

Malcolm was born in Nebraska and while an infant moved with his family to Lansing, Mich. When Malcolm was six years old, his father, the Rev. Earl Little, a Baptist minister and former supporter of the early black nationalist leader Marcus Garvey, died after being hit by a streetcar, quite possibly the victim of murder by whites. The surviving family was so poor that Malcolm's mother, Louise Little, resorted to cooking dandelion greens from the street to feed her children. After she was committed to an insane asylum in 1939, Malcolm and his siblings were sent to foster homes or to live with family members.

Malcolm attended school in Lansing but dropped out in the eighth grade, when one of his teachers told him that he should become a carpenter instead of a lawyer. As a rebellious youngster, Malcolm moved from the Michigan State Detention Home, a juvenile home in Mason, Mich., to the Roxbury section of Boston to live with an older half sister, Ella, from his father's first marriage. There he became involved in petty criminal activities in his teenage years. Known as "Detroit Red" for the reddish tinge in his hair, he developed into a street hustler, drug dealer, and leader of a gang of thieves in Roxbury and Harlem (in New York City).

While in prison for robbery from 1946 to 1952, he underwent a conversion that eventually led him to join the Nation of Islam, an African American movement that combined elements of Islam with black nationalism. His decision to join the Nation also was influenced by discussions with his brother Reginald, who had become a member in Detroit and who was incarcerated with Malcolm in the Norfolk Prison Colony in Massachusetts in 1948. Malcolm quit smoking and gambling and refused to eat pork in keeping with the Nation's dietary restrictions. In order to educate himself, he spent long hours reading books in the prison library, even memorizing a dictionary. He also sharpened his forensic skills by participating in debate classes. Following Nation tradition, he replaced his surname, "Little," with an "X," a custom among Nation of Islam followers who considered their family names to have originated with white slaveholders.

After his release from prison Malcolm helped to lead the Nation of Islam during the period of its greatest growth and influence. He met Elijah Muhammad in Chicago in 1952 and then began organizing temples for the Nation in New York, Philadelphia, and Boston and in cities in the South. He founded the Nation's newspaper,

Muhammad Speaks, which he printed in the basement of his home, and initiated the practice of requiring every male member of the Nation to sell an assigned number of newspapers on the street as a recruiting and fund-raising technique. He also articulated the Nation's racial doctrines on the inherent evil of whites and the natural superiority of blacks.

Malcolm rose rapidly to become the minister of Boston Temple No. 11, which he founded; he was later rewarded with the post of minister of Temple No. 7 in Harlem, the largest and most prestigious temple in the Nation after the Chicago headquarters. Recognizing his talent and ability, Elijah Muhammad, who had a special affection for Malcolm, named him the National Representative of the Nation of Islam, second in rank to Muhammad himself. Under Malcolm's lieutenancy, the Nation claimed a membership of 500,000. The actual number of members fluctuated, however, and the influence of the organization, refracted through the public persona of Malcolm X, always greatly exceeded its size.

An articulate public speaker, a charismatic personality, and an indefatigable organizer, Malcolm X expressed the pent-up anger, frustration, and bitterness of African Americans during the major phase of the civil rights movement from 1955 to 1965. He preached on the streets of Harlem and spoke at major universities such as Harvard University and the University of Oxford. His keen intellect, incisive wit, and ardent radicalism made him a formidable critic of American society. He also criticized the mainstream civil rights movement, challenging Martin Luther King, Jr.'s central notions of integration and nonviolence. Malcolm argued that more was at stake than the civil right to sit in a restaurant or even to vote—the most important issues were black identity, integrity, and independence. In contrast to King's strategy of nonviolence,

Malcolm X.

civil disobedience, and redemptive suffering, Malcolm urged his followers to defend themselves "by any means necessary." His biting critique of the "so-called Negro" provided the intellectual foundations for the Black Power and black consciousness movements in the United States in the late 1960s and '70s. Through the influence of the Nation of Islam, Malcolm X helped to change the terms used to refer to African Americans from "Negro" and "coloured" to "black" and "Afro-American."

In 1963 there were deep tensions between Malcolm and Eiljah Muhammad over the political direction of the Nation. Malcolm urged that the Nation become more active in the widespread civil rights protests instead of just being a critic on the sidelines. Muhammad's violations of the moral code of the Nation further worsened his relations with Malcolm, who was devastated when he learned that Muhammad had fathered children by six of his personal secretaries, two of whom filed paternity suits and made the issue public. Malcolm brought additional bad publicity to the Nation when he declared publicly that Pres. John F. Kennedy's assassination was an example of "chickens coming home to roost"—a violent society suffering the consequences of violence. In response to the outrage this statement provoked, Elijah Muhammad ordered Malcolm to observe a 90-day period of silence, and the break between the two leaders became permanent.

Malcolm left the Nation in March 1964 and in the next month founded Muslim Mosque, Inc. During his pilgrimage to Mecca that same year, he experienced a second conversion and embraced Sunni Islam, adopting the Muslim name el-Hajj Malik el-Shabazz. Renouncing the separatist beliefs of the Nation, he claimed that the solution to racial problems in the United States lay in orthodox

Islam. On the second of two visits to Africa in 1964, he addressed the Organization of African Unity (known as the African Union since 2002), an intergovernmental group established to promote African unity, international cooperation, and economic development. In 1965 he founded the Organization of Afro-American Unity as a secular vehicle to internationalize the plight of black Americans and to make common cause with the people of the developing world—to move from civil rights to human rights.

The growing hostility between Malcolm and the Nation led to death threats and open violence against him. On Feb. 21, 1965, Malcolm was assassinated while delivering a lecture at the Audubon Ballroom in Harlem; three members of the Nation of Islam were convicted of the murder. He was survived by his wife, Betty Shabazz, whom he married in 1958, and six daughters. His martyrdom, ideas, and speeches contributed to the development of black nationalist ideology and the Black Power movement and helped to popularize the values of autonomy and independence among African Americans in the 1960s and '70s.

IAN PAISLEY

(b. April 6, 1926, Armagh, County Armagh, Northern Ireland—d. Sept. 12, 2014, Belfast, Northern Ireland)

Ian Paisley, a militant Protestant leader in the factional conflict that divided Northern Ireland from the 1960s, was first minister of Northern Ireland from May 2007 to June 2008. He also served as a member of the British Parliament (1970–2010) and the European Parliament (1979–2004).

The son of a maverick Baptist minister, Paisley was ordained by his father in 1946. He cofounded and became moderator of his own church, the Free Presbyterian Church, in 1951. In 1969 he founded the Martyrs Memorial Free Presbyterian Church in Belfast, Northern Ireland. From 1961 to 1991 membership in his churches increased 10-fold, though the 1991 census indicated that they attracted less than 1 percent of Northern Ireland's population. Paisley's strength lay in his ability to combine the language of biblical certainty with that of politics at a time when many Protestants were uncertain about their constitutional identity and fearful of their physical security. His ideological message combined militant anti-Catholicism with militant unionism.

From the 1960s Paisley strove to become the leader of extreme Protestant opinion in Northern Ireland by organizing street protests and rallies. These activities led to frequent confrontations with the authorities and a brief prison term for unlawful assembly in 1966. That year he established the Ulster Constitution Defence Committee and the Ulster Protestant Volunteers, which served as paramilitary adjuncts to his churches.

In 1970 Paisley was elected to the parliaments of Northern Ireland and the United Kingdom. In 1971, in an attempt to broaden his electoral base, he led a split in the Ulster Unionist Party (UUP), cofounding the Democratic Unionist Party (DUP). Throughout the 1970s and '80s he tried to turn the DUP into the largest unionist party, but with the exception of one local council election in 1981, it always finished second, behind the UUP. Although his personal following was never in doubt (in elections to the European Parliament in 1999 he received more votes than any other candidate in Northern Ireland), his popularity showed some signs of waning after 1994.

Paisley's career was one of consistent protest against the Roman Catholic Church and ecumenism, against British concessions to the Irish government and Irish nationalists, and against members of the Ulster unionist establishment, whom he criticized for their upper-class backgrounds and their perceived willingness to compromise the interests of Northern Ireland's Protestant community (he demanded the resignation of each UUP leader from Terence O'Neill in 1966 to David Trimble in 1997). His methods were also consistent: a combination of parliamentary opposition and extraparliamentary street protest. He was identified with shadowy private armies such as the Ulster Volunteer Force (UVF), the Third Force, and the Ulster Resistance.

Despite his considerable oratorical skills, his huge personal following, his vibrant churches, and a well-organized political party, Paisley failed to impede attempts at a negotiated settlement of the conflict in Northern Ireland, a process that he maintained was driving the province in the direction of Irish unity and away from the United Kingdom. In April 1998 eight political parties signed the Good Friday Agreement on steps leading to a new power-sharing government in Northern Ireland. Although Paisley had earlier refused to participate in multiparty talks that included Sinn Féin (SF), the political wing of the Irish Republican Army (IRA), and campaigned against the accord in a popular referendum held in May 1998, he ran for election the following month and won a seat in the new Northern Ireland Assembly.

In subsequent years the DUP supplanted the UUP as the leading unionist political party in Northern Ireland. In 2003 it became the largest unionist party in the Northern Ireland Assembly, which would have made Paisley first minister, but devolved power to Northern Ireland had been suspended in 2002. Thereafter Paisley made modest overtures to Sinn Féin and took part in multiparty talks, though he insisted the negotiations were with the British government rather than Sinn Féin.

He expressed cautious optimism over Sinn Féin's vote in January 2007 to support the Protestant-dominated police force in Northern Ireland. In the elections to the Northern Ireland Assembly in March 2007, the DUP finished first, capturing 30 percent of the vote and 36 seats in the 108-member Assembly (compared with 15 percent and 18 seats for the UUP); Sinn Féin was second with 28 seats. The DUP and Sinn Féin subsequently agreed to form a power-sharing government. On May 8, 2007, as devolution returned to Northern Ireland, Paisley was sworn in as first minister, with Sinn Féin's Martin McGuinness as deputy first minister. Despite concerns over their ability to govern jointly, Paisley and McGuinness worked together amicably. In January 2008 Paisley stepped down as moderator of the Free Presbyterian Church, and in June he resigned as first minister and as DUP leader. He stood down from the British House of Commons at the 2010 general election and was succeeded by his son. Later in 2010 Paisley was made a life peer.

THOMAS SPENCER MONSON

(b. Aug. 21, 1927, Salt Lake City, Utah, U.S.)

Thomas Spencer Monson was an American religious leader who became the 16th president of the Church of Jesus Christ of Latter-day Saints (LDS), also known as the Mormon church, in 2008.

Monson was the second of six children. He joined the U.S. Naval Reserve at age 17 and served one year of active duty, including a few weeks at the end of World War II. He completed a business degree cum laude at the University of Utah in 1948. In the same year, he married and began his career in publishing; he eventually rose to the post of general manager of Deseret Press, then the largest publishing company west of the Mississippi River.

Monson's rise in church affairs was equally notable. He was made bishop of a ward (ecclesiastical jurisdiction) in Salt Lake City at age 22, and in 1959 he became president of the Canadian Mission. In 1963 he was elevated to the Quorum of the Twelve Apostles, the LDS's second highest executive body. In later years Monson was active with LDS mission work in the South Pacific and especially in eastern Europe, where he helped in the construction of a temple (dedicated in 1985) in Freiberg, E.Ger., and in gaining permission for the LDS to proselytize behind the Iron Curtain. He also was active in LDS church publishing activities, including the preparation of new versions of basic Mormon texts. He served for many years on the National Executive Board of the Boy Scouts of America and received numerous awards from national and international scouting bodies.

In 1985 Monson was appointed to the church's highest executive body, the First Presidency (consisting of the president and two counselors), for which he served as second counselor (1985–95) and then as first counselor (1995–2008). From 1995 he also served as president of the Quorum of the Twelve Apostles, a position that placed him in line for the presidency of the denomination. He was appointed president of the LDS following the death of his predecessor, Gordon B. Hinckley, on Jan. 27, 2008. He assumed office on February 3 of that year.

MARTIN LUTHER KING, JR.

(b. Jan. 15, 1929, Atlanta, Ga., U.S.—died April 4, 1968, Memphis, Tenn.)

Inspired by the belief that love and peaceful protest could eliminate social injustice, Martin Luther King, Jr., became one of the outstanding black leaders in the United States. He aroused whites and blacks alike to protest racial discrimination, poverty, and war. A champion of nonviolent resistance to oppression, he was awarded the Nobel Peace Prize in 1964.

Martin Luther King, Jr., was born in Atlanta, Georgia, on Jan. 15, 1929. His father, Martin, Sr., was the pastor of the Ebenezer Baptist Church, a black congregation. His mother, Alberta Williams King, was a schoolteacher. Martin had an older sister, Christine, and a younger brother, Alfred Daniel.

Martin encountered racism at an early age. When he was 6, his friendship with two white playmates was cut short by their parents. When he was 11 a white woman struck him and called him a "nigger."

A bright student, he was admitted to Morehouse College at 15, without completing high school. He decided to become a minister and at 18 was ordained in his father's church. After graduating from Morehouse in 1948, he entered Crozer Theological Seminary in Chester, Pennsylvania. He was the valedictorian of his class in 1951 and won a graduate fellowship. At Boston University he received a Ph.D. in theology in 1955.

In Boston King met Coretta Scott. They were married in 1953 and had two sons, Martin Luther III and Dexter Scott, and two daughters, Yolanda Denise and Bernice Albertine.

King had been impressed by the teachings of Henry David Thoreau and Mahatma Gandhi on nonviolent resistance. King wrote, "I came to feel that this was the only morally and practically sound method open to oppressed people in their struggle for freedom." He became pastor of the Dexter Avenue Baptist Church in Montgomery, Ala., in 1954.

In December 1955 King was chosen to head the Montgomery Improvement Association, formed by the black community to lead a boycott of the segregated city buses. During the boycott King's home was bombed, but

Martin Luther King, Jr.

he persuaded his followers to remain nonviolent despite threats to their lives and property. Late in 1956 the United States Supreme Court forced desegregation of the buses. King believed that the boycott proved that "there is a new Negro in the South, with a new sense of dignity and destiny." In 1957 King became the youngest recipient of the Spingarn Medal, an award presented annually to an outstanding black person by the National Association for the Advancement of Colored People.

In 1958 King became president of a group later known as the Southern Christian Leadership Conference (SCLC), formed to carry on civil-rights activities in the South. King inspired blacks throughout the South to hold peaceful sit-ins and freedom rides to protest segregation.

A visit to India in 1959 gave King a long-awaited opportunity to study Gandhi's techniques of nonviolent protest. In 1960 King became copastor of his father's church in Atlanta. The next year he led a "nonviolent army" to protest discrimination in Albany, Ga. King was jailed in 1963 during a successful campaign to achieve the desegregation of many public facilities in Birmingham, Ala. In a moving appeal, known as the "Letter from Birmingham Jail," he replied to several white clergymen who felt that his efforts were ill timed. King argued that Asian and African nations were fast achieving political independence while "we still creep at a horse-and-buggy pace toward gaining a cup of coffee at a lunch counter."

In 1964 King became the youngest recipient of the Nobel Peace Prize. He regarded it not only as a personal honor but also as an international tribute to the nonviolent civil-rights movement. In 1965 King led a drive to register black voters in Selma, Ala. The drive met with violent resistance. In protest of this treatment, thousands of demonstrators conducted a five-day march from Selma to the capitol in Montgomery.

King was disappointed that the progress of civil rights in the South had not been matched by improvements in the lives of Northern blacks. In response to the riots in poverty-stricken black urban neighborhoods in 1965, he was determined to focus the nation's attention on the living conditions of blacks in Northern cities. In 1966 he established a headquarters in a Chicago, Ill., slum apartment. From this base he organized protests against the city's discrimination in housing and employment.

King combined his civil-rights campaigns with a strong stand against the Vietnam War. He believed that the money and effort spent on war could be used to combat poverty and discrimination. He felt that he would be a hypocrite if he protested racial violence without also condemning the violence of war. Militant black leaders began to attack his appeals for nonviolence. They accused him of being influenced too much by whites. Government officials criticized his stand on Vietnam. Some black leaders felt that King's statements against war diverted public attention from civil rights.

King inspired and planned the Poor People's Campaign, a march on Washington, D.C., in 1968 to dramatize the relationship of poverty to urban violence. But he did not live to take part in it. Early in 1968 he traveled to Memphis, Tenn., to support a strike of poorly paid sanitation workers. There, on April 4, he was assassinated by a sniper, James Earl Ray. King's death shocked the nation and precipitated rioting by blacks in many cities. He was buried in Atlanta under a monument inscribed with the final words of his famous "I Have a Dream" address. Taken from an old slave song, the inscription read: "Free at Last,/ Free at Last,/ Thank God Almighty,/ I'm Free at Last."

King's brief career greatly advanced the cause of civil rights in the United States. His efforts spurred the passage of the Civil Rights Act of 1964 and the Voting Rights Act of 1965. His energetic personality and persuasive oratory helped unite many blacks in a search for peaceful solutions to racial oppression. Although King's views were challenged by blacks who had lost faith in nonviolence, his belief in the power of nonviolent protest remained strong. His writings include *Stride Toward Freedom: The Montgomery Story* (1958); *Strength to Love* (1963); *Why We Can't Wait* (1964); and *Where Do We Go from Here: Chaos or Community?* (1967).

In 1977 King was posthumously awarded the Presidential Medal of Freedom for his battle against prejudice. In 1986 the United States Congress established a national holiday in King's honour to be observed on the third Monday in January.

DESMOND TUTU

(b. Oct. 7, 1931, Klerksdorp, South Africa)

Desmond Tutu was a South African Anglican cleric who in 1984 received the Nobel Prize for Peace for his role in the opposition to apartheid in South Africa.

Tutu was born of Xhosa and Tswana parents and was educated in South African mission schools at which his father taught. Though he wanted a medical career, Tutu was unable to afford training and instead became a schoolteacher in 1955. He resigned his post in 1957. He then attended St. Peter's Theological College in Johannesburg and was ordained an Anglican priest in 1961. In 1962 he moved to London, where in 1966 he obtained an M.A. from King's College London. From 1972 to 1975 he served as an associate director for the World Council of Churches. He was appointed dean of St. Mary's Cathedral in Johannesburg in 1975, the first black South African to hold that position. From 1976 to 1978 Tutu served as bishop of Lesotho.

In 1978 Tutu accepted an appointment as the general secretary of the South African Council of Churches and became a leading spokesperson for the rights of black South Africans. During the 1980s he played an unrivaled role in drawing national and international attention to the iniquities of apartheid. He emphasized nonviolent means of protest and encouraged the application of economic pressure by countries dealing with South Africa. The award of the 1984 Nobel Prize for Peace to Tutu sent a significant message to South African Pres. P.W. Botha's administration. In 1985, at the height of the township rebellions in South Africa, Tutu was installed as Johannesburg's first black Anglican bishop, and in 1986 he was elected the first black archbishop of Cape Town, thus becoming the primate of South Africa's 1.6 million-member Anglican church. In 1988 Tutu took a position as chancellor of the University of the Western Cape in Bellville, South Africa.

During South Africa's moves toward democracy in the early 1990s, Tutu propagated the idea of South Africa as "the Rainbow Nation," and he continued to comment on events with varying combinations of trenchancy and humour. In 1995 South African Pres. Nelson Mandela appointed Tutu head of the Truth and Reconciliation Commission, which investigated allegations of human rights abuses during the apartheid era.

Tutu retired from the primacy in 1996 and became archbishop emeritus. In July 2010 he announced his intention to effectively withdraw from public life in October, though he said he would continue his work with the Elders, a group of international leaders he cofounded in 2007 for the promotion of conflict resolution and problem solving throughout the world. On Oct. 7, 2010—his 79th birthday—he began his retirement.

Tutu authored or coauthored numerous publications, including *The Divine Intention* (1982), a collection of his lectures; *Hope and Suffering* (1983), a collection of his sermons; *No Future Without Forgiveness* (1999), a memoir from his time as head of the Truth and Reconciliation Commission; *God Has a Dream: A Vision of Hope for Our Time* (2004), a collection of personal reflections; and *Made for Goodness: And Why This Makes All the Difference* (2010), reflections on his beliefs about human nature. In addition to the Nobel Prize, Tutu received numerous honours, including the U.S. Presidential Medal of Freedom (2009), an award from the Mo Ibrahim Foundation that recognized his lifelong commitment to "speaking truth to power" (2012), and the Templeton Prize (2013).

LOUIS FARRAKHAN

(b. May 11, 1933, Bronx, N.Y., U.S.)

L ouis Farrakhan was an African American leader (from 1978) of the Nation of Islam, an African American movement that combined elements of Islam with black nationalism.

Louis Walcott, as he was then known, was raised in Boston by his mother, Sarah Mae Manning, an immigrant from St. Kitts and Nevis. Deeply religious as a boy, he became active in the St. Cyprian's Episcopal Church in his Roxbury neighbourhood. He graduated with honours from the prestigious Boston English High School, where he also played the violin and was a member of the track team. He attended the Winston-Salem Teachers College from 1951 to 1953 but dropped out to pursue a career in music. Known as "The Charmer," he performed professionally on the Boston nightclub circuit as a singer of calypso and country songs. In 1953 he married Khadijah, with whom he would have nine children.

In 1955 Walcott joined the Nation of Islam. Following the custom of the Nation, he replaced his surname with an "X," a custom among Nation of Islam followers who considered their family names to have originated with white slaveholders. Louis X first proved himself at Temple No. 7 in Harlem, where he emerged as the protégé of Malcolm X, the minister of the temple and one of the most prominent members of the Nation of Islam. Louis X was given his Muslim name, Abdul Haleem Farrakhan, by Elijah Muhammad, the leader of the Nation of Islam. Farrakhan was appointed head minister of Boston Temple No. 11, which Malcolm had established earlier.

After Malcolm X's break with the Nation in 1964 over political and personal differences with Elijah Muhammad, Farrakhan replaced Malcolm as head minister of Harlem's

Temple No. 7 and as the National Representative of the Nation, the second in command of the organization. Like his predecessor, Farrakhan was a dynamic, charismatic leader and a powerful speaker with the ability to appeal to the African American masses.

When Elijah Muhammad died in February 1975, the Nation of Islam fragmented. Surprisingly, the Nation's leadership chose Wallace Muhammad (now known as Warith Deen Mohammed), the fifth of Elijah's six sons, as the new Supreme Minister. Disappointed that he was not named Elijah's successor, Farrakhan led a breakaway group in 1978, which he also called the Nation of Islam and which preserved the original teachings of Elijah Muhammad. Farrakhan disagreed with Wallace Muhammad's attempts to move the Nation to orthodox Sunni Islam and to rid it of Elijah Muhammad's radical black nationalism and

Louis Farrakhan.

separatist teachings, which stressed the inherent wickedness of whites.

Farrakhan became known to the American public through a series of controversies that began during the 1984 presidential campaign of the Rev. Jesse Jackson, whom Farrakhan supported. Farrakhan withdrew his support after Jewish voters protested his praise of Adolf Hitler, and he has been embroiled in a continuing conflict with the American Jewish community because of his making allegedly anti-Semitic statements; Farrakhan has denied being anti-Semitic. In later speeches he blamed the U.S. government for what he claimed was a conspiracy to destroy black people with AIDS and addictive drugs.

In 1995 the Nation sponsored the Million Man March in Washington, D.C., to promote African American unity and family values. Estimates of the number of marchers, most of whom were men, ranged from 400,000 to nearly 1.1 million, making it the largest gathering of its kind in American history. Under Farrakhan's leadership, the Nation of Islam established a clinic for AIDS patients in Washington, D.C., and helped to force drug dealers out of public housing projects and private apartment buildings in the city. It also worked with gang members in Los Angeles. Meanwhile, the Nation continued to promote social reform in African American communities in accordance with its traditional goals of self-reliance and economic independence.

In the early 21st century, the core membership of Farrakhan's Nation of Islam was estimated at between 10,000 and 50,000 — though in the same period Farrakhan was delivering speeches in large cities across the United States that regularly attracted crowds of more than 30,000. Under Farrakhan's leadership, the Nation was one of the fastest growing of the various Muslim movements in the country. Foreign branches of the Nation were formed in Ghana, London, Paris, and the Caribbean islands. In order to strengthen the international influence of the Nation, Farrakhan established relations with Muslim countries, and in the late 1980s he cultivated a relationship with the Libyan dictator Muammar al-Qaddafi. After a near-death experience in 2000 resulting from complications from prostate cancer (he was diagnosed with cancer in 1991), Farrakhan toned down his racial rhetoric and attempted to strengthen relations with other minority communities, including Native Americans, Hispanics, and Asians. Farrakhan also moved his group closer to orthodox Sunni Islam in 2000, when he and Imam Warith Deen Mohammed, the leading American orthodox Muslim, recognized each other as fellow Muslims.

JERRY FALWELL

(b. Aug. 11, 1933, Lynchburg, Va., U.S.—d. May 15, 2007, Lynchburg)

J erry Falwell, an American religious leader and televangelist, was the founder of the Moral Majority, a political organization for the promotion of conservative social values.

Although his grandfather and father were atheists, Falwell accepted Jesus Christ in 1952, perhaps through the influence of his mother, a devout Christian. A good student and athlete—he turned down the opportunity to play professional baseball—Falwell entered Lynchburg College but later transferred to Baptist Bible College in Springfield, Mo., and graduated in 1956. In that year he founded Thomas Road Baptist Church in Lynchburg; the congregation grew from some 35 members to more than 20,000 by the time of Falwell's death. In 1956 Falwell also began broadcasting his sermons on a radio program, the

Jerry Falwell.

"Old-Time Gospel Hour." Six months later the program began appearing on a local television network; eventually it went into national and even international syndication and claimed more than 50 million regular viewers.

In 1971 Falwell founded Lynchburg Bible College—later Liberty University, a fundamentalist Christian university—which he led until his death. In the late 1980s he unsuccessfully sought to revive the PTL (Praise the Lord) Club, the conservative Christian organization and television network of the disgraced televangelist Jim Bakker. Falwell advocated a conservative Christian faith and condemned what he perceived as the sinfulness and godlessness of contemporary society. A segregationist in his early years, he later abandoned that view. He opposed abortion, feminism, gay rights, and other causes associated with the social and cultural transformations of the 1960s and '70s.

A successful minister, Falwell was perhaps best known for his political activism and the founding in

1979 of the Moral Majority, which he characterized as pro-family and pro-American. The organization, which quickly grew to several million members, was credited with playing an important role in the election of Republican Ronald Reagan as president in 1980; it remained a force in American politics during the first half of the 1980s but was disbanded in 1989 after Falwell declared that it had accomplished its mission.

In the 1990s, despite fading somewhat in the public eye, Falwell was an outspoken critic of the Democratic Party and especially of Democratic President Bill Clinton. Throughout his career Falwell was a staunch supporter of the State of Israel as well as the Republican Party; his Liberty University became an important stop for Republican presidential candidates in the early 21st century. In 2004, buoyed by the electoral victories of George W. Bush, Falwell founded the Faith and Values Coalition—now the Moral Majority Coalition—as a successor to the Moral Majority.

Throughout his career Falwell engendered controversy with remarks that many Americans perceived as intolerant or bigoted. He declared that AIDS was a divine punishment for homosexuality; he blamed "abortionists," gays and lesbians, feminists, and others for the Sept. 11, 2001, attacks on the United States (a statement he subsequently retracted); he identified Muhammad, the Prophet of Islam, as a terrorist; and he asserted that the Antichrist was a currently living Jewish male. Despite the hostility he sometimes provoked, Falwell was largely responsible for making American Christian conservatives politically active, and he had a marked impact on other aspects of American religious and political life in the late 20th century.

DALAI LAMA XIV

(b. July 6, 1935, Tibet)

Dalai Lama XIV was the title of the Tibetan Buddhist monk Bstan-'dzin-rgya-mtsho (Tenzin Gyatso), the 14th Dalai Lama but the first to become a global figure, largely for his advocacy of Buddhism and of the rights of the people of Tibet. Despite his fame, he dispensed with much of the pomp surrounding his office, describing himself as a "simple Buddhist monk."

It is a tenet of Tibetan Buddhism (which traditionally has flourished not only in Tibet but in Mongolia, Nepal, Sikkim, Bhutan, and parts of India and China) that highly advanced religious teachers return to the world after their death, motivated by their compassion for the world. At the time of the Chinese invasion of Tibet in 1950, there were several thousand of these teachers, often referred to in English as "incarnate lamas" (the term in Tibetan is *sprul sku*, which literally means "emanation body"). The most important and famous of these teachers was the Dalai Lama, whose line began in the 14th century. The third incarnation, named Bsod-nams-rgya-mtsho (1543–88), was given the title of Dalai Lama ("Ocean Teacher") by the Mongol chieftain Altan in 1580. His two previous incarnations were posthumously designated as the first and second Dalai Lamas. Until the 17th century the Dalai Lamas were prominent religious teachers of the Dge-lugs-pa sect (commonly called Yellow Hats), one of the four major sects of Tibetan Buddhism. In 1642 the fifth Dalai Lama was given temporal control of Tibet, and the Dalai Lamas remained head of state until the flight of the 14th Dalai Lama into exile in 1959. It is said that the previous incarnations of the 14th Dalai Lama extend not only to the previous 13 but further back into Tibetan history to include the first Buddhist kings (*chos rgyal*) of the 7th, 8th, and 9th centuries. All the Dalai Lamas and these early kings are considered human embodiments of Avalokiteshvara, the bodhisattva of compassion and the protector of Tibet.

The 13th Dalai Lama died in Lhasa, the capital of Tibet, on December 17, 1933. According to custom, executive authority was given to a regent, whose chief task was to identify and educate the next Dalai Lama, who would typically assume control at about the age of 20. After consulting various oracles, the regent sent out search parties to locate the child. One party made its way to Amdo, in the far northeast region of the Tibetan cultural domain, where it encountered a young boy named Lha-mo-don-grub, the son of a farmer. After passing a number of tests (including the selection of personal items that had belonged to the 13th Dalai Lama), he was proclaimed the next Dalai Lama. He and his family were then held for ransom by a powerful Chinese warlord. The ransom was paid by the Tibetan government, and the child and his family made the long trip to Lhasa, where he was enthroned on February 22, 1940.

Ordained as a Buddhist monk, the young Dalai Lama moved (without his family) into the vast Potala Palace (the residence of the Dalai Lamas and the seat of Tibetan government), where he began a rigorous monastic education under the tutelage of distinguished scholars. Affairs of state remained, however, in the hands of the regent, who preserved Tibet's neutrality during World War II. Although removed from international affairs, the Dalai Lama learned something of the outside world from magazines and newsreels, as well as from the Austrian mountaineer Heinrich Harrer during the latter's seven years in Tibet.

After they took control of China in 1949, the communists asserted that Tibet was part of the "Chinese motherland" (the non-Chinese Qing rulers of China had exercised suzerainty over the region from the 18th century until the dynasty's fall in 1911/12), and Chinese cadres entered Tibet in 1950. With a crisis looming, the Dalai Lama was asked to assume the role of head of state, which he did on Nov. 17, 1950, at the age of 15. Attempts by the Chinese to collectivize monastic properties in eastern Tibet met with resistance, which led to violence and intervention by the People's Liberation Army that year. On May 23, 1951, a Tibetan delegation in Beijing signed a "Seventeen-Point Agreement" (under duress), ceding control of Tibet to China; Chinese troops marched into Lhasa on September 9, 1951. During the next seven and a half years, the young Dalai Lama sought to protect the interests of the Tibetan people, departing for China in 1954 for a year-long tour, during which he met with China's leader Mao Zedong.

In 1956 the Dalai Lama traveled to India to participate in the celebration of the 2,500th anniversary of the Buddha's Enlightenment. Against the advice of some members of his circle, he returned to Tibet, where the situation continued to deteriorate. Guerrillas fought Chinese troops in eastern Tibet, and a significant number of refugees flowed into the capital. In February 1959, despite the turmoil, the Dalai Lama sat for his examination for the rank of *geshe* ("spiritual friend"), the highest scholastic achievement in the Dge-lugs-pa sect.

As tensions continued to escalate, rumours that Chinese authorities planned to kidnap the Dalai Lama led to a popular uprising in Lhasa on March 10, 1959, with crowds surrounding the Dalai Lama's summer palace to protect him. The unrest caused a breakdown in communications between the Dalai Lama's government and Chinese military authorities, and during the chaos the Dalai Lama (disguised as a Tibetan soldier) escaped under cover of darkness on March 17. Accompanied by a small party of his family and teachers and escorted by guerrilla fighters, the Dalai Lama made his way on foot and horseback across the Himalayas, pursued by Chinese troops. On March 31 he and his escorts arrived in India, where the Indian government offered them asylum.

In the wake of the Lhasa uprising and the Chinese consolidation of power across Tibet, tens of thousands of Tibetans followed the Dalai Lama into exile. In 1960 he established his government-in-exile in Dharamsala, a former British hill station in the Indian state of Himachal Pradesh, where he continued to reside. The government of India, however, was reluctant to allow all the Tibetan refugees to concentrate in one region and thus created settlements across the subcontinent, where the Tibetans established farming communities and built monasteries. The welfare of the refugees and the preservation of Tibetan culture in exile, especially in light of reports of the systematic destruction of Tibetan institutions during China's Cultural Revolution (1966–76), were the primary concerns of the Dalai Lama during this period.

The Dalai Lama traveled little during the early part of his exile and published only two books, an introduction to Buddhism and an autobiography. In later years, however, he traveled quite extensively, visiting Europe for the first time in 1973 and the United States for the first time in 1979. He subsequently traveled to dozens of other countries, delivering addresses at colleges and universities, meeting with political and religious leaders, and lecturing on Buddhism.

His activities focused on two main goals, one of which was to build and sustain international awareness of the plight of Tibet. In 1988, at a session of the European Parliament in Strasbourg, France, he set forth a plan in which Tibet would be an autonomous region of China rather than an independent state. He continued to advocate what he called a "middle way approach" between the complete independence of Tibet and its complete absorption into the People's Republic of China. He also sent numerous delegations to China to discuss such proposals, but they met with little success. In recognition of his efforts, he was awarded the Nobel Prize for Peace in 1989.

His other goal was to disseminate the central tenets of Buddhism to a wide audience. He is the author of dozens of books on Buddhist themes, many of which are derived from public lectures or interviews. Some of these works are written in the traditional form of commentaries on Buddhist scriptures, while others range more widely over topics such as interreligious dialogue and the compatibility of Buddhism and science.

Throughout his life, the Dalai Lama has fulfilled his traditional roles for the Tibetan community: he is revered by Tibetans both in Tibet and in exile as the human incarnation of the bodhisattva Avalokiteshvara and as the protector of the Tibetan people. In the latter role he consulted with oracles in making major decisions and made pronouncements on the practice of Tibetan Buddhism, as in 1980 and again in 1996, when he spoke out against the propitiation of the wrathful deity Dorje Shugden, one of the protectors of the Dge-lugs-pa sect.

After the Dalai Lama reached the age of 70, the question of his successor was repeatedly raised. In the 1980s his public speculation about whether there would be a need for another Dalai Lama was taken by some as a call to the Tibetan community to preserve its culture in exile. During the first decade of the 21st century, he declared that there would be a 15th Dalai Lama and that he would be discovered not in Chinese-controlled Tibet but in exile. Yet he subsequently suggested that he might appoint his successor. The Chinese government rejected this idea and insisted that the tradition of selecting a new Dalai Lama by determining the reincarnation of the predecessor had to be maintained. In 2011 the Dalai Lama stepped down as the political head of the Tibetan government-in-exile.

Previous Dalai Lamas were often figures cloaked in mystery, living in isolation in the Potala Palace in Lhasa. The 14th Dalai Lama, in contrast, achieved a level of visibility and celebrity that would have been unimaginable for his predecessors. He became the most famous Buddhist teacher in the world and is widely respected for his commitment both to nonviolence and to the cause of Tibetan freedom. In 2012 he won the Templeton Prize.

FRANCIS I

(b. Dec. 17, 1936, Buenos Aires, Argentina)

Francis I was the bishop of Rome and the leader of the Roman Catholic Church (2013–). He was the first pope from the Western Hemisphere, the first from South America, and the first from the Jesuit order.

Jorge Mario Bergoglio was the son of Italian immigrants to Argentina. After studying in high school to become a chemical technician, he worked briefly in the food-processing industry but felt called to the church. When he was about 21 years old, he suffered a severe bout of pneumonia that led to the removal of part of his right lung. He entered the Jesuit novitiate in 1958 and then turned to academics, studying humanities in Santiago, Chile, and earning a licentiate (equivalent to a master's degree) in philosophy in Buenos Aires province. After graduation he taught literature and psychology in high school while pursuing a degree in theology. He was ordained a priest in 1969, took his final vows in the Jesuit order in 1973, and subsequently served as superior (head) of the Jesuit province of Argentina (1973–79).

Bergoglio's tenure as head of the country's Jesuits coincided with the military coup in Argentina (1976) led by Lieut. Gen. Jorge Rafael Videla. During the ensuing Dirty War (1976–83), a campaign by the country's military dictatorship against leftists and other perceived subversives, between 10,000 and 30,000 people were disappeared (kidnapped, tortured, and usually killed) by the military and police. Bergoglio later claimed to have hidden several people from the authorities, even helping some of them to flee the country. In 1976 two Jesuit priests who had worked in poor neighbourhoods disappeared; they were found alive, but drugged, in a field five months later. Years after the Dirty War, Bergoglio's role in the priests' kidnapping and release generated controversy. Some critics faulted Bergoglio for failing to protect the priests and even accused him of turning the men over to the regime. Others accepted Bergoglio's claim that he covertly interceded with the regime to secure their eventual release. A lawsuit against Bergoglio charging him with complicity in the priests' disappearance was ultimately dismissed.

In the 1980s Bergoglio served as a seminary teacher and rector and pursued graduate studies in theology in Germany. In 1992 he was appointed an auxiliary bishop of Buenos Aires. He was named archbishop of Buenos Aires (a post he held until his election to the papacy) in 1998 and was consecrated a cardinal in 2001. During the economic crisis in Argentina beginning in the late 1990s, which culminated in 2002 in the rapid devaluation of the country's currency, Bergoglio acquired a public reputation for humility, living in a simple downtown apartment rather than in the archbishop's residence and traveling by public transportation or by foot rather than in a chauffeured limousine. He became an outspoken advocate for the poor and an able politician, deftly promoting the church's position on social matters in meetings with government officials. His theological conservatism, however, set him at odds with the centre-left administrations of President Néstor Kirchner (2003–07) and his wife and successor, Cristina Fernández de Kirchner (2007–). Bergoglio was a particularly vocal critic of Fernández's social initiatives, including the legalization of same-sex marriage in 2010. Fernández in turn depicted Bergoglio as a right-wing extremist and a supporter of the Videla dictatorship.

In February 2013 Pope Benedict XVI resigned, citing old age and health concerns. A conclave was convened in early March, spurring hopes that Benedict's replacement could be elected and installed before the impending Easter holiday. Bergoglio was elected on the fifth ballot and chose the name Francis, in honour of St. Francis of Assisi (1181/82–1226), who lived a life of humble service to the poor, and also recalling St. Francis Xavier (1506–52), a founding member of the Jesuits. Although he was the first Pope Francis and was widely referred to as "Francis I," he declined to use the Roman numeral I to indicate that he was the first to use his papal name. (Traditionally, the numeral I is not added to a pope's name until after a second pope of the same name has been elected. John Paul I [1978] was the first pope to use the numeral during his reign.)

Francis took charge of a church at a crossroads. In the early 21st century Roman Catholics constituted more than one-sixth of the world's population, many of them in Latin America and Africa. Yet scandals, particularly the clergy sexual-abuse scandals that first arose in the 1980s and '90s, had undermined the church's stature, particularly in the United States and Europe. In his earliest public addresses and in his first public mass, Francis called for spiritual renewal within the church and increased attention to the plight of the poor, and he sternly condemned the forces that diverted the church from its ministry and set it at risk of becoming a "pitiful NGO." He also reached out to his political opponents, including Fernández, whom he invited to his first official papal address. Yet he incensed some traditionalists by appearing on that occasion in a simple tunic rather than in the more traditional papal garments. He further drew traditionalists' ire when he washed the feet of two young women, including a Muslim, in a juvenile detention centre during the traditional Maundy Thursday reenactment of Jesus' washing of the feet of the Twelve Apostles. (Church tradition held that women could not participate in the ceremony because the Apostles were men.) He also took the unprecedented step later in 2013 of appointing a council of eight cardinals to advise him on church policy.

ROWAN WILLIAMS

(b. June 14, 1950, Swansea, Wales)

Rowan Williams was the 104th archbishop of Canterbury (from 2002), a noted theologian, archbishop of the Church in Wales (2000–02), and the first archbishop of Canterbury in modern times chosen from outside the Church of England.

Williams was born into a Welsh-speaking family. After attending the Dyvenor Secondary School, he entered Christ's College, Cambridge, where he earned bachelor's and master's degrees in theology; he was awarded a doctorate of philosophy in theology by Wadham College, Oxford, in 1975. After teaching at the College of the Resurrection, Mirfield, he held a series of academic and ecclesiastical appointments, culminating in his professorship of divinity at Oxford (1986–92). He became bishop of

Monmouth in 1992 and was enthroned as archbishop of Wales in 2000. His nomination as archbishop of Canterbury in 2002 generated significant controversy because of his liberal views on homosexuality and other matters, though he was supported by stalwarts of the church such as the Rev. Desmond Tutu. Williams opposed the war against the Taliban regime in Afghanistan in 2001 and harshly criticized the Iraq War in 2003.

Upon assuming office, Williams faced numerous challenges concerning interfaith relations and internal discipline. He made efforts to improve relations between Christians and Muslims, and he strove to maintain good ties with the Roman Catholic Church, meeting early in his reign with Pope John Paul II in Rome. Although warmly welcomed by the pope, Williams was cautioned by Rome over the consecration of homosexuals as bishops (Williams himself once ordained an openly gay man). Despite differences, Rome and Canterbury continued to work toward better relations. Williams attended John Paul's funeral in 2005—the first archbishop of Canterbury since the 16th century to do so—and he also attended the installation of Pope Benedict XVI. He visited Benedict at the Vatican in 2006, and they issued a declaration of friendship and continued dialogue while recognizing important differences between the two churches.

Within the Church of England the ordination and consecration of openly homosexual individuals remained a controversial issue that threatened to divide the Anglican Communion (the worldwide association of Anglican churches). In 2003 Williams appointed a special commission to address the matter. The commission also explored how Williams could more effectively implement his moral authority over the communion of churches. The issue, however, continued to trouble the church and its archbishop in the following years, as the Episcopal church in America ordained homosexuals, including an openly gay man as bishop, while the Anglican church in Africa staunchly opposed the practice.

In 2008 Williams faced further controversy when he suggested that the English legal system should adopt parts of Sharīʿah, or Islamic law, as a means to promote social cohesion. He argued that Muslims in England might feel more comfortable addressing financial or marital issues in a Sharīʿah court than in a secular court. Although Williams found support among members of the church hierarchy who recognized his right to raise the matter even if they disagreed with his opinion, others interpreted his remarks as undermining the long tradition of English secular law.

In 2011 Williams was an officiant at the royal wedding of Prince William and Catherine Middleton. In March 2012 he announced that he would step down as archbishop of Canterbury at the end of the year and would become master of Magdalene College, Cambridge, in January 2013.

A fellow of the British Academy since 1990, Williams has published collections of articles, sermons, and poetry. He is the author of *On Christian Theology* (2000), *Arius: Heresy and Tradition* (2002), *Writing in the Dust: After September 11* (2002), and *Tokens of Trust: An Introduction to Christian Belief* (2007).

RICK WARREN

(b. Jan. 28, 1954, San Jose, Calif., U.S.)

Rick Warren was an American pastor who, as founder of Saddleback Church and as the author of *The Purpose-Driven Life* (2002), became one of the most influential Evangelical Christians in the United States.

Warren, a fourth-generation Southern Baptist pastor, earned a Bachelor of Arts degree from California Baptist

College, a Master of Divinity from Southwestern Baptist Theological Seminary in Fort Worth, Texas, and a Doctor of Ministry from Fuller Theological Seminary in Pasadena, Calif. Turning down an offer to become pastor of a 5,000-member church in Texas during his last year in seminary, he and his family arrived in California's Saddleback Valley in January 1980 to establish a church.

On Easter Sunday, 1980, Saddleback Church held its first public service in Lake Forest, Calif., with 205 people, most of whom had never been churchgoers. Less than three decades later, the church numbered more than 20,000 members and conducted Sunday services at 6 times and 10 locations on its 120-acre (49-hectare) campus. The congregation subsequently started more than 30 daughter churches and sent nearly 5,000 members on mission projects around the world.

Warren's 1995 book, *The Purpose-Driven Church,* won him renown by focusing on worship, evangelism, fellowship, discipleship, and ministry. It was translated into more than 20 languages and used in more than 120 countries by hundreds of thousands of pastors who adapted its principles to their cultural and denominational settings. His next work, *The Purpose-Driven Life,* encouraged individuals to ask, "What am I here for?" and told them that they were planned for God's pleasure, formed for God's family, created to become like Christ, shaped for serving God, and made for a mission. Within six years of its publication, the book sold some 25 million copies and spurred 40-day studies (one day for each chapter) in more than 20,000 congregations representing 80 denominations. In addition to churches, the message was popular with a wide range of readers, including members of Pres. George W. Bush's administration and corporate officials.

In 2003 Warren stopped taking his $110,000 annual salary from Saddleback and returned the money the church had paid him for the previous 23 years. He pledged to donate 90 percent of his book royalties to the church and the three foundations he had created with his wife to promote evangelism and to fight poverty, illiteracy, and disease. His influence was noted in 2008, when he held a church forum attended by John McCain and Barack Obama, the Republican and Democratic presidential nominees, respectively. On Jan. 20, 2009, Warren delivered the invocation at the inauguration of President Obama.

JOEL OSTEEN
(b. March 5, 1963, Houston, Tex., U.S.)

Joel Osteen was an American televangelist, theologian, and popular speaker and author.

Osteen's parents founded the nondenominational, charismatic Lakewood Church in Houston in 1959. His father, John Osteen, was pastor and over the years had built a regional following. In 1981 Osteen left Oral Roberts University after less than one year of study to help his father develop Lakewood's growing national television ministry, working behind the cameras as a producer of the church's broadcasts.

After his father's death in 1999, Osteen took over as pastor. Under his leadership, Lakewood soon became the largest and fastest-growing congregation in the U.S. He rapidly expanded the church's media presence by purchasing advertisements on billboards and in other venues, doubling the church's budget for television airtime, negotiating with different networks for optimal time slots, and targeting the largest media markets. Within a few years his weekly television broadcast reached households in more than 100 countries and became the top-rated inspirational program on the air. His 2004 book, *Your Best Life Now: 7 Steps to Living at Your Full Potential*, was a best seller. In 2005 he conducted a 15-city U.S. tour, preaching to large crowds at virtually every stop. That year Lakewood opened a new 16,000-seat mega-church in Houston's Compaq Center, a former basketball and hockey arena. Weekly attendance at Lakewood rose from 6,000 in 1999 to more than 25,000 by 2005. His second best seller, *How to Become a Better You: 7 Keys to Improving Your Life Every Day,* was published in 2007.

Joel Osteen.

An affable youthful-looking man who had earned the nickname "the smiling preacher," Osteen typically avoided dense or orthodox theology in his sermons. Instead, he delivered simple, upbeat messages that emphasized his oft-repeated belief that "God wants us to have a better life." While this approach struck an obvious chord with the public, it also drew sharp criticism from those who viewed Osteen as little more than a motivational speaker offering a watered-down interpretation of Christianity. Others accused him of promoting a "prosperity gospel" designed to justify the accumulation of wealth. Osteen responded that he wanted to remain focused on the "goodness of God" and that he did not define prosperity in purely materialistic terms. He defended Lakewood's unabashedly commercial approach to attracting new members, arguing that churches that opposed "changing with the times," as he put it, risked losing members or folding altogether.

GLOSSARY

apologist A person who defends or supports something (such as a religion, cause, or organization) that is being criticized or attacked by other people.

Buddhism A religion of eastern and central Asia growing out of the teaching of Gautama Buddha that suffering is inherent in life and that one can be liberated from it by mental and moral self-purification.

cardinal A high ecclesiastical official of the Roman Catholic Church who ranks next below the pope and is appointed by him to assist him as a member of the college of cardinals.

crucifixion An act of killing someone by nailing or tying his or her hands and feet to a cross, or an act of crucifying someone.

Daoism (also spelled Taoism) A Chinese philosophy based on the writings of Lao-tzu that stresses living simply and honestly and in harmony with nature.

deity A god or goddess.

dharma The basic principles of cosmic or individual existence; divine law.

dispossess To put out of possession or occupancy.

divine Of, relating to, or proceeding directly from God or a god.

doctrine A set of ideas or beliefs that are taught or believed to be true.

dogma A belief or set of beliefs that is taught by a religious organization.

eschatology A belief concerning death, the end of the world, or the ultimate destiny of humankind; specifically any of various Christian doctrines concerning the Second Coming, the resurrection of the dead, or the Last Judgment.

eunuch A castrated man placed in charge of a harem or employed as a chamberlain in a palace.

exegesis An explanation or critical interpretation of a text.

historiography The writing of history based on the critical examination of sources, the selection of particulars from the authentic materials, and the synthesis of particulars into a narrative that will stand the test of critical methods.

Islam The religious faith of Muslims including belief in Allah as the sole deity and in Muhammad as his prophet.

Judaism A religion developed among the ancient Hebrews and characterized by belief in one transcendent God who has revealed himself to Abraham, Moses, and the Hebrew prophets and by a religious life in accordance with Scriptures and rabbinic traditions.

Muslim A person whose religion is Islam, or a follower of Islam.

polemic An aggressive attack on or refutation of the opinions or principles of another.

presbyter A member of the order of priests in churches having episcopal hierarchies that include bishops, priests, and deacons.

prophecy The power or ability to know what will happen in the future.

prophet A member of some religions (such as Christianity, Judaism, and Islam) who delivers messages that are believed to have come from God.

FOR FURTHER READING

Abdel Haleem, M.A.S. *The Qu'rān: A New Translation.* Oxford, England: Oxford University Press, 2008.

Aslan, Reza. *No God but God: The Origins, Evolution, and Future of Islam.* New York, NY: Random House Trade Paperbacks, 2011.

Botton, Alain De. *Religion for Atheists: A Non-believer's Guide to the Uses of Religion.* London, England: Hamish Hamilton, 2012.

Brodd, Jeffrey. *Invitation to World Religions.* New York, NY: Oxford University Press, 2012.

Dawood, N.J. *The Koran: Translated with Notes by N.J. Dawood.* London, England: Penguin Books, 2014.

Doniger, Wendy. *The Hindus: An Alternative History.* New York, NY: Penguin Press, 2009.

Glossop, Jennifer, and John Mantha. *The Kids Book of World Religions.* Toronto, ON, Canada: Kids Can Press, 2003.

Goldstone, Nancy Bazelon. *Maid and the Queen: The Secret History of Joan of Arc.* New York, NY: Penguin Books, 2013.

Hexham, Irving. *Understanding World Religions.* Grand Rapids, MI: Zondervan, 2011.

Hinnells, John R. *The Penguin Handbook of the World's Living Religions.* London, England: Penguin, 2010.

Keller, Timothy. *Prayer: Experiencing Awe and Intimacy with God.* New York, NY: Penguin Books, 2016.

Laozi, and D. C. Lau. *Tao Te Ching*. London, England: Penguin Books, 2009.

MacCulloch, Diarmaid. *Christianity: The First Three Thousand Years*. New York, NY: Penguin, 2011.

Miles, Jack, Wendy Doniger, Donald S. Lopez, James Robson, David Biale, Lawrence S. Cunningham, and Jane Dammen McAuliffe. *The Norton Anthology of World Religions. Judaism, Christianity, Islam*. New York, NY: W.W. Norton & Company, 2014.

Prothero, Stephen R. *God Is Not One: The Eight Rival Religions That Run the World--and Why Their Differences Matter*. New York, NY: HarperOne, 2011.

Roebuck, Valerie J. *The Dhammapada*. London, England: Penguin Books, 2010.

Wade, Nicholas. *The Faith Instinct: How Religion Evolved and Why It Endures*. New York, NY: Penguin Books, 2009.

Wong, Eva. *Taoism: An Essential Guide*. Boston, MA: Shambhala, 2011.

INDEX